"YOUNG MAJORS WERE IN GREAT DEMAND . . ."

The author at Shanghai, February 1919

Frontispiece

BRITMIS

A GREAT ADVENTURE OF THE WAR

Being an account of Allied intervention in Siberia and of an escape across the Gobi to Peking

BY

MAJOR PHELPS HODGES

The Naval & Military Press Ltd

Published by
The Naval & Military Press Ltd

In reprinting in facsimile from the original, any imperfections are inevitably reproduced and the quality may fall short of modern type and cartographic standards.

BRITMIS

CONTENTS

LIST OF ILLUSTRATIONS

MAPS

TO

MY COMPANIONS

BRITISH, FRENCH, GERMAN

HUNGARIAN AND RUSSIAN

ON THE UNEXPECTED JOURNEY ACROSS

THE GOBI

BRITMIS

CHAPTER I

IN SIBERIA

Early in the afternoon of 2nd December 1919, three rough country carts, driven by bearded peasants in tattered sheepskins, entered the small steppe town of Karkaralinsk in southern Siberia. As they made their way slowly through the wide, snow-covered streets, they attracted many a furtive, curious glance from groups of idlers scattered here and there, or from some scared white face pressed close to a window-pane. For this was a time when no man trusted his neighbour, and the rumours of strange happenings in the north made men uneasy, and suspicious of newcomers.

The carts and their occupants were certainly a sorry sight. The small, wiry steppe ponies that pulled them were obviously exhausted. The long hair on their heaving flanks was frozen in patches where the sweat had turned to ice, and their laboured breathing shot smoke-like jets of vapour into the frosty air, a vapour which formed into tiny icicles in nostrils and about drooping muzzles. They pulled weakly, with heads low and ears flapping dejectedly, staggering and pausing as the heavily laden carts rocked and skidded over the rough surface of the streets.

Battered and patched almost beyond belief, the carts were of the most primitive description – a number of light poles lashed across two low wooden axles. Piled high on each was a motley assortment of luggage, covered with coarse strips of camel's hair felt, and perched uncomfortably on top of all these bags and boxes sat the drivers and five weary travellers.

It was the appearance of two of these men that attracted the curiosity of the Cossacks and Kirghiz grouped at gateways and street corners, for they wore clothing that was strange to this part of the country, and their faces were not the faces of Russians. The Cossacks did not know it, but the fur caps and sheepskin coats of the two strangers were of the regulation pattern issued to British soldiers serving in cold climates, and the two tired faces, burnt by the sun, chapped by the icy wind, and bristling with almost a week's growth of beard, were those of British officers.

Arrived at the house where the Town Commandant had his quarters, the carts stopped, and the travellers descended slowly and painfully to the ground. Their limbs were stiff and half frozen, and it was some minutes before any of them could move about freely without an expression of pain, or a muttered curse in any one of five languages. As they stamped about in their awkward felt boots, or swung arms encumbered by many layers of clothing beneath their sheepskin coats, a small crowd of White Russian officers, Cossacks, peasants, and Kirghiz gathered round and stood staring at the strangers, hoping for news from the outside world.

As a few of the boldest pushed closer, a young Russian, dressed in the khaki uniform of a British soldier, except for his long leather boots, emerged from the Commandant's house, and recognised the leader of the newcomers. He pushed his way importantly through the crowd, halted a couple of paces in front of the Englishman, and saluted.

Keeping his right hand stiffly to the peak of his cap, Russian fashion, he said a few words rapidly in French. The words were few, but they contained news so surprising and so grave that for a moment there was silence, while onlookers glanced uneasily at one another, suspicious of the strangers and their foreign dress, unable to understand what had been said, yet straining forward to catch each word and gesture.

To the Englishman, this news was as disturbing as it was unexpected. If it were true, and he did not doubt it for a moment, he and his companions were in the devil of a mess, far worse than anything he had imagined possible. The Bolshevik net, which he had hoped to slip through without much difficulty, in order to rejoin his comrades of the British Military Mission Headquarters somewhere on the Trans-Siberian Railway, east of Omsk, was drawing swiftly round him, and he could see little or no chance of escape.

North, west, and south of this little Cossack settlement, an outpost of Russian colonisation in the wild Kirghiz steppe, the country was in the hands of the Bolsheviks. Only to the east, where, across hundreds of versts of desolate prairie, loomed the mysterious frontier of Mongolia and Chinese Turkestan, was there the remotest chance of safety. Isolated from the world, hemmed in on almost every side by rapidly approaching enemies, without proper winter clothing or sufficient money, ignorant of the country through which a difficult and dangerous journey would have to be made, and faced with the possibility of capture and death, the situation looked, and was, distinctly serious. How serious, only the events of the next few days could tell.

There was just a possibility, however, that a way out could be found, and if that were so, untold opportunities for adventure lay ahead. Adventures which, if he survived, would bring honour and glory, but best of all, perhaps, the romance of wanderings through strange and primitive countries, of hairbreadth escapes from death, of privations endured cheerfully with stout-hearted companions, and of living with and meeting in out-of-the-way places all sorts and conditions of men from the little-known tribes and races of this very heart of Asia.

These thoughts flashed quickly through his mind in the few seconds that followed the receipt of the news. Then noticing that the Russian was still standing at attention, he thanked him, and turning to the other officer at his side, said smiling:

'Well, Moss. It looks as if we were going to get some scrapping after all.'

*

The five travellers, who reached Karkaralinsk on this December afternoon, made up the personnel of the British Military Mission, attached to the Orenburg Army, a force which had been operating against the Reds south of the Trans-Siberian Railway. The members of the Mission consisted of myself, then a captain in the Royal Field Artillery (acting as liaison officer between the general commanding the Army and British Mission Headquarters at Omsk), and my assistant, Temporary Lieutenant Paul Moss, of the York and Lancaster Regiment. With us were three ex-enemy prisoners of war, a Saxon, a Magyar, and a Ruthenian (or some such nationality, I never really knew what he was), who acted as servant, cook, and groom respectively.

Before giving an explanation as to what had brought up to this desolate part of the Siberian steppes, it is necessary to describe the peculiar sequence of events, which led to Allied intervention in Russia at the end of the war, and scattered British officers and soldiers from Archangel to Ekaterinodar, from Omsk to Merv, and from the Pamirs to Vladivostok.

It is strange that more has not been written of this extraordinary period, which began with the Bolshevik *coup* in November 1917, and ended with the defeat of General Wrangel in the Crimea. And yet no phase of history is more full of material for the historian and the novelist than those four years of bitter civil war in Russia. How many people to-day, who read their morning paper and their magazines, and who take an intelligent interest in current events, have heard of that epic struggle of the Czechoslovaks in their effort to return home around the world? How a hundred thousand men, through countless difficulties and dangers, fought their way from the Ukraine to Vladivostok, held Siberia for almost a year, and finally reached their own country by way of the Pacific, Canada, the Atlantic, and Germany? What of the intrigues and bloodshed in Mongolia with Semenov and Ungern-Sternberg as the villains of the piece; of British gunboats fighting on the Volga and the Caspian; of the very grave French mutiny at Odessa, and the Russian mutiny on the Dvina, where British officers were murdered in their beds by their own men? Who has told of the German and Hungarian ex-prisoners who wandered through the ancient cities of Turkestan, or of the German troops that seized the Ukraine in the south, and swaggered through the streets of Helsingfors in the north? Someone has yet to describe the heroic march of General Kappel through the Siberian winter from Omsk to Irkutsk, when at the end of thousands of versts on foot, his soldiers found the enemy before them, and the General, both of whose legs had been amputated after frostbite, died, at the end of this long journey, as stoically as he had lived. Perhaps no one will ever adequately tell of the sufferings and despair of thousands of homeless refugees, who fled into the wilderness of Central Asia to escape the advancing Red armies, and who died by the wayside or endured miserably in mud hovels on the Kirghiz steppes or in the barren lands across the Chinese border.

In Siberia, awkward young peasants in the khaki of King George fought half-heartedly against their own countrymen, or deserted in droves to the enemy. Japanese Divisions strung out along the bleak reaches of the Amur waged a bitter guerrilla warfare against armed bands of Red raiders. Thousands of refugees lived for months in trains on railway sidings in indescribable filth and misery. Czech cavalry swaggered through the streets of many a town and village, or rode on punitive expeditions through the dense forests to some bandit stronghold. More than once, Americans and Japanese faced each other with rifles and machine guns ready for a 'scrap,' which was only averted at the last moment by perspiring staff officers. British troops paraded through the streets of Omsk, and British-trained cadets arrived from the base to officer Kolchak's levies. Hordes of German, Austrian, and Turkish prisoners of war starved and endured in wretched prison camps, hoping against hope for the hour of repatriation. While through it all, the sturdy peasants tilled the land and tended their cattle, praying for peace, and, as often as not, for the return of the Tsar and a Republic!

Volumes can and will be written of the various phases of this gigantic struggle, which, for all its tragedy and suffering, contains much that is comic and futile. So much inefficiency, senseless waste, spineless leadership, bigotry, cowardice, and treachery can seldom have been witnessed anywhere in recent years. Only the rarer case of heroism, the appalling tragedy of the refugees, and the widespread misery caused by an upheaval on such a scale, can rescue the period of Allied intervention in Russia from the realm of comic opera.

Although the part I played in the general scheme of things was a very humble one, my experiences are worth recording, for I not only saw a great deal of Siberia under exceptional conditions, but during the final Bolshevik attack, which caused the collapse of Kolchak, I became involved in a retreat that very nearly finished my career. Only by escaping across the Kirghiz steppes in the dead of winter with a few companions, taking refuge over the Chinese border, and traversing the great desert of Gobi, did I succeed in reaching civilisation again in safety. For seven months, on foot, on horseback, and by cart, we wandered more than three thousand miles across some of the most desolate country in the world, until one glorious day in May 1920, we reached the gates of our goal, the old Imperial City of Peking.

Looking back on this journey, which is probably unique in many ways, I forget the dangers, the hardships, and the monotony, only to remember those moments of elation when, conscious of youth and well-being, I rode forward into the unknown across Siberian plains, and the mountains and deserts of China. The intense feeling of complete freedom, of limitless space, and of glorious adventure yet to come, gave life a zest and a joy which I have never experienced since, in those countries where the spread of industrial civilisation has crowded men into cities, and the land is covered with a network of railways, roads, canals, and telegraph wires.

Happily, the world still contains great tracts where life still goes on as it has done for many thousands of years, and my story should be of interest to those who find pleasure in reading of travels and adventure in strange out-of-the-way places of the earth, where one can ride care free, with a good horse between one's knees, to recapture for a space the spirit of the knights-errant of a more chivalrous age.

CHAPTER 2

INTERVENTION

Often I like to look back and trace the trivial sequence of events that entangled me eventually in the turmoil of the Russian Revolution. In March 1918, after three and a half years' service with different field batteries in France, the Germans shot me in a clean and gentlemanly way, so that I was honourably relieved of any further active participation in the war for some months. The middle of June found me convalescing strongly in Lady Beaumont's delightful house in Sussex, and my shoulder was so far repaired by that time that I was able to play a little tennis with a gentleman whose wounded leg was also coming along nicely. My weakened condition made strenuous exercise rather unwise, but unwise I was; an awkward return tore a muscle in my back, and I was once more deposited in bed. The immediate result was my dispatch to Harrogate Spa for a special course of treatment, much to my disappointment, as I had made friends at Slindon, and was sorry to leave the lovely house on the Downs overlooking the sea. The change from a quiet and beautiful country home to a great barrack of a hospital, which held some two hundred strange officers, was so depressing that I began thinking seriously of wangling a return to the front, as being more bearable than life at the Grand Hotel.

I remember so well, lying in bed one night at about ten o'clock, and throwing down with disgust a magazine I had been reading. Soon it would be 'Lights Out,' and then the long night with its sleepless hours before me, and the ever-recurring dreams with their screaming shells and chattering explosions. (I hadn't had shellshock by any means, but my nerves had been frayed pretty thoroughly.) Fiction in every form had ceased to amuse or interest. I suddenly felt the need of work of some kind, something to turn my thoughts in a new direction, something interesting and difficult that would stir the stagnation of my mind and start again those currents of mental activity still dammed by the terrible monotony of war. In spite of being one of the worst Latin scholars that ever construed a line of Virgil, I had always been interested in languages, and as I lay thinking out this problem it struck me that I might take up a new one – not French or German, for they were both familiar – but Spanish, Italian, or possibly Russian? Like a flash the idea showed a fascinating possibility. Russian of course! I had read a day or so previously of British officers being sent to South Russia to aid the anti-revolutionaries. If I could only succeed in being ordered on one of those 'side-shows,' where war at least pretended to be romantic, and not such a brutal business as in France!

Next day I wrote to Hugo's school for a correspondence course in Russian, and when the little books arrived, settled down manfully to master the formidable alphabet, and then plunged on in an ever-victorious pursuit of words, phrases and sentences.

Some time in July I was passed by a Medical Board as fit for Home Service and after a month's leave, posted to a battery in the north of England. Despite encouraging news from France, the end of the war seemed as far away as ever, and the prospect of a return to that dreaded existence spurred me on to fresh efforts in my language study. I wrote to the War Office, asked to be sent back to the Black Sea, and said (modestly) that I spoke a little Russian!

Early in November, when I was finally fit for active service, I received a reply saying that they would keep me in mind, but that no more officers were being sent out for the time being. Soon after came the Armistice and in the excitement that followed I forgot all about my application for service in Russia.

*

To those who have read little of the part played by the Allies in Russia during and after the revolution, and are a bit hazy as to why the British officers were being sent to that country, a short résumé of the situation will give an idea as to what was going on at that time.

The intervention of the Allies at the end of the war has been, and still is, severely criticised by both extremes of political opinion. From the conservative, militarist or royalist point of view, far too few troops were sent to help the anti-Bolshevik forces and no concerted action was taken to drive the Soviet leaders from power. On the other hand, liberal and socialist opinion condemns the whole episode as an unjustifiable adventure, which did nothing but inflict added hardships on the population of Russia, and had no object but to replace a hated oligarchy in authority.

Both these points of view are easy to understand as they are founded on sympathy with one side or the other, and not on a real knowledge of the situation. To anyone who knows the facts and has troubled to read something of the military situation at the end of 1917 and the beginning of 1918, it is obvious that Allied intervention of some sort was inevitable. A study of subsequent events fully justifies the landing of small detachments of Allied troops at various important points in Russia and the support given to the local anti-Red forces, while at the same time it is quite evident that it would have been a very grave mistake to have intervened in Russia's internal affairs to any further extent, as, for example, by the dispatch of an Allied army to drive the Bolsheviks from Moscow. Whether we stayed too long in Russia after the end of the war is a question of opinion, but to have withdrawn our forces immediately after the Armistice would have been unwise from a military point of view, and a flagrant betrayal of the Czechs and our White Russian comrades.

This tale does not pretend to be a history of the intervention period, but I intend to give a short account of the series of events which led to the dispatch of British officers and men to Murmansk, Siberia and South Russia; not only are they interesting in themselves but at the same time they will give the reader a clear idea as to what I and my companions of the British Military Mission were sent to accomplish out there. The following chapters, while they describe my own personal adventures, will also show what difficulties we had in carrying out our duties, and how ridiculous it would have been to send really large forces to support the armies of Kolchak and Denikin.

As every one knows, the first or Kerensky Revolution in Russia occurred early in 1917. However, in spite of some ill-advised speeches to the soldiers, Kerensky managed to maintain some sort of discipline in the army, and General Brussilov was able to attack the Austro-German front with considerable success. This was short-lived, counter attacks drove back the Russians and in November the Bolshevik *coup* completely demoralised the troops. Deserters streamed back from the front in ever-increasing numbers, leaving much war material in the hands of the enemy, and, more serious still, allowing many German divisions to be transferred from the crumbling eastern front to the west.

The early days of 1918 were gloomy ones for the French and British. The initiative had passed to the Germans, who, freed from all anxiety on the east, were massing troops for the great Spring Offensive, which was to crush the Allies, then much exhausted by the bloody fighting of 1917, before the long-expected reinforcements from America could arrive in sufficient strength to be of real assistance.

In the same month that saw the smashing of the Franco-British lines near St. Quentin, the Treaty of Brest-Litovsk was signed between Germany and the Soviet. Following this, German troops poured into Finland, Lithuania and the Ukraine, ostensibly to assist the governments of these newly independent states to preserve order, actually to obtain as much war material and food as possible, in order to minimise the effect of the Allied blockade from which Germany suffered severely during the war.

While German soldiers occupied Helsingfors, Kiev and other towns, German officers appeared in various parts of Russia collecting bands of prisoners of war. They co-operated with the Turks early in 1918, assisting them to overrun Georgia, Armenia and other parts of the Caucasus.

They occupied most of the northern shore of the Black Sea and even in Siberia seized parts of the railway and confiscated valuable stores.

The Soviet was powerless, as the whole country was in chaos, and it seemed to the Allies that this vast territory would soon be in the hands of the Germans. Not only were they in control of the granary of the Ukraine, but the enormous resources of Siberia lay almost within their grasp. Besides food supplies, there were great stores of war material of all kinds at Archangel, Murmansk, Vladivostok, and other towns in the interior. Practically all of this material had been sent from England and America for transfer to the front, and was now lying in godowns or on railway cars at the disposal of our enemies.

With the final struggle going on in France, it was of vital importance to prevent Germany from gaining any further advantage from the downfall of Russia, and ways and means of intervening for this reason were discussed by the various Allied Powers. As early as March 1918 a British naval force was landed at Murmansk to guard the stores accumulated there from the danger of attack by German and Finnish forces, but no general plan was decided on, until a very unexpected and surprising development took place, which altered the whole situation in our favour.

As early as 1914, a number of Czechs, living in Russia, obtained permission to raise a force to fight against Austria. This force from a small beginning had grown into an army corps by the time the revolution broke out, and the question arose as to what was to be done with this large body of men, many of whom had deserted to the Russians during the war, with the hope that the Allies would help in the creation of a Czech state. Willing to fight for the Allies, fearing the demoralising effects of Bolshevik propaganda, and yet unable to join hands with the French or British owing to the military situation, it was decided that they should be transported across Russia and Siberia to Vladivostok and thence in Allied vessels to France. This was confirmed by the Treaty of Brest-Litovsk.

Even in normal times, the transfer of such a large body of men across a continent would have presented certain difficulties, and trouble soon occurred between the Czechs and the Soviet. The Czechs were supposed to be unarmed, but for their own safety they had been allowed to retain a fixed number of rifles and other arms per unit, and this caused continual friction and delay as they moved slowly eastward from the Ukraine. Local Red commanders placed many difficulties in the way of the various échelons, and Trotsky, egged on by the Germans, who had no wish to see another 100,000 men added to the western front, tried to disarm certain detachments by force.

Some of the Czechs had already reached Vladivostok, when fighting broke out between the Bolsheviks and the scattered Czech regiments. The daring and resourcefulness of the latter made up for their lack of arms and small numbers, for although hostilities began only in May, in about two months they had seized Samara, Kazan, and Simbirsk on the Volga, and all the important towns on the Trans-Siberian Railway as far east as Irkutsk. This effectively cut off Siberian food supplies from Russia. Further east, they occupied Vladivostok and several towns on the Amur. In August, the region around Lake Baikal was cleared of Reds, and early in September, the young

General Gaida, whose exploits along the railway had been very spectacular, joined hands near Chita with his fellow-Czechs from Vladivostok, and certain Allied detachments.

Encouraged by the successes of the Czechs and alarmed at the growing entente between the Germans and the Bolsheviks, the Allies had decided in the spring to land a British force (with a few French and Americans) at Archangel and on the Murmansk coast to protect the railway from the attacks of Germans and Finns, and to prevent the establishment of submarine bases and the shipment of war material to the enemy. This landing took place in June 1918.

A further expedition was to occupy Vladivostok, police the Trans-Siberian Railway and help the Czechs. This force was nomin lly under General Otani and consisted largely of Japanese, with smaller detachments of British, Americans, French, Chinese, and Italians. The troops disembarked in August, and in about a month had cleared the regions along the Ussuri and Amur rivers, and the railway as far as Lake Baikal where they joined up with the Czech forces coming from the west.

By this time the Soviet power in Siberia had collapsed.

Meanwhile, as early as February 1918, anti-Bolshevik governments began to spring up all over the country. The first was the Temporary Government of Autonomous Siberia, proclaimed at Tomsk. This was later dispersed, when Reds and German prisoners seized the town, and in July, General Horvath set up an independent anti-Bolshevik régime for the Maritime Provinces.

With the support of the Czechs, various provisional governments were first formed at such places as Samara and Orenburg, but their leaders were soon persuaded to establish a central directorate at Chelyabinsk and later at Omsk. This directorate consisted of five men under the presidency of Aksentiev, and was by no means popular, as it was neither reactionary enough for the officer class, nor radical enough for the republicans. Relying as it did on the support of the Czechs, it had little chance of survival, and was soon replaced by Kolchak.

Admiral Kolchak had had a distinguished career in the Russian Navy, and soon after the commencement of the Bolshevik revolution he offered his services to the British Government and received a temporary commission. He was actually on his way to Mesopotamia, having reached Singapore, I believe, when he was ordered to Peking to assist the Russian Minister in the organisation of White troops on the Manchurian border. He went to Peking and then proceeded to Omsk to look over the situation. There he was received enthusiastically by the Russian officers who apparently hailed him as the saviour of the country, and he was guarded carefully from harm by a battalion of the Middlesex Regiment, whose commanding officer was a Labour M.P., one Colonel John Ward.

Apparently fearing that the Japanese would support the claims of Ataman Semenov, of whom more later, and desiring a reliable 'strong man' in power, the British Government allowed Kolchak, backed by Colonel Ward's battalion, to overthrow the directorate and to declare himself dictator on 18th November 1918. Although this *coup* was effected without serious opposition, and Kolchak was eventually acknowledged Supreme Ruler by Denikin in South Russia, Semenov on the Manchurian border, and the other semi-independent leaders, he was hardly the man for the job, and unfortunately incurred the enmity of the Czechs, a fact which cost him his life a year later.

While the Czechs were fighting in Siberia, and Allied troops landing in the north and far east, the anti-Bolshevik movement among the Russians themselves gained ground rapidly. In midsummer at about the time that Germany's principal envoys were assassinated in Moscow and Kiev, the Don Cossacks rose against the new régime, and officers' corps, partisans, and other irregular formations sprang up in many parts. The growing disorder in Russia, the arrogance of the Germans, the atrocities and confiscations of the Bolsheviks or of peasants and deserters, and the successes of the Czechs gave heart to the counter-revolutionaries, and they were further encouraged when the Allies announced that they would supply credits for arms and equipment, and would send out military missions to advise and help in the training of the new units in order to restore stable government in a country that was drifting into anarchy. England took under her wing all the Russians, while France became responsible for the Czechs and Poles, and for a number of military organisations raised from among the Serbs and Rumanians who had been prisoners of war.

In addition to the arming of these forces, the dispatch of military missions for instructional purposes, and the landing of small bodies of troops, an International Railway Mission was formed under the command of the well-known American engineer, General Stevens. This mission, with headquarters at Harbin, had as its object the efficient operation and maintenance of the Trans-Siberian Railway, and in spite of countless difficulties, they did their job very well.

The northern, or Amur, branch of the railway, which runs from Chita to Nikolsk-Ussurisk, was heavily guarded by Japanese troops, who had a hard task in keeping the line open, and suffered many casualties in skirmishes and expeditions against the Red bands, which lurked in the forests and mountains near the Manchurian border. The Japanese were the only nation which sent a really large expeditionary force to Siberia, their total strength at one time reaching 75,000 men, and they were the only Allied troops which saw any serious fighting, excepting, of course, the Czechs.

At Chita, the end of the Japanese section of the line, was a Russian force under Ataman Semenov, a cruel and unscrupulous Cossack, who was a thorn in the side of the Allies, and of little real assistance to the White Russian cause. From Baikal to Omsk, the railway was guarded by Czechs and Russians, most of the Czechs having been withdrawn from the front as soon as newly formed Russian divisions could replace them. These troops were largely armed and equipped by us, as the military mission commanded by General Knox had begun to arrive in September 1918, and British officers were soon hard at work distributing guns, harness, uniforms, and so on, and instructing the Russian soldiers as to how to use them. We had agreed to equip a Russian army of 100,000 men in Siberia alone, and the entire work was to be done by our small mission, assisted by the British officers of the International Railway Mission.

All the wheels of the organisation had been put in motion before the Armistice, and when that came on 11th November it was not possible or even advisable to stop the machine at once. However, in January the Allies proposed a conference of all the Russian factions at Prinkipo Island in the Sea of Marmara, and this was accepted by the Bolsheviks, Esthonians, Letts, Lithuanians and Ukrainians. Unfortunately the anti-Bolsheviks were too strong in Paris, the Allies hesitated and the psychological moment passed. Intervention was then declared to aim at relieving the distress of the Russian people, but an economic blockade was maintained until January 1920.

The real truth of the matter was that every one was afraid of the Bolshevik menace, and hoped to overthrow the Soviet by giving moral and material support to the counter-revolutionists. Actual military support in any strength was out of the question owing to the political situation at home, and to the fact that an attempt to settle Russia's internal affairs by foreign troops could never have succeeded. At the same time, to have abandoned our White Russian friends completely, as soon as the Armistice was signed, would have been a betrayal, especially when one remembers the feeling against the Bolsheviks at that time, for having let us down during the war.

CHAPTER 3

JOINING BRITMIS

AT the beginning of 1919, after the abortive attempt at a peace conference on Prinkipo Island, the situation was roughly as follows:

The Bolsheviks, with headquarters at Moscow, were opposing the advance of an Anglo-Russian force from Archangel and Murmansk on the north, of a White Russian force on the west close to Petrograd, of the Volunteer Army under Denikin on the south, of Dutov's Cossacks on the south-east near Orenburg, and of Kolchak's troops on the east. Russian Turkestan was Bolshevik, but there was a small Anglo-Indian force operating near Merv. The British were keeping some semblance of order in the Caucasus, and becoming increasingly unpopular thereby. The Ukraine was a seething mass of revolt and counter-revolt, where the outstanding figure was Petlura, whose politics I have never been able to discover, but who seemed both anti-Red and anti-White, with good reason but little success. Russia was therefore in an unhappy state, her Communist rulers organising, driving, cursing, terrorising as their French predecessors had before them, licking a spoiled, disorganised mob into soldiers again, sending them out to fight with a sinister commissar at each commander's elbow and the promise of an unpleasant end in case of failure; Communist Russia encircled by a wall of enemies, a wall imposing in its length and in the supports that propped it up behind, but very tottery at the base and lacking continuity. At the great capitals of Europe men watched the movements of the coloured pins that meant the advance or retreat of armies, but if they thought in terms of the Great War, they were sadly mistaken. Here were no unbroken miles of trenches, with aircraft and artillery, tanks and gas, but great stretches of limitless steppe, where no-man's-land was maybe fifty versts wide and the high-sounding designations of Division and Brigade meant a handful of wild-looking Cossacks on shaggy ponies, or a few score awkward young peasants armed with Japanese rifles, who patrolled a hundred versts or more, and seldom fired a shot in battle. The ebb and flow of the armies was very largely due to propaganda and in the uncertain morale of the troops – of which more later.

If Kolchak had under his immediate command at the front, one hundred thousand men to cover a line over five hundred miles long, he was luckier than I believe, and if the Bolsheviks had that number opposed to him I should be still more surprised. Big distances were covered by small forces, and a few shots made a big noise. Given the right time of year, a British, French or American cavalry division would have gone straight to Moscow, or anywhere else it pleased in Russia, so demoralised and panicky were both Reds and Whites at this juncture.

If the Allies had decided on the downfall of Lenin and Trotsky, they could easily have chased them out of Moscow with Allied troops, but they had to keep up a pretence of neutrality, and armed the White troops to do the work for them. Of course the Allies were in an awkward position, for having assisted the Whites to resist and having succeeded in preventing the Bolsheviks from handing over great quantities of stores to the Germans *before the war ended*, they could not very well drop their Russian friends without giving them some further assistance, while at the same time they wished to see the speedy downfall of the Communist Government whose propaganda was having such a disturbing effect all over the world, without openly engaging in hostilities. Not only would the advance of an Allied army on Moscow have caused serious disturbances in the Allied countries, but this crude attempt of foreigners to settle domestic disputes would undoubtedly have greatly strengthened the Bolsheviks, and made Lenin's return to power sooner or later a certainty.

*

As already mentioned this story does not pretend to be an accurate and detailed account of Allied intervention in Russia, nor a history of the Kolchak adventure in Siberia. It is a tale of one of the most curious and extraordinary adventures that any young officer has ever had the luck to experience, and if the telling of it fails to interest the reader, the fault lies not in the subject but in the author's failure to present it in an attractive form. Some years have passed since these events occurred, and I am glad to have waited all this time before setting the story down, as I feel so much more competent to handle it, more tolerant and understanding, less swayed by the passions of the hour. Since returning from that mission in Siberia, I have again completed the circle of the globe, lived for two years in the Far East, and later started once again at the bottom of the ladder in the unfamiliar sphere of New York business.

More recently, my work has taken me to Scandinavia, Germany and France, where I have rubbed shoulders with so many types and conditions of men, and seen so many things that my point of view has altered a great deal, and in writing this tale I know it will be better done than in those months following my return to England.

The first days of December 1918 found me in London on a week's leave from my Battery in the north of England, and I had placed such little hope in being sent abroad now that the Armistice had been signed, that I was both astonished and elated to receive instructions from my Division to hold myself in readiness to embark for Vladivostok at short notice. The Brigade granted immediate embarkation leave, and I was soon busy overhauling my kit and buying winter clothing, for which a special allowance of £20 was made by the War Office. Thinking that it would be better to get most of the necessary things on the spot, where one could soon find out what was really needed, I limited my purchases to heavy underwear, a pair of fur gauntlets, fur cap, and a wonderful pair of rubber-soled, sheepskin thigh-boots, as worn by the Flying Corps.

Having been ordered to Vladivostok, which was the last place on earth I should have guessed, and remembering vaguely, from studies of the Russo-Japanese War, where to find it on the map, it was obvious that there was no time to lose in enjoying life, as it might be many long months before I should see London again. I expected to sail in under a week, and started giving farewell parties to all and sundry, dashing madly from theatre to night club, and from dinner to dance, just as all the other young idiots were doing about that time. London was a City of

Delights in those crazy days, and I enjoyed every minute of it, revelling in the realisation that the war was over, that the nervous strain of the last few years was gone for ever, and that instead of having to settle down to the drudgery of reconstruction, here was a glorious adventure before me, with a voyage round half the world, and all sorts of romantic possibilities at the journey's end.

The first week of leave passed, and then another, my farewell parties had to be repeated, and still the days went by and no orders came, nor could any information be obtained from the War Office. New Year came and went, London began to pall, and funds in the exchequer were beginning to look remarkably low, while I began to fear that the whole scheme would be cancelled and no more officers sent out. With an air of playing a practical joke, the War Office finally sent me orders on the 10th to embark at Liverpool on the *Empress of Russia* at 10 a.m. on Sunday the 12th. My instructions arrived late on Friday so that Saturday was a mad rush of packing, of making last minute purchases, and finally of catching the midnight train at Euston Station.

An acquaintance, Leeson, of the East Lancashire Regiment, and Bunnett, a temporary officer of the same regiment, were on board, both on the same business as myself, and so full of high spirits at the thought of leaving England again for a while, that they were soon rolling round on the floor of the compartment in a light-hearted way, most undignified for two veteran officers of His Majesty's forces.

Liverpool received us with weeping eyes, and after various formalities at the A.M.L.O.'s office, and a dreary breakfast at the famous Adelphi, we were glad to take a taxi to the docks, and leave behind the dirty streets and grimy buildings. By three o'clock the bustle on the quay was over, the gangway hauled ashore, and soon our fine-looking *Empress of Russia* was dropping down the Mersey, and heading for the Irish Sea.

The *Empress*, after many months of war service, was now on her way back to Hong-Kong for refitting, and then she would resume her normal trans-Pacific voyages. Her passengers consisted of some thirty officers like myself bound for Vladivostok, and forty or fifty civilians, returning to Malayan or Chinese ports. Some of them were business men demobilised, others missionaries, and a fortunate few travelling for pleasure only.

CHAPTER 4

THE VOYAGE

At Havre, the *Empress of Russia* stopped long enough for us to saunter through streets full of memories of 1914, to drink a *bock* at a familiar café, and to buy Leeson a fur cap. The only thing that Havre had to offer was a small, round black cap, such as the French *cochers* wear, and this Leeson purchased, wearing it with great success later in Siberia adorned with his regimental badge. It seemed to suit his cheery red face.

While we explored the town, the *Empress* filled her hold with a couple of thousand Chinese coolies, who were being sent back to Wei-hai-wei, after several months' service behind the front in Labour Battalions. Half a dozen of their British officers also came aboard, and proved a welcome addition to the passenger list.

Three uneventful days brought us to the Pillars of Hercules. It was close on midnight, as the silent ship ploughed her way steadily through the dark waters, across whose calm expanse stretched a silver ribbon of moonlight. I stood forward, watching impatiently for the first glimpse of that almost legendary Gibraltar.

At last it came. At first a crouching shape in the darkness, the great Rock slowly raised its blunt head as we slid by, until it towered above us outlined in frosted silver, as though peering down like some fine old watchdog, which eyed us distrustfully, and then, reassured, sank back again to interrupted slumbers. Perhaps that old Mohammedan warrior, Jebel Tarik, first saw his rock on such a night as this. Even in Paradise, he must be pleased that his name is commemorated on earth in such a place.

I love that first picture of Gibraltar. It satisfied me as few sights of famous places have done since. Its quiet strength and massive beauty, seen thus in the softening light of the moon, with the calm waters of the Atlantic and the Mediterranean stretching away to east and west were strangely comforting after the many disillusionments of the past few years. A reawakened feeling of pride and faith in England's empire came to me, and I felt more than proud to belong to the Regiment that had held the famous Rock against all comers for over two hundred years.

Port Said and my first glimpse of the East. The Canal. El Kantara, where the Turks actually reached the Canal's banks in 1915. The immense sweep of the desert. Suez. The Red Sea. *Sola topees*, proudly purchased for the first time at Port Said, at ruinous prices. Khaki drill. Deck sports. Russian lessons. Long, lazy hours in a deckchair, idly reading or gazing contentedly at the sun-kissed waves. Dolphins. Dancing to a gramophone in the dismantled saloon. Quiet rubbers of bridge in the smoking-room. Selling sweeps on the day's run. And above all, the blissful knowledge that the seemingly endless war was really over, and that I was alive to taste the full savour of this life of unaccustomed luxury and pampered ease. No irksome discipline, no mud, no dangers, no horrors, no shells, and no vermin. Life and hope were born again in the long days of the voyage, and the mind quickened by new sights, new sounds, new colours, and new experiences.

Our ship's company was small, and on the whole congenial. In addition to the military members, there were a number of passengers returning to Malayan or Chinese ports, where they were in business, and also some missionaries, who kept much to themselves and did not emerge very often on to the upper deck. Fortunately, there were enough young women to make life interesting, and altogether we had a very cheery time.

The members of the British Mission included regulars, territorial and temporary officers, and a few Colonials. Major Sydenham of the Royal Warwicks was in command. Most of us were in the middle twenties, and all, of course, had seen active service. Most of us regulars had been acting-Majors during the war when holding certain commands, but had been demoted to our substantive rank on embarkation. Many of the others, however, had been Lieutenants until the Armistice, but were given the temporary rank of Captain while seconded for service in Siberia. Thus with one or two exceptions we were now all of equal rank, and this caused a good deal of good-natured grousing on our part. In fact, three of us, who had been acting-Majors until the ship sailed, ripped the three stars from our cuffs and sewed on the crowns again, to assert our seniority, quieting our consciences by the fact that the War Office had vaguely promised one of our number that he should keep his majority while with the Mission. This self-promotion was brought to an ignominious end in Vladivostok, but it was well worth the risk, for young Majors were in great demand in Hong-Kong and Shanghai, and we were able to lord it over the humble Captains for the entire voyage.

An irrepressible youngster called Bunnett, of Leeson's

regiment, was by no means impressed, however, and became so cheeky that we decided to give him a lesson. One hot night, when we were in the Bay of Bengal, Leeson, Carthew of the Bedfords, and I raided Bunnett's cabin, seized him in his bunk, and hustled him out on deck, our object being to duck him in the canvas swimming tank aft. Bunnett fought like a cat. A crowd of officers, attracted by the racket, pressed around us, as we strove to hold the slippery form, which writhed, kicked and cursed, as we carried it with difficulty along the deck. The din was tremendous – shrieks, curses, and laughter mingled and echoed in the narrow space. A number of missionaries, who occupied cabins there, grew alarmed, and white faces appeared at port-holes, anxiously watching the struggling forms dimly seen in the semi-darkness. Suddenly our victim's pyjamas came off, and as we clutched wildly at his perspiring limbs, I heard a stentorian voice shout, 'Halt!' and at the same moment, a large Service revolver was thrust into my face from a cabin port. There was a shriek of laughter from the crowd, a scurrying of forms, and the wrathful Bunnett was alone, searching for his night clothes.

We learnt afterwards, that a certain R.A.M.C. Major, waking to the sound of bedlam we were causing, thought that the Chinese coolies had mutinied and were overpowering the passengers and crew, and prepared to sell his life dearly with a pistol in each hand. It was lucky he didn't fire.

We had lots of fun. There were the gallant officer and his lady love, who discovered a secluded spot aft for their deck-chairs one evening, and had been in transports for a considerable time, before they discovered that a delighted

Sergeant was an eager witness of the scene from a dim hammock, slung not far away. There was another gallant officer, who recognised an old flame among the passengers, cut her dead for two days, and was caught kissing her outside my cabin port-hole. There was the night Leeson dressed as a Turkish lady with yashmak complete and danced with me in the saloon, while every one ached to know who 'she' was.

Colombo passed like a dream, with lunch (now we must call it tiffin) and dinner at the Galle Face, rickshaw rides along the water front past feathery palm trees, a dance at the hotel, and many long, cool, Tom Collins to slake the thirst. Then two days to Singapore. An excursion across the island through miles of rubber plantations, to Johore, dinner at Raffles's, a call on the Gunner Mess, rickshaw rides again, this time through crowded, narrow streets full of shrill cries and the mixed races of the Orient, and then to bed with a 'Dutch wife.'

The night before the end of the voyage, half a dozen of us gave a special dinner, and invited several married ladies, without their husbands. The latter were furious, but we had a good time. In fact three or four of us had too good a time and the Captain threatened us with irons!

At Hong-Kong, which was reached on 15th February, we said good-bye to the *Empress*, and disembarked to await further orders, while our good ship sailed away to land her coolie cargo at Wei-hai-wei.

Hong-Kong is one of the most beautiful places in the world, and he who has missed the gorgeous views from the Peak by day, and the myriad lights of Victoria, seen from above by night, should make haste to complete his education. I was billeted at the Peak Hotel, and spent as much time as I could in exploring the beauties of the island, but we were the first 'heroes' to arrive from the battlefields of the late war, and were fêted accordingly. Eastern hospitality is proverbial, but during our four days it was overpowering. Every house was thrown open to us, and every one wished to stand drinks, until we were literally reeling from too much kindness.

Alas, for the stately cabins of the *Empress of Russia*! Our next ship was the coastal steamer *Sunning* on which the naval authorities abruptly embarked us for Shanghai. I often wondered whether our prompt departure was due so much to efficiency as to the fact that we were being given too good a time by all the fair ladies, who, heretofore, had had eyes only for the sailors!

Our new ship had cabins for seven first-class passengers, and we were thirty odd. Naturally, the seven senior officers were in luck. I was, unfortunately, the eighth senior, and led the grousing in what we called the 'Coolie Mess.' Our cabins were noisome rabbit warrens aft, immediately over the propeller, and our dining saloon a narrow passageway with a rough trestle table or two. Add some dirty Chinese 'boys' who actually tossed the meat from pan to plate with their fingers, and the picture is almost complete. It was too much for me, especially after Hong-Kong, and I made strenuous efforts to worm my way forward. Luckily there was a spare seat at the saloon table, so I persuaded one, Lacey of the King's Royal Rifles and an Old Shirburnian like myself, to let me sleep under his bunk on the floor at night, and thus became one of the élite.

On the 25th we entered the Yangtze, crossed the Woosung Bar, and steamed up past the mud-flats to Shanghai.

Hong-Kong's welcome paled beside the one accorded to us by the Paris of the East. I tremble to think of the enormities we committed, and wonder at the charity of our hosts. Luckily for me, I met a number of people who were keen on riding, and so spent much of my time astride that stout-hearted little beast, the Mongolian pony. Delightful days chasing paper over the dikes and soggy fields around the International Settlement. Grey English mornings when I jogged or galloped round the famous racecourse. The evenings were more hectic.

After our long voyage, what little money most of us had had at the start was gone. Shanghai was expensive, and at that time the premium on silver was so high that our pay did not begin to cover our bare hotel bills. There was no Paymaster or Field Cashier there, so we all descended on the only British officer in residence, who happened to be on recruiting duty. He was a stout fellow and advanced us all he dared, but our demands for more money were so insistent, that he cabled to Britmis, Vladivostok, for instructions. Meanwhile we were almost destitute, when the local British Red Cross came to the rescue with an allowance of six dollars a day 'billeting allowance.' This generous action put us on our feet, and enabled us to meet our living expenses. In fact, when I left the Shanghai Club at the end of our stay, and asked for my bill, which not only included room, meals, and 'boy,' but many drinks at the bar, the Secretary told me I was in credit, and we compromised on two bottles of whisky, which I carried off with his blessings!

The Shanghai people not only entertained us royally, paid us an allowance during our stay, but the British Women's War Work Society (or some such name, I forget the correct one), loaded us down with Shantung silk underclothes, padded waistcoats, socks, and other comforts. No wonder we were sorry to leave.

The Recruiting Officer's wires to Vladivostok finally produced an effect, but not in the way we expected. Instead of money, we were ordered to embark at once, and our delightful three weeks' stay was brought to an abrupt close.

Anchored in midstream, the Russian Volunteer ship, *Penza*, awaited us. Aboard all was dirt and confusion. A semi-mutinous crew, a powerless captain, disorder, insubordination, horrible food.

When I reached my cabin, it was locked – from inside. Two Russian women had taken possession of it and refused to be ejected. As they probably had friends among the crew, I could not get them out. We sailed. Again I slept under a bunk on the floor, but this time it was in Sydenham's cabin.

At breakfast in the morning, when the sea was inclined to be boisterous, I sat opposite to an imposing-looking Chinese merchant, dressed in the usual black silk, whose table manners were, to say the least, trying. The cloth was dirty, the steward frowsy, and the food far from tempting. I was considering some greasy eggs and bacon with a jaundiced eye, when the polite Oriental, to show appreciation of the fare, belched heartily in my direction. I rose hastily and made for the windswept deck.

Half an hour later, I turned from the silent contemplation of white-capped seas, to confront my late companion of the dining saloon. He was clad in a rich fur-lined coat of brocaded silk, his hands were thrust comfortably into his long sleeves, and he was in the act of expectorating throatily on the slippery deck. This time, I dived past him, and sought shelter and solitude under my commander's bunk.

A glimpse of Nagasaki, on the 16th of March, where the Elizabethan sailor, Will Adams, was cast ashore in 1660, and where he became Master Shipbuilder to the Yedo Government. We bought tortoiseshell objects, drank tepid Asahi beer while watching some even worse *geisha* dancing, motored over to the little fishing village of Moji in a decrepit Ford, to lunch, and returned in time to sail that evening. Then came two days more of rough weather across the Sea of Japan.

At last, in the darkness, we crept into the harbour of Vladivostok and anchored off-shore amid the drifting ice-floes. Our nine weeks' holiday was over, and most of us looked back regretfully on many happy or amusing moments during that time, as we leant against the rail and stared shorewards. Another milestone past and a less pleasant stretch of road ahead.

CHAPTER 5

VLADIVOSTOK

VLADIVOSTOK, or, as its name implies, Lord of the East, became Russian in 1858 by the Treaty of Aigun with China. This was soon after the Crimean War, during which a strong Anglo-French naval squadron failed miserably in an attack on Kamchatka. Established as a naval base in 1872, her growth has been rapid, and during the World War she became a vital link in Russia's chain of communications.

Occupied by the Allies in August 1918 to prevent the seizure of vast quantities of war material and their probable shipment to Germany by the Bolsheviks, she was soon the base of operations against Revolutionary Russia from the East, an Allied camp, a training ground for Kolchak's armies, a great asylum for refugees from all over Siberia, and a hotbed of political intrigue.

On the sparkling waters of the Golden Horn, foreign warships rode at anchor, merchantmen and troopships lay alongside the wharves, military and refugee trains crowded the noisome railway sidings at the water's edge, while rising one above the other on the steeply sloping hills around the bay, stood tier after tier of low wooden houses, broken to the north and east by pine-clad crests still powdered here and there with glittering snow.

Two cobbled avenues, lined with stone buildings, ran

at right angles to each other along the western and northern sides of the Golden Horn, but beyond them the streets were innocent of metal, filled with deep ruts, yawning holes, and rivers of mud and slush where droshkies sank up to their axles, and often drove their long-suffering fares to the comparative safety of the rotting wooden sidewalks.

Trade was almost at a standstill. Penniless refugees thronged the town, crime and licence grew unchecked, and there was universal and feverish speculation in foreign exchanges. On the streets an extraordinary motley of races, creeds, and tongues passed and repassed. Allied soldiers, carefree and with money to spend – Americans, British, Canadians, French, Italians, Japanese, Chinese, and Serbs – British, French and American sailors, tanned by the open sea and now ashore in search of a girl or a scrap; ex-Tsarist officers in grey greatcoats lined with scarlet silk; Russian soldiers in the homely drab supplied by the British Government; a sprinkling of soberly dressed foreign consuls and business men; soldiers of the new nations, Poles, Letts and Czechoslovaks, many of them ex-prisoners of war, now clad in fresh uniforms; fat Chinese merchants and lean coolies; Koreans in flowing white with strange stove-pipe hats; bearded Russian priests trailed by numerous offspring; fierce-looking Cossacks in mighty fur caps; tight-lipped American nurses in hard blue hats and billowing cloaks; pretty ladies with scarlet lips, high French heels, and expensive furs; Jews in gabardines and Jews in soiled frock-coats; hook-nosed Armenians; ragged refugees; indescribable beggars; lean-faced Turks, Germans and Austrians – prisoners of war awaiting repatriation; fat speculators;

decent bourgeois; hooligans; grey-clad militiamen; a never-ending stream of polyglot humanity.

Into this dirty, evil-smelling seaport, our happy band of thirty odd officers was dumped, and left to twiddle its collective thumbs in discomfort and apathy for a fortnight. Billeted for want of better accommodation in the West Barracks, hard by British Mission H.Q. and the railway station, we remembered regretfully the fleshpots of Shanghai.

The upper storey of a long, two-storeyed brick building was roughly partitioned with pine boards which formed cubicles large enough to hold two officers. Into each cell had been thrown a table and two iron cots, whose mattresses were planks. In the dim corridor, a couple of rusty iron stoves were supposed to heat the place, but as there was little fuel they were seldom lit and in any case proved totally inadequate. Most of the windows were broken and were now stuffed with rags or paper. The rear view from them disclosed a bleak hillside covered with refuse and latrines.

On the day of our arrival, shivering in our British Warms and seated on our hard beds, Leeson and I surveyed the dismal scene with jaundiced eyes. At the door, appeared Sydenham's dark but cheerful face.

'What are you two looking so glum about?' he asked, grinning at our forlorn appearance. 'This looks like home to me. It's just like a Boche prison camp. I spent four years in one, so you young fellahs ought to stand a week or two, without its killing you.'

'*C'est la guerre*, I suppose,' assented Leeson mournfully.

'Old stuff,' I put in. '*C'est la révolution.*'

Sydenham was not the only member of our party who

had spent unhappy years as a prisoner. Several others had undergone varying periods of enforced idleness in Germany, and not a few had made use of their time in studying Russian from fellow-prisoners. Their thirst for glory having been sharpened by absence from the front had made them eager volunteers for any expedition which offered an opportunity to earn distinction and promotion. The regular officers particularly felt that they had missed the chance of a lifetime when they saw their contemporaries who had survived the war, covered with honours and decorations. Here was a last chance to regain lost ground.

Nearly all the officers selected for service with the Mission, including myself, had few qualifications for the job. Most of us knew very little or no Russian, and this was to prove our most serious handicap, for an officer, unlike a business man, cannot effectively perform his duties with the help of an interpreter. As far as I have been able to discover, there were plenty of Russian-speaking soldiers, who could have been sent out, but the War Office made no serious attempt to use them, unless they happened to offer their services. As it afterwards turned out, most of my party, together with many others who came later, were sent to Ekaterinburg to officer an Anglo-Russian Brigade, which was not allowed to go into action. The officers were then sent home, having been in the country about six months without accomplishing anything. In fact we were nearly all useless, and most were heartily glad to go when the time came.

In Vladivostok on our arrival, there was no place for us in the Mission Mess, but we were directed to an 'excellent restaurant.' It proved to be the Zolotoi Rog (meaning Golden Horn) on the Svetlandskaya, famous to the soldiers of two nations as the 'Solitary Dog.' William Gerhardi, at that time a member of Britmis, in his excellent novel *Futility*, has given a very slightly exaggerated description of its 'service.'

It was our first introduction to the Russian's complete contempt of time. After giving our order, we waited with ever-increasing impatience for the appearance of food. Entreaties, prayers, threats, curses, all brought the same answer from the waiter. 'Seichass' – immediately. Our waiter went home. Another was dragged from the kitchen. Exactly two hours and five minutes from the time we sat down dinner arrived. I had asked for a cutlet, but a platter, bearing what looked like four young shoulders of mutton, was placed before me. I couldn't finish even one. It was a meal for an Elizabethan trencherman. Thereafter we ordered one portion for four and found it enough. It was the same with everything. Even the oysters conformed to the gargantuan nature of the fare. They were as big as soup plates, and so, after one attempt at dissection, I gave them up. It was too much like drawing and quartering.

No special arrangements, no bribes, no threats, could lessen the time necessary for ordering a meal. Two hours, almost to the minute, was the recognised period. If one ordered and then went away, expecting to return later and find it nearly ready, one's waiter had probably disappeared or had forgotten all about one. In self-defence, to pass the time, we took to vodka and liked it. Perhaps that was the idea. Make your guests as drunk as possible, and they won't care whether they eat beef, horse, mutton or dog. But no, that is a gross libel. The truth is that for the Russian, time does not exist.

After a few days of this, Leeson and I had had enough, and politely but firmly invaded the Mission Mess, where the fact that we were Regulars, and battle-scarred veterans to boot, soon overcame all opposition.

We were even welcomed by some, after both of us had been summoned in front of a Brass Hat and ordered to remove from our shoulders those crowns, which we had re-sewn on our tunics on board the *Empress of Russia* over two months before. However, those few extra weeks as Majors (self-appointed) had been well worth the wigging we received, for youthful officers of Field rank had been in great demand in Hong-Kong and Shanghai, and I can say from experience, that to be in demand in those hospitable Treaty Ports (at that time) meant something.

The Mess enjoyed the joke, and we soon became one of the family. There were many pleasant cynics among them, who delighted in tales of unvarnished truth, which made us wonder why we had come. Chiefly our short stay was valuable from the information we got from the smaller fry as to what was going on. The senior officers took no notice of us whatever, and we literally had no idea what we had been sent for. No statement of policy, no instructions as to the aims and objects of the Mission, no information as to our future employment, and no effort to keep us employed, properly housed, or fed. Not even a talk from General Blair, or one of the Staff, on what to do or what not to do.

The only hint of the Official Mind was contained in a confidential typewritten statement handed to us when we were taken one day to the Russian Island Cadet School. This was a school officered by British and Russians, for the training of the future officers for Kolchak's armies, and run on the lines of our schools behind the lines or in England at the end of the war. We were shown over the place one day, and incidentally given this paper to read. Who wrote it, or was responsible for its opinions, I don't know, and probably never shall. At any rate, we officers were instructed to be patient and tactful in our handling of the Russians until the situation was ripe and then we could step in and take complete command of the White forces. We would then be in a position to do as we pleased.

If that represented the official military point of view as regards the Russian situation, then whoever was responsible for that point of view wasn't fit to hold his job, because even we insignificant pawns in the game knew that British officers never would and never could take actual command in Russia. When we read the paper, there was a general groan from the whole party (we were on a small steamer going over to Russian Island at the time), and by more or less common consent I collected the typewritten sheets and consigned them to the waves. That was the last we heard of British control.

While waiting for orders, we learnt something of the situation, and heard that General Knox, with Mission H.Q., were at Omsk, where also was a Territorial Battalion of the Hampshire Regiment. We would probably go to Omsk ourselves shortly to help in the training of the newly formed White regiments, especially as regards the uses of British arms and equipment issued to them, and supplied by British credits granted to the Kolchak Government. We had already small missions at Irkutsk and at Tomsk, and our Railway Mission officers were established at certain important stations of the Trans-Siberian, chiefly from Omsk to the front.

The tales of inefficiency and corruption that we heard were enough to make the most optimistic doubt the success of our effort to help the Whites, whose difficulties were of course considerable. Their financial troubles alone were formidable, and the quantity of paper roubles which they printed in such large numbers never seemed to keep up with the depreciation and the consequent demand for more notes. As one man put it, 'Kolchak can't turn the handle fast enough, and he doesn't trust anyone else to do it.'

This paper money shortage gave rise to an amusing tale, which had a certain amount of truth in it.

The Russian police in Vladivostok arrested a Japanese passenger on his arrival on a steamer from Nagasaki, as he was found to be carrying two suit-cases containing 2,000,000 Omsk roubles in forged notes. Owing to diplomatic relations with Japan, the Vladivostok authorities wired to Omsk reporting the case and asking for instructions.

The reply came back immediately.

'Urgent stop Deport Japanese subject stop Put notes in circulation immediately.'

In the shabby ante-room of the Mess, we heard many stories of the Allied occupation and rumours from the front, served out by those who had already been in the country a few months. Listening to the talk around us, some conception of the magnitude of the task we had so lightly undertaken, began to creep into our minds, for the inefficiency and general unpopularity of the Kolchak régime was no secret. The only force that kept the many anti-revolutionary parties in outward harmony was fear of the Reds, and, of course, hope of Allied support.

As we were to find later, most of the local population, even the refugees whose safety depended on our presence, eyed us with ill-concealed dislike or open hatred. Poor devils, I suppose our well-fed, carefree faces, and the money in our pockets, excited more envy than gratitude, while our financial and moral support, only visible in our weak forces, did not satisfy the followers of the old régime. As for Bolshevik sympathisers they would naturally have put us all out of the way with pleasure, but we were too numerous for assassination, and they had to bide their time.

To anyone who has never been in a country during the throes of revolution, it is impossible to realise the feeling of uneasiness and suspense that hung over a town like Vladivostok. No one could trust his neighbour; trade was at a standstill; half the population was starving; and crime increasingly prevalent. Personal security was a thing of the past; justice, mercy, and fair play a memory. Endless plotting went on in secret; violence had replaced law; all the peace and order of a civilised community was suddenly replaced by terror and chaos. The mass of the population had sunk back to a primitive condition of life, where the survival of the fittest became a stern reality. Every man went armed. Political murders and brutal slayings for money went unpunished. The bold and the unscrupulous overawed the better element. Everywhere was the uneasy current of fear, suspicion and evil. It was to me a new and somewhat terrifying experience, and I began to take a more serious interest in the job ahead.

But I soon had little time for speculation, as we received orders to proceed up-country to Omsk, and I was asked by Sydenham to be adjutant of the train then being assembled, which was to take us some three thousand odd miles across Siberia. We were allowed two old first-class coaches as sleeping-carriages. A dining, or mess, car was improvised from a second-class coach, one end of which was partitioned off to form a kitchen, while rough wooden tables at the other end were installed by German prisoners. A carriage for our servants and baggage, and yet another for a detachment of the Hampshire Regiment, armed with a Lewis gun, who were to act as a guard for the train, together with a heavy closed car containing ammunition for the White troops at the front, completed the échelon.

Supervising German carpenters and arranging the various petty details necessary to prepare for our long journey, which might take a week or a month, was not thrilling work, but it occupied my time, and I had been bored stiff doing nothing. There being no spare British soldiers in Siberia, we had to look elsewhere for our batmen, and took the only ones we could find. These were Chinese 'boys,' and, as may be imagined, the best house 'boys' were not loitering around the streets of Vladivostok, so our choice was from necessity, not inclination. A mess cook, a helper, and one 'boy' for every two or three officers were all that we engaged.

Leeson and I secured the services of a diminutive Chinaman, called Li Yen Ching, a perfectly useless individual, who spoke only a few words of Russian, looked like a coolie, and only consented to honour us with his company as he felt safe under our wing and hoped to reap a rich reward by smuggling several rolls of cotton goods into the interior, where high prices were paid for manufactured articles. This was how the hated 'speculator' waxed fat.

Having engaged his services at so many roubles a week and his food, we invested in a large sack of rice, imagining that the Chinese ate nothing else. Every time he came to us uttering unintelligible sounds and rubbing his stomach to indicate hunger, we produced the rice, until he gave us up in disgust and did his own foraging.

During the last few days in Vladivostok, I was kept busy laying in stores, not only for the Mess, but for my own use, as most of the common necessities of life were unobtainable up-country. Besides a few tinned meats, I invested in coffee, tea, sugar, chocolate, salt, tooth paste, boot polish, soap, collar studs, and suchlike, as I did not expect to be able to buy any of them, once away from the coast, and it was lucky that I laid in a good supply, for this was the case, with a few minor exceptions. I also bought some whisky and wine. The latter from the ward-room of H.M.S. *Kent*, as they had a surplus stock of excellent South African brands.

At last, on 3rd April, all was ready. We dined at the Mess, drank the King's health, and, with the snow softly falling on the sleeping town, drew slowly away from the station towards the great plains of the interior.

CHAPTER 6

ON THE TRANS-SIBERIAN

We were setting out on the same road that thousands of comfortable bourgeois (or bourgeouy as the Bolsheviks now called them) had travelled on their way to a few months' vacation at home, but the circumstances were very different. We were starting on a three-thousand-mile journey into the heart of a really hostile country. While nominally not at war with the Soviet Government, the British were sending arms, ammunition and other stores to Omsk for the use of Admiral Kolchak's forces, and we were not only guarding these stores but were destined to train the White troops and assist them in every way to defeat the Bolsheviks and re-establish a reactionary form of government. Although a train service was maintained between Omsk and the coast, it was only made possible by strong forces of Allied, Czech and White Russian troops, as Red bands from points all along the route made constant attacks on stations and fortified posts, tore up rails and burnt bridges at every opportunity. In fact the whole country was in a state of smouldering rebellion, which burst forth into the flames of guerrilla warfare at widely separated points, and kept the garrisons of the larger towns, and the troops along the railway, in a continual state of alarm and uncertainty. While the majority of the population, both intelligentsia and peasant, lived in constant fear and prayed for any Government that would bring peace, the two extreme parties who fought for power used every means to discredit and destroy the other, and in the struggle forced the unhappy moderates to take sides or be denounced as traitors. Where the presence of Allied troops brought at least a feeling of security to the inhabitants of a town, even those who profited most by the occupation soon turned against their protectors and taunted them with being lukewarm allies and even Bolshevik sympathisers. It was the fixed belief of most White Russians, that the Allies owed it as a duty to their country to oust the Soviet régime by force, and place a tsar or dictator in power. While this was going on, presumably the grateful Allies would support the many thousands of able-bodied Russians, who preferred the security of Vladivostok or foreign countries to the dangers of fighting for the cause about which they talked so much.

If our position with the people we were trying to help was so uncertain, the pink-shaded portion of the population made it doubly unpleasant, for they had good reason to hate and fear us as the active backers of counter-revolution. The nature of our reception, therefore, seemed a little doubtful, and we were quite prepared for it to be unpleasant.

As Adjutant of the train, I was responsible for the detailing each day of an orderly officer from among our number, and two sentries from the guard of Hampshires. As soon as the train stopped one sentry would patrol on each side and prevent anyone from coming on board or approaching the car carrying the ammunition. The orderly officer was on duty for twenty-four hours and had to see that the sentries were at their posts as ordered. In addition, whenever a particularly dangerous section of the line was to be traversed, two officers with loaded revolvers rode in the engine cab to keep the driver and fireman on the job in case of attack. We had no intention of letting these men get away and leave us stranded on a lonely stretch of country, possibly surrounded by gleeful Bolsheviks.

Before leaving Vladivostok I was warned that a great many people would try to board our train, or ask permission to have their coaches attached, as they knew we would afford the best protection available, but that I was not to permit this as spies were everywhere, and women were just as likely to be dangerous as men. This warning was the cause of rather an amusing incident, which got me quite a reputation. Our first stop was at Razdolnoy, which we reached at 7.30 a.m. on the 4th of April, after a little over six hours' travelling. Here we halted for over an hour while a semi-armoured train with forty men and two machine guns was sent ahead to see if the road was safe, as this district was full of Red bands, which constantly attacked the railway. The local commandant then put a guard of six Russian officers on board our train (much to our disgust), and we set out for Nikolsk-Ussurisk, which we reached about eleven. This town, which was surrounded by a stout wooden stockade, was the centre of the disturbed area and had a Japanese garrison of some strength, as it was here that the northern branch of the railway went to Kharbarovsk, turned westwards along the Amur River, passed Blagovyeschensk, and eventually rejoined the main line at Chita. This section of the railway was entirely guarded by Japanese troops to the tune of about fifty thousand men.

After half an hour's delay, we left Nikolsk and travelled on uneventfully across the snow-covered countryside, dropping our Russian officers early in the afternoon at a small station whose name I can't remember, and crossing the Manchurian border soon after dark. Some time early next morning, while I was sleeping peacefully, we stopped at a place called Mulin. Here the orderly officer was accosted by a Russian woman, who asked to be allowed to ride on our train, and he being unable to refuse rudely, for she was quite good to look upon, brought her on board and referred her to me. I was wakened by a hand shaking my shoulder, and sat up slowly to find a pair of very attractive blue eyes brimming with tears, looking beseechingly at me. After recovering from the shock, I scrambled out of my 'flea' bag, and found an apparently unhappy young woman, clad only in an overcoat, nightdress and a pair of slippers. We stood confronting each other, while the door of the compartment was filled with interested and sympathetic faces, and she told her story. She, a passenger on the preceding train, had descended to buy some food at the station, and her train had gone off and left her without anything but the clothes she had on, and a few roubles in her purse. She had spent the night at the station in constant fear of the Chinese soldiers, and asked permission to ride with us to Harbin, or until she could transfer to a regular passenger train. With the warning about spies, and the instructions not to take any unauthorised person on board, and finding it hard to believe that a woman of her standing would get off a train in so few clothes to buy food, and let it start without her, I politely told her that I was sorry but that my duty prevented me from granting her request, and that she must wait for the next train to arrive. A howl of protest came from the group of officers at the door, which encouraged the damsel to further tears and heartrending appeals, which made me feel the most awful brute in the world, but I continued to refuse, until I was overruled and the lady, with a stalwart band of supporters, left me for the more august but weaker presence of my commanding officer. His heart melted in his breast at the first sight of beauty in distress, and my decision was reversed without any argument, so that in a few minutes all traces of tears had vanished, breakfast was ready for her, and a portly but gallant officer undertook to entertain her until she left us at three o'clock the next morning just outside of Harbin. Needless to say my reputation for callousness and being G.S.[1] travelled from one end of the land to the other.

Our journey through Manchuria was uneventful except that at Mulin our engine staff had 'gone sick,' which resulted in a six-hour delay while another driver and fireman were found.

We reached Harbin just before noon on the 6th, waited five hours, during which two cars under Kendall of the Railway Mission were hitched on to us, and pushed on, reaching Tsitsikhar next morning, and leaving an hour and a half later. As we moved inland it became appreciably colder, and whenever we popped out of the train at one of the frequent halts, we were glad of fur caps and sheepskin coats. I played a lot of bridge, studied a little Russian, and got off the train as often as possible to stretch my legs or kick around a football, which appeared like magic whenever there was enough flat ground near by

[1] G. S. in the British Army means General Service. In slang, as in this case, it means martinet.

to serve as a 'field.' At midnight on the 9th we reached Manchuria Station, where there was another five hours' delay due to engine trouble. On leaving here we were in Siberia once more, and the really dangerous part of the journey lay ahead. The scene was peaceful enough, for the road ran across a wide level plain on which were grazing great herds of horses and cattle watched over by Buriat horsemen and women clad in picturesque blue and red. At one place where we stopped, two of them came galloping up to us, reined in their ponies at a distance of fifty yards, and gazed at us with unblinking curiosity. When we tried to get closer to them, they wheeled suddenly and sped away. All that day and night we puffed along, reaching Chita soon after eight o'clock next morning.

This was the Headquarters of Ataman Semenov, commander of the Trans-Baikal Cossacks, who acknowledged the claim of Kolchak to be Supreme Ruler, but afforded him no assistance, except to hold the country between Lake Baikal and the Manchurian border and thus keep open communications. Semenov was reputed to have Mongol blood in his veins, and at one time aspired to rule an independent Mongolia as its King or Prince, while his cruelty in repressing the local uprisings and his high-handed methods in dealing with all and sundry who came within his territory, made him a thorn in the side of the Kolchak régime, and an object of suspicion and dislike on the part of the Allies, and of all those Russians whom he did not directly benefit. Chita is where the Amur branch of the Trans-Siberian railway joins the main line, so the Japanese had troops at this point, and although they may not have actually subsidised Semenov, their presence practically assured his safety. The Japanese garrison prevented any serious attack from the local Red bands, and Semenov was therefore able to live under their protecting wing, and send forth his Cossacks to murder and pillage, without fear of reprisals, while his control of the frontier served as an excuse to relieve both speculator and refugee of a great part of their worldly goods. He had unearthed an old Russian law that forbade anyone to cross the frontier with more than 250 roubles, and this he enforced with considerable profit to himself.

We only stayed about an hour at Chita, but had time to inspect a very efficient-looking armoured train, which was used to patrol the line; and also a more primitive one, which had a couple of light field guns mounted on open trucks for more long-distance scrapping.

Two more uneventful days, and then on the morning of the 12th we skirted the south shore of Baikal, caught glimpses of wide expanses of the frozen lake, and steamed into the station. Across the river, the white houses and gilded domes of the churches of Irkutsk shone in the brilliant sunlight, and as we were assured of a two hours' halt, Leeson and I set off to see the town. Having reached the river bank, we saw that a wooden bridge built on the ice connected the station side with the town, but the ice was breaking up rapidly and it looked as if it was only a matter of minutes before it would be swept away. As peasants and soldiers were still crossing, we walked about half-way over, but finally decided not to risk being left behind and returned to the train.

Again we pushed on just before noon, but had hardly gone three miles before we were held up by railway officials for ten hours, as they wanted to know all about our carful of ammunition before they would let us proceed. This car was the object of the greatest curiosity all the way up the line, and it was firmly believed by many that we were guarding a great shipment of gold from the British Government to Kolchak.

On the 13th, at 5.30 p.m., we reached Tulun and remained there until 4.30 a.m. on the 16th, a slight delay of two and a half days. The reason for this was an apparently heavy attack by Red bands on the Czechs guarding the railway. Czech officers at Tulun kept us informed of the fighting, which seemed severe, as their reports indicated isolated actions eighty versts away, extending westwards for another three hundred versts. Four car loads of ammunition and four guns were said to have been captured by the Bolsheviks, when they succeeded in derailing a train and driving off the guard. Losses did not seem very heavy, perhaps twenty or thirty a side, which was not surprising as some of the captured arms shown us were so antiquated and rusty that a hit must have been pure luck. I really felt sorry for the Bolsheviks when I saw some of those muzzle-loading bits of scrap iron. The Czechs seemed a fine body of men with good morale, but anxious to get home, which was not to be wondered at as they had practically cleaned up Siberia for the Whites, and were now getting little thanks for the unpleasant job of guarding the most dangerous section of the railway.

Nijni Udinsk was reached at 10 a.m. on the 16th, but affairs were not yet right further along, and we spent another thirty-six hours cooling our heels. As the situation seemed rather uncertain, it was arranged that two of us should remain constantly in the engine cab, and keep the crew at their job in case of attack, while the Hampshires'

ON THE TRANS-SIBERIAN RAILWAY

Major Gardner, Captains Leeson, Carthew and Hodges

Facing p. 70

Lewis gun was mounted on one of the coach platforms to keep hostile fire down as much as possible should we have to run the gauntlet. It might have been very unpleasant in those wooden cars if a Red band, with a few modern rifles, let loose at close range from a belt of forest.

As all seemed peaceful, we pulled out late on the 17th and ran into the danger area next morning. Evidences of the fighting could be seen in a derailed train lying forlornly on its side, a smouldering and blackened station, and the smoke rising from the ruins of villages near the line. The Czechs told us we should see corpses a plenty hanging from the telegraph poles, but whether they were pulling our legs, or the peasants had removed the bodies, I don't know, for I didn't see any.

Those two-hour stretches in the cab remain among my most vivid impressions. Our antiquated wood-burning engine puffed along mile after mile through bleak and deserted country, where the melting snow dripped ceaselessly from the trees, and turned the cart tracks into rivers of liquid mud. Convict settlements long since deserted, burning or seemingly empty villages, and an occasional station guarded by a small detachment of Czech troops, were all the signs of human habitation, but back somewhere in those woods marauding bands were counting their losses on this latest raid, and planning further swift descents upon the railway. As darkness came on, our eyes strained forward yet more anxiously, fixed on the brightly polished rails ahead, hoping to detect any tampering with the sleepers or the rails themselves, and thus pull up in time and avert catastrophe. All blinds were drawn in the cars behind, and only the engine's headlight, and the occasional dancing firelight in the cab as the furnace door was opened, gave any mark to the sniper in the trees.

The recent fighting, however, seemed to have cleared the air for the time being, and we reached Taishet soon after dark on the 18th, remained there all night as travelling at night was not to be recommended, and left next morning for Krasnoyarsk, a town of considerable size on the banks of the Yenisei. It had been rumoured that some of us might be needed there, as they were fitting up river gunboats and needed instructors, but instead of that a telegram reached Sydenham that Major Patterson, R.G.A., Captain Slanin, Quebec Regiment, and myself should detrain at Novo Nikolaevsk and report to British Mission Headquarters there.

Our train reached Taiga, the junction for Tomsk, on the 21st, and Novo Nikolaevsk early next morning. Our kit was dumped on the station platform, we said goodbye to our companions and to our mud-splashed coaches which had been our home for close on three weeks, and found ourselves a forlorn group amidst a crowd of bearded peasants and youthful gaping soldiers in ragged greatcoats and awkward-looking boots.

CHAPTER 7

BARNAUL

THREE days later we were on our way to Barnaul, a hundred and fifty miles to the south, on the branch railway that runs from Novo Nikolaevsk to Semipalatinsk. At Barnaul, the artillery of the 11th and 13th Siberian Divisions was being formed, and we were destined to act as instructors there.

Our stay at Novo Nikolaevsk had been short and uncomfortable. The town was alive with Russian, Polish, and Czech troops, and also housed a French and a British Mission and an American Red Cross unit. Otherwise it was a dirty, uninteresting hole, with a faintly hostile population, discontented at the stagnation of trade, and the rapid depreciation of the currency. The local Bolsheviks had posted manifestoes, threatening all Allied officers with death if they did not leave within twenty-four hours, but the threat was not carried out. One British officer declared that he had been fired on one night in a lonely part of the town, but his story was discounted, as he had consumed much vodka before the event, and could hardly remember how he reached the Mission Mess.

Barnaul was the first definite halt in our long journey, which had already covered 15,000 miles. A tidy distance to come for the benefit of a few Russian artillerymen. It marked a fresh phase in the adventure, for here work was to be begun, and the three months of unfettered travel gave way once more to military routine.

I was therefore much interested in what the next few weeks would bring in the way of fresh experiences, and plunged into this new life with considerable enthusiasm.

Barnaul, we found to be quite a cheery little town on the left bank of the River Ob. The main part had been ravaged by a great fire in 1917, which every one naturally blamed on the Bolsheviks. Most of the best buildings had suffered, and remained in ruins at the time of our arrival.

Our own quarters consisted of the entire second floor of a two-storey brick building, which had been repaired that winter, and we found ourselves very comfortably off, though of course there was no furniture and our camp equipment was hardly enough to make the place luxurious.

Patterson, ten years or so my senior, and a very pleasant fellow, took over the 13th Division, and I the 11th. Slanin, a short dark Russian, who had settled in Canada, acted as interpreter. He was the backbone of the Mission, as Patterson spoke practically no Russian, and I almost as little. Without him, we were lost, and he did his job wonderfully well.

The British Government had already sent a number of 15-pr. B.L.C. guns and 5-in. howitzers, with equipment, harness and uniforms, and would send more.[1] It was our

[1] These guns and howitzers were of obsolete pattern, and had only been used by some Territorial Divisions at the beginning of the war until 18-prs. and 4·5-in. howitzers could replace them. This fact caused much dissatisfaction among the Russians, who accused us of supplying antiquated artillery. They forgot that when they requested a supply of arms early in 1918, we were in need of every gun we had and could not send them the most modern weapons.

job to explain the mechanism of the gun, demonstrate the gun drill, supervise the distribution of stores, and help in any other way we could.

We had been met at the station by a group of officers, headed by a Colonel, who welcomed us warmly. The first evening, we were invited to dine at one of the infantry messes, as our own domestic arrangements were not yet made. A carriage was sent for us and we arrived about eight. Dinner would be ready in a moment. We were tired, but gallantly strove to understand our hosts and appear convivial. At ten o'clock, a good two hours later, the meal was served! I almost forgave the Solitary Dog!

This introduction to life in Barnaul was only too typical. It was a warning of what was to come, and we were soon in the thick of difficulties. Not only was there no conception of the value of time, as understood by us Westerners, but there was an almost impassable gulf between our fundamental ideas and theirs. Our Russian allies were kind-hearted, generous to absurdity at times, laughter-loving frequently, devoted comrades at odd moments, delightful hosts and good talkers. Socially they were interesting and amusing companions. From a military or business point of view they were a flop. That is, as far as we were concerned. They could not get things done, they were lazy, untidy, pessimistic, boastful, ignorant, untruthful and dishonest. They had no patriotism, though they wept over Holy Russia. They bragged, but were incompetent and often cowardly. They were cruel. They hated the Allies for not sending enormous armies to settle their troubles, when the only people who could clean up the mess were themselves. They promised everything and did nothing. They carped at the arms and supplies sent them, made little attempt to make use of them, and often sold military stores for their own profit.

At that time I was not quite twenty-five, and had served in one of the finest armies the world has ever seen. I was impatient and intolerant. Now I can look back with a more unbiased opinion, realise the difficulties the Russians had to deal with, and recognise many of their truly splendid qualities, but then it was different. It was heartbreaking to fight inefficiency, ignorance, and corruption, and it is no wonder that most of the Allied officers felt far more sympathy with the Bolshevik enemy than with the White forces.

Our own difficulties began when we started lecturing in a hall to a group of officers. A 15-pr. gun had been brought in, and with Slanin as interpreter, we began.

Now one of the Russian's characteristics is that he knows all about a thing before he looks at it. Our audience was no exception, and in addition it was quite undisciplined. The senior officers had no control over their juniors. Before we could get started, all sorts of idiotic questions were hurled at us, arguments began all over the room, and finally a number of the most impatient ones began to take the gun to pieces. Our protests were unavailing. In a few moments the buffer-oil gushed out on to the floor, and the gun was out of action until a fresh supply could be brought from Vladivostok, three thousand miles away. Other attempts at direct instruction proved equally fruitless.

Despairing of accomplishing anything in this way, I suggested forming a demonstration section from each division, one under Patterson and another under myself. These we would train in gun-laying, fuze setting, gun drill, and the care and handling of equipment, so that we could teach the two Divisions correct methods by practical demonstrations given by men who were at all times under our direct command. This was finally agreed on, and I set to work to teach a score of awkward Russian soldiers the secrets of British gun drill. Slanin who naturally helped me a good deal was a marvel, and I soon picked up the drill by heart until I could put them through their paces alone.

The sections were a great success, as we were totally independent, and therefore able to train our men without interference.

I grew quite fond of the men, who worked hard and became remarkably efficient. Under good officers they would have made fine troops, but for the most part they were badly led. The majority of the officers unfortunately were of poor quality – lazy, inefficient, and dispirited. They had no heart in their work or in the cause they fought for, and although I despised and disliked them at the time, I can hardly blame them now. Some had tasted the bitter humiliation of Brest-Litovsk, had seen their men melt away by desertion on the German front, and had been hunted and hounded from one hiding-place to another.

When one's own men have turned against one, it can always happen again. And I have often wondered since, had I been in their shoes, would I have been any better? A shot in the back at any moment is not a pleasant or encouraging prospect.

I must say I got very fed up with the Russian officer, but acquired a great liking for his womenfolk. They were far braver and more intelligent. I spent nearly all my spare time with friends, both soldiers and civilians, and made quite astonishing strides in the language. I also discovered a very delightful young teacher, whom I took to the Gardens almost every night, where a local troupe of actors, refugees from Moscow, gave a different play each evening. It was often pathetic to watch the efforts of the better class to recall the happy and prosperous pre-war days, the women clad in all the ancient finery they could muster, and the men in dilapidated uniforms, their badges of rank often marked in indelible pencil. Times were hard and would be harder, but for a few short months the old days came back, and I for one enjoyed them.

The warm, dark nights seemed all too short, as we strolled by the banks of the Barnaulka, or sat in the shadows somewhere, on a bench against the house wall or under the trees of one of the wide silent streets. I made love clumsily in bad Russian, and was not offended at the mocking laughter that greeted my jerky sentences, or I listened dreamily for hours to interminable discussions over countless glasses of tea. Russian voices are so soft and charming, one never tires of listening to them. Then there were occasional picnics in the forests, and rides on shaggy ponies to far-off clearings where we bathed in some rocky pool, shouting and singing 'Tipperary,' or some other war-time favourite. The Russians liked to hear them.

The short spring gave way to summer, and I changed to khaki drill and a sun helmet. Each morning I put my gunners through their paces, and watched them doing physical training under Slanin. Outside the yard where the section drilled, the measured tramp of Siberian infantry shook the earth as, preceded by their singers, they

AT BARNAUL. RUSSIAN ARTILLERYMEN WITH BRITISH UNIFORMS, HARNESS, AND A 15-PR. B.L.C. GUN

roared out those melancholy soldier songs that are famous throughout Europe. The music of a brass band crossing the square announced the arrival of a batch of conscripts, shambling, stupid peasant lads from Bisk and the slopes of the Altai, clad in felt boots and home-made fur caps, and gazing with wonder at the churches and brick buildings. Some had wept with terror at their first sight of a train.

In a few days they would be tramping the streets in drab uniforms, on the brass buttons of which appeared the Royal Arms of Great Britain. In a few months, most of these youths had deserted to the Bolsheviks, and fought with the badge of the Hammer and Sickle on their caps, and the Lion and the Unicorn on their hearts.

Rough country carts laden with produce ploughed through the dust, drawn by a couple of dejected ponies, and driven by a flat-faced peasant woman, her head bound up in a bright coloured kerchief, while her spouse strode clumsily alongside, eyeing the vodka shops as he passed. By nightfall he would be lying dead drunk across the cart, unconscious of the cuffs and kicks administered by his irate wife.

Cossacks and Czech cavalrymen trotted and galloped along the streets, wheeling sharply at the corners, and cursing the unwary, as they scuttled to safety on the wooden sidewalks.

In the evening life was gay enough in spite of old clothes and slim purses. Besides the plays in the Gardens, balls were given by the Russian officers, and we even essayed one at the Mission. My Chinese 'boy,' Li Yen Ching, had disappeared in Novo Nikolaevsk the night we left, so we were servantless on our arrival. This want was speedily remedied by the local prisoner-of-war camp, which still held many Austrian and German soldiers waiting to be repatriated. An excellent cook and two batmen arrived, one of whom spoke fluent English. They did nobly, and our dance was quite a success. It started off rather flat, but good supplies of vodka and beer carried the day, and we ended by trying to teach some of the Russian girls the one-step, without too much adverse comment. The Russians thought our dancing immoral, which is not surprising, as at that time lots of provincial English and Americans did too.

Colonel Steel, who had joined us early in May, was an enthusiastic banjoist and insisted on my doing a foxtrot, while he played, as the Russian band could only blare out a noisy march. I seized a trembling but proficient partner and managed to give a fair exhibition, but the audience was politely hostile and we gave it up.

With the spring, hope was born anew that in a few months the end of civil war would be in sight. The hardships and sufferings of the past winter were forgotten, and all those whose salvation lay with Kolchak and the Allies took courage and did their best to further the cause. In spite of poverty and the shortage of all the luxuries and many of the necessities of life, a few honest attempts were made to aid the troops. Charity concerts and balls took place continually, socks and comforts were fashioned somehow, and attempts were even made to supply books for the soldiers, though most of them couldn't read.

The military situation was better than it had ever been, and the optimists prophesied the speedy downfall of Lenin and Trotsky. On our own front Kolchak's armies were beyond the Urals, held Perm and had taken Ufa.

Gunboats, with British officers, steamed down the Volga, to the discomfiture of the Red flotilla. To the south, Kolchak was in touch with Dutov's Orenburg Cossacks, and in South Russia Denikin's Volunteer Army seemed within striking distance of Moscow itself. The Ukraine was in revolt, and Yudenitch threatened Petrograd from the west. To make the circle complete an Allied force based on Archangel and Murmansk and supported by local Russians, pressed slowly southwards, until it was almost in touch with Kolchak's right wing. In fact a Sergeant and thirty men of the Durham Light Infantry managed to cross and recross the desolate region to and from Ekaterinburg, after suffering considerable hardships.

To all appearances victory was on our side. Everywhere could be seen French and British officers drilling, instructing, issuing equipment, and putting new heart into the raw levies behind the line. In two or three months they would reinforce the front and press on irresistibly to Moscow.

Our own prestige was high, for Germany's defeat, especially after Russia had withdrawn from the war, was an amazing thing to the Russians in general. Many acknowledged to me that when war was declared in 1914, they regarded Germany as invincible and had no hope of victory. They had no idea that England had played any great part on land in the struggle, and were astounded when we told them the number of men we had put into the field on various fronts.

Hope was in the air, and optimistic rumours replaced tales of death and defeat. The Allies were to 'recognise' Kolchak; the blockade of Soviet Russia was to be stiffened; British and French troops were to be sent out to take a hand; the Bolsheviks were already defeated; their troops were deserting in masses; and the commissars were preparing to flee from Moscow.

In Ekaterinburg, where most of my late comrades and a number of other British officers now were, together with a battalion of the Hampshire Regiment, an Anglo-Russian Infantry Brigade was formed. Officered by us, it was hoped that this force would stiffen the other troops, and for a time it was expected to go to the front. A similar experiment in North Russia, with a regiment of Bolshevik deserters, proved unsuccessful however, as the men mutinied, and murdered several British officers. This affair and the jealousy of Kolchak's officers decided the War Office not to risk a similar tragedy, and the Brigade was eventually handed over to the Russians, unfortunately at a time when Ekaterinburg was threatened by a Bolshevik advance. In fact, the Hampshires and all my late companions were hurriedly entrained for Omsk at a critical moment, much to their own chagrin, leaving an impression of cowardice and desertion in the minds of the men they left behind.

I received a couple of letters from Leeson, who was at Ekaterinburg at the time (this was before the evacuation). He was thoroughly fed up with the whole show, as were most of the others. That the Russians' reputation for incompetence, procrastination and negligence was well deserved was only too evident. Cowardice and corruption, intrigue and delay sapped the strength of the Government and the army. The Allied Generals were hard put to it to get anything done, and must have threatened often to withdraw from the country entirely. Promises meant nothing, supplies were stolen and sold, ammunition and equipment sent from the base never reached their destination, staffs and back areas were crowded with surplus officers while the front cried out for men, and we were blamed openly for every disaster or mistake.

In Barnaul the artillery was just about ready to carry out practice shoots, preparatory to leaving for the front, when early in June I was stricken with typhus, the day after we had a visit from General Knox. He had come down to see what progress we were making. As he was on his way to Vladivostok, he took one of our officers with him to procure and bring back certain essential stores, which we had not been able to obtain for our artillery brigades.

Typhus was very prevalent, and filled the local hospitals with both officers and men. I was pushed off to one of them, as typhus is contagious, and remained semi-delirious for several days. Two German prisoners looked after me, insisted on keeping the windows tightly closed although the town was sweltering, and invariably forgot to obtain enough ice for my head, so that the nights became long hours of torment. Slanin soon got me moved to another hospital, where a young German boy looked after me tenderly, delighted at finding I spoke a little of his language. One morning I woke up to find a circle of curious but kindly Boches staring down at me as a specimen of the British officer they had probably fought against far away in Flanders. With my shaven head and sunken cheeks I must have looked a poor creature.

In three weeks I was sufficiently recovered to return to the Mess, where a very efficient Kansas City lady of the American Red Cross, sent down from Novo Nikolaevsk, looked after me.

On 4th July, we heard that peace had at last been signed

in Europe, and on the same day our two artillery Divisions left for the front, my place being taken by Captain Cook, who had arrived in Barnaul just before I caught typhus.

There was no further need of us in Barnaul, and we made our preparations to leave for Omsk. Colonel Steel and Slanin departed *via* Semipalatinsk; Patterson and the American nurse *via* Novo Nikolaevsk, leaving myself and Major Newbery, another newcomer, to follow in a few days. I was gradually regaining my strength, and it was probable I should be sent down to Vladivostok to recuperate.

With the departure of most of the troops, the local Bolsheviks began to lift their heads, and but for the presence of a Czech cavalry regiment, a rising would undoubtedly have taken place. As it was the last few days were quite tense with excitement, guns were trained on the town from a nearby hill, and the remaining troops were kept in constant readiness to quell any disturbance.

The uncertain sympathies of the Russian soldiers added to the danger, and the news from the front looked threatening. Already the imposing circle of Soviet Russia's foes was giving back. Before I left for Omsk in the middle of July, we had lost Ufa and Perm, and Ekaterinburg was being evacuated. The Hampshires and our Mission there had to beat a hasty and undignified retreat, for the rapid retirement of the front had placed the British War Office in a dilemma. Should the battalion and a few score officers hold on to be sacrificed to National pride, or should they be ordered back to Omsk in a manner that looked uncommonly like running away? The War Office swallowed the pill and wisely ordered evacuation, although to the men on the spot it was a bitter humiliation.

One enthusiastic young officer confronted General Blair, and expressed his determination to remain behind with the Brigade to save England's honour, and probably many would have done so, but their discouragement was too great, and they climbed sullenly into the waiting trains.

To make up for our sudden retreat, the British officers of the Railway Mission did wonders during the evacuation and earned the eternal gratitude of many families threatened by the Bolshevik advance.

I said good-bye to Barnaul sadly, for I felt I should never see it again. In spite of disappointment and disillusionment in the work of the past three months, I had caught something of the spirit of the Russian people, a something which cannot be explained by mere words. Beauty, melancholy, patience, simplicity, combined or singly do not describe it. It is something which once appreciated can never be forgotten, and combined with the beauty of their language, and the wild sadness of their music, make the Russians the most tragic and the most fascinating people in the world.

CHAPTER 8

OMSK–VLADIVOSTOK–OMSK

MAJOR NEWBERY, a temporary soldier of parts, with no small sense of humour, was the proud possessor of a little blue railway coach, in which he had been wont to visit the various British Missions scattered along the Trans-Siberian Railway. It consisted of a small sitting-room with two bunks, another sleeping compartment for two, a diminutive kitchen, and servant's bunk.

Leaving Barnaul behind us, we reached Novo Nikolaevsk on 18th July, were coupled on to a west-bound train, and set out for Omsk, where it would soon be decided whether I was to return to the base for convalescence or to remain on light duty.

The extent of the recent reverses suffered by Kolchak's forces immediately became apparent. The railway was almost blocked with train loads of wounded and refugees. Hour after hour, as we lurched onward, the long lines of *teplushkas* crept by, with their pitiful freight of bandaged forms, and despairing families.

Packed thirty, forty or even fifty to a truck, with others clinging precariously to roofs and buffers, some of these unfortunates had already been on the road for three weeks or a month. What was their destination, what could be their fate? Why had they abandoned homes and possessions to make this hopeless, ineffectual journey? These were not all officers or bourgeois, by any means, but peasants, and the poor of the towns, flying in terror before the oncoming tide of the revolutionary armies.

Poor cattle and cannon fodder, they little knew that their journey could have but one end – submission to the Soviets – for within the year the Red armies held Siberia from end to end. All these trials and hardships were in vain. Sooner or later, the Red tide must submerge them. Better if they had stayed at home, and risked the first fury of Bolshevik conquest, than endure it destitute and in rags in some strange far-off town on the steppes.

From our jolting coach, which swayed and snapped like the tail of a kite as we rattled along at the end of the train, I watched the never-ending procession. *Teplushkas*, battered third-class coaches, and antiquated wood-burning engines. Wounded soldiers; refugees from Perm and beyond; terror-stricken traders and peasants from Omsk and Ekaterinburg; lean cattle and shaggy ponies; feather-beds, sticks of furniture, pots and pans. Old men and women, girls and boys, tiny children, and many a stalwart man too. They slid past as their cars crept eastward, or halted hours and days at crowded sidings to let expresses and troop trains pass.

Late on the 19th, we reached Omsk, and next day moved our car to the Vedka siding, where the Allied Generals and many of the most important Russian officers and officials lived in their special trains.

Omsk was hot and dusty, full of troops and refugees. Its pre-war population had been 100,000, but it was now estimated at half a million. Our own battalion of Hampshires was there, and also most of the Mission. Borrowing a horse, I rode out to the camp, where many of my old companions were under canvas.

After the congratulations on my recovery and the jeers at my shaven head were over, I heard all the news. Kolchak's troops had not fought at all and were still retreating; there had been wholesale desertions to the enemy, and an epidemic of self-inflicted wounds; the retirement of the fighting troops had been so rapid that the handing over of the Anglo-Russian Brigade to Russian officers and the entrainment of the Hampshire Regiment for Omsk were necessarily accomplished with such speed that it looked as if the British Mission was running as hard as anyone else, and so it was, but by command and much against the will of all our officers and men; our Railway Mission had worked wonders evacuating Ekaterinburg, and many of the officers were still missing, presumably still at work on the line, helping on the many train loads of refugees and soldiers that had not yet reached Omsk.

Things were in a pretty bad way. We were disgusted with the Russians and they with us. I think most of us were secretly in sympathy with the Bolsheviks, after our experience with the corruption and cowardice of the other side. It was revolting to see wounded men dragging their way from station to hospital over dirty streets for perhaps a mile or two, while officers rode scornfully by in droshkies or motor cars.

While the front-line troops needed officers badly, Kolchak in Omsk had a military staff of nine hundred officers, and there were probably five thousand others doing petty jobs in addition. Not only was it the aim of most officers never to go to the front but those already there looked longingly to the rear. One story which I believe to be true, was told concerning a General with a distinguished name in Russian history. In May, while commanding the Second Ural Corps, he wired to Omsk, 'Front quiet request few days leave.' *On the following day*, his Chief of Staff wired frantically to Omsk, 'Situation grave. Have been fighting superior forces equipped with heavy artillery for three days. Have retreated fifteen kilometres.' Whether the General got his leave is not reported but he retained command of his corps.

I was still weak from typhus, and Newbery was being sent home, so on the evening of the 22nd we boarded the express for Vladivostok, it having been decided by the authorities that I was to recuperate there. This time we rode luxuriously in a *wagon-lit* compartment, with a dining-car and a *provodnik*. My last impression of Omsk was the crowded station platform, thronged with refugees, waiting patiently for a train to take them eastwards. It might be days before they could fight their way into a cattle-truck. Sullen sentinels with fixed bayonets guarded the doors and patrolled the yards, while officers with loaded revolvers stood ready to suppress any sign of trouble.

Just before we pulled out a smartly dressed but over painted blonde, escorted by an anxious-looking young Russian wearing pince-nez, boarded the train. The lady had evidently secured a *wagon-lit* berth for she deposited her various belongings in the compartment next to ours, but her young *ami* had no such luck and departed to his place in an ordinary first-class coach further back.

Standing at the door of her compartment, the lady was using her brilliant eyes quite freely in our direction, when suddenly she stiffened and gazed past us horrified. A tall, bearded man brushed by, stared at her without a word, and disappeared through her door. Until her young man reappeared, she leant limply against the partition, and then came a perfect torrent of abuse and despair. To our delight we learnt that the bearded gentleman was a recently discarded lover, forsaken for the younger man, and now she had to sleep in the same compartment with him all the way to Vladivostok! But even that prospect was not enough to make her give up the luxury of the *wagon-lit*, and so for weeks we watched the comedy, the past lover and the lady, never speaking, but sleeping one above the other, and the poor tormented one in pince-nez haunting the corridor in an agony of disappointed rage.

Eastwards we sped past the endless crowded trains, over flat steppe country parched in the summer heat, and through shady woods where purple foxgloves made pleasant splashes of colour in an otherwise dusty landscape.

There were several French officers on board. One had been caught in Russia during the revolution, joined the Reds, served on Trotsky's staff, escaped to the Caspian, joined the White forces in that region and eventually reached Omsk. Another, Captain Sourbibiel, and a very superior private soldier named Jacobi, had just been up to Omsk with dispatches and were returning to France. With a couple of other British officers and some of the young Russian women on board we managed to pass the time quite pleasantly.

All went well until we reached Krasnoyarsk on the 25th. We had now to cross the dangerous section of the line, that had been so unsettled on our way up. Sure enough, after several hours' travelling we reached a small station, where the Czech guards told us that the previous train had been derailed by Bolsheviks a few miles away. We were for pushing on, and offered to ride in the engine cab as we had done on the journey up-country, but the majority of the passengers were fat speculators and their wives, and they had the 'wind-up' properly. Nothing would do but to spend the night there, which we did, reaching Irkutsk safely the next evening. I've never seen such a panicky crowd. I would have booted the whole lot into the arms of the Bolsheviks with the greatest of pleasure.

Once more we plunged into the tunnels by Lake Baikal, and steamed on over dusty plains and by rugged mountains. The heat was sweltering and the dust crept through every nick and cranny. The dining-car was like a steam bath, and the flies settled in swarms on every particle of food, on hands, face and clothing, until one fled in disgust to wile the weary hours with bridge and attempts at sleep.

Soon after passing Chita, the train halted at a little place called Olovanaya on the Onon River. Here we stayed for three days. For some time it was impossible to learn what the delay was, but finally we discovered that the train in front of us had been struck by a cloud-burst. We laughed at first, but this tale turned out to be true for once.

The train, made up of *teplushkas* and carrying refugees and peasants, had been puffing peacefully over the plain, when the cloud-burst struck the engine and the first few carriages. In a moment the engine and cars were derailed and overturned, road bed and sleepers swept away, rails twisted, carriages smashed, and people killed and injured. Some bodies were said to have been washed hundreds of yards away. The survivors must have thought the Day of Judgment had really come.

The line had been destroyed for about a hundred yards, and it was cluttered with debris, so we kicked our heels, waiting for repairs to be made, and spent most of the time bathing in the pleasant Onon. In Russian fashion we bathed naked, the women a couple of hundred yards downstream. Russians, French, British and Chinese all disported themselves in the cold, clear water, while some ungallant souls raised field glasses surreptitiously to get a hurried 'close up' of the various female forms, which had only been visible, so far, decorously clad in dining-car or corridor. Some of the 'close ups' must have been worth while, for prolonged strolls *à deux* along the river bank became the thing to do after dinner.

The great steel bridge over the river had been destroyed during the civil war, but was cleverly repaired by Kolchak's men, who worked unceasingly all winter, in fifty degrees of frost sometimes, until a wooden framework rose from the river bed and once more opened the spans to traffic.

Nearly eight hundred years before, the great Genghis Khan, then but a boy fleeing before his enemies, must have crossed these hills and gazed on the swift waters of this very river. For just to the south on the extreme northern outskirts of the Great Gobi, between the Rivers Onon and Kirulen, had been the Mongol grazing grounds. These very hills had looked down upon the tents of these fierce nomads, whose armies spread terror from the Yellow Sea to the Adriatic, and from Moscow to the Indus.

On the 31st, when we should have been in Vladivostok, we crossed the bridge and soon after came to the scene of the recent cloud-burst. On all sides stretched the gently rolling steppe, so that no mountain torrent could have caused the wreck. The new rails and sleepers had been relaid hastily over the parched earth, and as we crawled slowly by, I saw a litter of smashed wood, wheels and machinery, and close to the line deep furrows of earth as if a giant plough had churned the virgin plain. It was here that the sudden mass of water had struck against the train and hurled it from the rails!

On reaching Manchuria Station at the border, a fresh obstacle appeared. There was a strike of the Russian employees on the Chinese Eastern Railway, and it looked as if we should be held up indefinitely. After strenuous efforts, we secured a driver and fireman, who agreed to go on if a guard of foreign officers was kept in the cab, and we succeeded in getting away some twelve hours later. There was more trouble at Tsitsikhar next day, which was settled by a fat bribe and we eventually reached Harbin.

There all was confusion. The railway workers were on strike, the Japanese and Chinese were ready for open warfare, and two Chinese factions were scrapping together as well. To add to the turmoil, bands of Hunghuses had attacked the railway at various points, and a passenger train arriving from Moukden had been heavily fired on by panicky Chinese troops. The express, which had left Omsk two days ahead of us, had been derailed in the Manchurian mountains, and two British officers, who were in the dining-car next the engine, had miraculously escaped unhurt, when the engine left the rails and the diner turned completely over.

Travelling at that time was not devoid of possible excitement.

Harbin station was full of trains waiting to go east, while a train from Vladivostok had just arrived after eight days on the road. General Gaida, a Czech who had commanded one of Kolchak's armies at Perm, was there in his special, unable to get an engine.

Every one was very jumpy, and the station yard was an inferno of noise, smells and flies. It was impossible to sleep at night, so every one was driven to seek relief in the town at the Garrison Club or the numerous cabarets that thronged a certain quarter of the Russian city.

4th August was the anniversary of our declaration of war on Germany and also the birthday of one of our number, so we celebrated it at the Palermo, where we dined sumptuously and watched the Café Chantant which was in progress. The French officers were with us and we toasted each other endlessly in vodka and cheap champagne, until one of our Allies turned a sickly green and fell forward on the table. Friendly arms supported him to the outer air and returned to continue the celebration. I became anxious when half an hour had passed, and tottered past innumerable tables to a sort of yard at the rear of the building. Passing through a gate, I came suddenly on the unfortunate Frenchman, stretched out on a Chinese wheelbarrow with his pale face turned upwards to the open sky. Looming over him in the darkness was the shadowy form of a large but peaceful old horse, which was sympathetically licking the pallid features on the barrow. I rescued our Ally and took him back to the station.

After three days in the heat and stench, we pulled out, passed the scene of a battle between Chinese troops and Hunghuses, which had taken place the day before and reached Yahminkoo, where we stopped for the night. The express behind us now came up, was coupled to us and we set off again with two engines to cross the mountains. The grades are steep and there are many hairpin bends, just the place for an ambush or derailment, so when we were going down one of the worst grades, and the shrill whistles of the two engines began to shriek suddenly and warningly, the passengers went crazy. Men and women rushed up and down the corridors weeping and yelling, expecting every moment to crash over a precipice, and had it not been for the presence of mind of one of the *provodniks* who applied the emergency brakes, we might have done so. The engine-drivers had found that the weight of the two trains was too much for the engines' brakes, and the whole échelon began to run away, until the warning whistles told the guard what to do.

At the next station we stopped to separate the trains, and learnt first-hand one of the causes of unrest among the railway workers. About a week before, a Russian officer, for some unknown reason had shot and killed a railwayman. The latter's comrades rose, attacked some fourteen officers in a train there, and killed eight before they were driven off. A few hours before our arrival, General Rozanov, who was on his way to Vladivostok and had passed us at Harbin, reached the station, seized the entire railway staff, shot seven of the men, cleared the station with whips, and gave the remainder two hours to return to work. Such was justice in Siberia, and all was quiet when we appeared upon the scene. Another night was spent at Nikolsk, owing to 'wind up' on the part of the passengers, and we reached Vladivostok on 9th August, exactly ten days late. I heaved a sigh of relief when I left that train.

The journey had taken so long that I was practically well and strong again and began work in the Intelligence branch of the Mission. News continued to be bad. On our front, west of Omsk, the retreat continued. Kolchak lost Tobolsk and Tyumen in the north, and General Belov, who had succeeded Ataman Dutov in command of the Southern Army near Orenburg, retreated further and further to the south-east along the Tashkent Railway. Denikin in South Russia had some minor successes, but seemed to be making little headway. Towards the end of September the news from Omsk improved somewhat. Dutov was sent to rally the Orenburg Cossacks again, and it seemed that if we could only hold our own, Denikin would reach Moscow and crush the Soviet Government.

In Vladivostok, General Rozanov, who had succeeded Horvath, vacillated between a reactionary policy backed by the Japanese, and a secret liaison with the old Social Revolutionary party, which detested Kolchak. On several occasions the political situation was quite tense, especially as some of the Allied officers were dabbling in politics, when they should have known better. There were rumours of a Social Revolutionary *coup*, and Rozanov filled the town with his troops, he himself forsaking his railway carriage for safer headquarters on an old steamer in the harbour. General Gaida, the Czech, was caught intriguing against his old master Kolchak and deprived of his Russian rank and orders. A couple of months later he led an uprising in the town, but was defeated and only escaped with difficulty.

Not only was there plot and counterplot among the Russian factions, secretly aided by the various Allies, but there was much bad blood between the Allies themselves.

The Japanese and Americans only avoided open conflict on several occasions by the merest accident, especially as the latter detested one Kalmikov, a brutal Cossack, whose headquarters lay in the Japanese zone along the Amur River. The Japanese supported him and the Americans were after his blood. Two of Kalmikov's officers had the cheek to kidnap a Colonel Fevralov in a motor car in broad daylight on the main street in Vladivostok. They carried him off to First River just outside the town, where he was found murdered a few hours later. No one was punished.

Our Mission H.Q. was just opposite the station, where several 'international incidents' occurred, and it seemed our duty to rush out and make peace. Once it was a Russian general who shot an American private, then a drunken Russian who shot an inoffensive Czech, or next a couple of doughboys intent on murdering a handful of excited Japanese. Except for occasional sailors' scraps on the docks, we got on well with every one, and I believe helped most to keep peace.

During September, the 25th Battalion Middlesex Regiment, together with a great many officers of the Mission, embarked for home, Leeson being among them. This was the beginning of the Allied withdrawal from Russia as decided by the Big Four in Paris at about this time.

In view of the political situation, during the last week in September, General Otani, nominal Commander-in-Chief of all the Allied troops in Vladivostok, issued a proclamation that he intended to keep the peace and that any disorders would be put down by him at once. Things quieted down for a few days and then for some reason

Otani ordered Rozanov to clear all his troops out of the town by noon on Monday, the 29th. Rozanov refused and we had to climb down.

What happened thereafter I don't know, as I received a telegram to return to Omsk forthwith to join Colonel Steel's Jaeger Artillery Brigade. I do know that several high Allied officers lost their jobs and departed for home wishing they had left local politics alone.

Early on the 29th, with a *wagon-lit* compartment to myself, as I was carrying mail and dispatches, I set out once more for Omsk, and reached there without incident in eight days, very glad to have crossed those three thousand miles again in safety.

CHAPTER 9

UNEXPECTED ORDERS

AFTER a three-thousand-mile journey through semi-hostile country, it is not very amusing to be told that one's presence is not really required after all, and that one will probably be sent back to the base in a few days.

Such was my reception at Omsk. The Jaeger Artillery Brigade was about to leave for the front, so that artillery instructors were no longer needed. I was rather annoyed, and now that I had reached Omsk once more I was determined not to leave without a struggle.

I soon discovered that a number of temporary officers who would be demobilised on their return to England were being retained, while Regulars were being sent home. After all, the army was my profession and the experience to be gained while serving with the Mission would be of far more importance to me in my career than to a T.G., who would soon be out of the Army altogether.

Armed with these arguments, I proceeded to lay siege to Major Cameron, also a Gunner, who was General Knox's Brigade-Major, and to all and sundry who had any influence in higher quarters. Soon after this, I had the satisfaction of hearing that one morning General Knox had demanded somewhat peevishly of Cameron, 'Who is this fellow Hodges?' I felt proud! My humble name was at least known to the General, and I redoubled my efforts!

One evening, an unshaven, travel-stained figure appeared in the Mess, and through the grime I recognised Captain Cook, who had taken my place at Barnaul, when I was in hospital, and had gone to the front with the 11th Siberian Division. We all crowded round him, and listened to his amazing adventures. He had gone with the Division to join the Southern Army under Dutov, and accompanied the artillery on the disastrous retreat along the Tashkent Railway until, attacked front and rear, the remnants had fled eastwards over the Hungry Steppe to Atbasar. He got away with the clothes he stood in, and considered himself lucky at that. I little knew that I should set out in a few days to join that very same army, and should have an even stranger experience.

Another evening a concert was given in aid of General Kappel's Corps. This formation had greatly impressed General Knox at the front, and it was said to be the best in Kolchak's Army. As usual the audience sat at tables while the show was in progress, and drinking was very heavy. At the end General Kappel rose to thank every one for the assistance this concert would give in providing comforts for the troops. He stood up bravely to face the half-drunk assembly, but his voice could scarcely be heard above the din of laughter, shouts, songs and the crash of breaking glass and crockery. In vain he called for silence, and his pale, bearded face clouded as he watched the tipsy officers and speculators, who cared no more for his Corps up at the front than they did for active service. It was hard for those few devoted Russians, who risked their lives for the rabble behind the lines. Months afterwards, I heard that on the fearful retreat from Omsk to Irkutsk in the winter of 1919-1920, Kappel had had his frostbitten legs amputated, and died as he would have wished, among his own men.

Our own ranks were thinned at Omsk that autumn by the death of Colonel Steel, who succumbed to pneumonia at the American Hospital. I was one of his pall-bearers, with Cameron and Faber, all of us being Gunners. Three Russian Artillery officers guarded and carried the flag-draped coffin with us, as we marched through the crowded streets, escorted by large bodies of troops and followed by Generals Knox and Janin, and by many Russian generals. At the graveside, a platoon of soldiers were drawn up to fire the last volley, while we pall-bearers rested on our swords on each side of the newly-dug hole. The rifles were raised, and just before the order to fire was given, General Knox ran forward and struck the muzzles upward with his cane. Had it not been for his prompt action three more Gunner officers would have been buried beside their gallant Colonel, for the soldiers were carelessly aiming at the backs of our heads!

The funeral took place on 19th October, and as I had had a tiring day, I went to bed early that evening. Next morning I slept late, but was wakened by Major Sydenham, who came in to my room and told me that I had been selected for liaison work with the Orenburg Cossack Army, and must leave Omsk that night.

Such a day of packing, collecting stores, money, papers, information, selecting horses, and acquiring servants! A lanky Saxon youth, called Albert Tigethoff, had acted as my batman since my arrival, and he volunteered to go gladly. I then secured two other prisoners-of-war, one Peter Rigo, a Magyar, as cook, and another Alexei, I think from the Hungarian border, as groom. Two fine horses, a bay gelding and mare, were supplied by the Royal North-west Mounted Police, and as companion and interpreter I was given Lieutenant Paul Moss, of the York and Lancaster Regiment, who had been born in Russia, and spoke the language better than he did English.

The Orenburg Cossacks, after their disastrous retreat along the Tashkent Railway at the end of the summer, were said to be reassembling their scattered forces at Atbasar, a small town in the Kirghiz steppe some 250 miles south of the Trans-Siberian Railway. They were again under the command of their old general, Ataman Dutov.

I was to take the train to Petropavlovsk, due west of Omsk, and then strike south across country until I reached the headquarters of the Army. Once there it would be my duty to report to the British Mission by wire and by letter whenever possible, keeping General Knox informed of the situation as fully as I could. I was given a code, and also told that it was important to use every means in my power to get information about the Tashkent Railway. This important line opened up the Soviets' communications with Central Asia, and might be used to threaten India. The War Office was anxious to have it cut, and I was to urge Dutov to do this if possible.

Finally all was ready. General Knox wished me good luck, and I jumped into a waiting motor car to be driven over the flat fields, which the first frosts were beginning to harden, to the ever-crowded, evil-smelling station. In a cattle truck, our two horses were contentedly munching hay, while Alexei sat on a pile of kit alert against possible thieves. Moss and the two batmen were in an old first-class coach used by our railway mission, in which two of its officers were returning to their duties at Petropavlovsk. Night had already fallen and the feeble rays of a hurricane lantern shed a pale glow over the grimy mess table.

Outside armed guards patrolled the station platform, and the huddled forms of refugees lay crowded close together on the ground, waiting patiently day after day for a train to take them eastwards. At last the station bell clanged for the third time and we drew out on a journey which for four of us was to be as strange, as unexpected and as interesting as the most ardent of adventurers could have wished.

I little thought, as the dim world slid by the carriage window, what surprises were in store. I was tired after the strenuous day, but my mind was active, and in the fantastic shapes and flitting shadows outside, I seemed to see a procession passing of all those who had trod the eastward road. Prehistoric forms in skins, drifting slowly to the far-off plains of North America; nomad horsemen of Mongol race; Mongol warriors in armour; bowmen; small bands of Cossack raiders; Russian trappers and traders of the sixteenth century; wretched bands of convicts struggling painfully in chains; a vast tide of peasant immigration; a grey column of slow-moving infantry; more Cossacks on their wiry ponies.

What a marvellous thing the history of this age-old Yugria, once the home of Alexander the Great's 'unclean people.' How closely linked with the lives of Genghis Khan, Timurlane, Yermak, Toktamish, leader of the Golden Horde, Ivan the Terrible, and many others almost unknown to the world at large. I wished I were not so ignorant myself, and looked forward eagerly to the next few weeks, when at last I should ride across the steppe, far from these iron rails and taste the freedom and the sunlight, where life was almost as it had been, unchanged for countless centuries. My dream of rescuing princesses was gone, but already I felt the saddle between my knees and the wind in my face as I galloped happily across a wide expanse of open country.

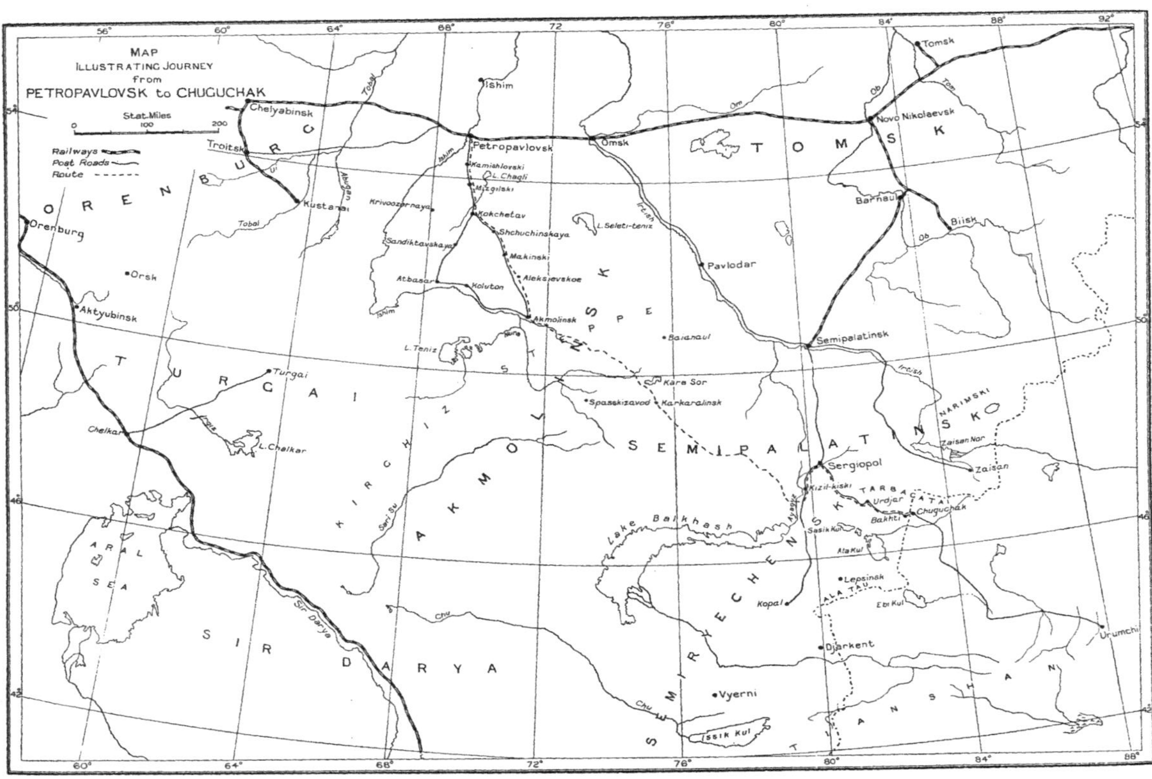
MAP
ILLUSTRATING JOURNEY
from
PETROPAVLOVSK to CHUGUCHAK
Stat. Miles
0
100
200
Railways
Post Roads
Route
Chelyabinsk
Troitsk
Kustanai
Orenburg
Orsk
Aktyubinsk
Turgai
Chelkar
L. Chelkar
Ishim
Petropavlovsk
Kamishlovski
L. Chagli
Mizgilski
Kokchetav
Shchuchinskaya
Makinski
Alekseevskoe
Krivoozernaya
Sandiktavskaya
Atbasar
Koluton
Akmolinsk
L. Teniz
L. Seleti-teniz
Omsk
Pavlodar
Baianaul
Kara Sor
Spasskizavod
Karkaralinsk
Semipalatinsk
Novo Nikolaevsk
Tomsk
Barnaul
Biisk
Sergiopol
Kizil-kiski
Urdjar
Bakhti
Chuguchak
Zaisan
Zaisan Nor
Lake Balkhash
Sasik Kul
Ala Kul
Lepsinsk
Ala Tau
Ebi Kul
Kopal
Djarkent
Vyerni
Issik Kul
Urumchi
Aral Sea
Sir Darya
Chu
Sari Su
Irtish
Ob
Om
Tom
Tobol
Abugan
Ishim
Nura
Irgiz
Ui
O R E N B U R G
T U R G A I
K I R G H I Z S T E P P E
A K M O L I N S K
S E M I P A L A T I N S K
T O M S K
S E M I R Y E C H E N S K
S I R D A R Y A
T I A N S H A N
NARIMSKI
TARBAGATAI
56°
60°
64°
68°
72°
76°
80°
84°
88°
92°
54°
50°
46°
42°

CHAPTER 10

THE FIRST OF THE STEPPE COUNTRY

PETROPAVLOVSK before the war was a prosperous town on the River Ishim, the centre of the hides and frozen meat trade of all Siberia, and the site of the ancient Barter Court, where the materials and Asiatic goods of the Kirghiz steppe found a ready market.

I found it a typical Siberian town, dirty, uninteresting, and woefully poor. Its former busy markets had vanished, and along its muddy streets only an occasional Cossack trotted past.

We had reached the town on the evening of 21st October, armed with all sorts of documents from the Russian staff to enable us to procure transport for our servants and kit, but it was not until five days later that we were able to set out. Every available horse and cart had been requisitioned by the troops, as the Second and Third Armies were again in full retreat, from further west, and it looked as if Petropavlovsk itself would soon be in danger.

Luckily, I met a Russian official, Baron von Tiesenhausen, who was also on his way to join Dutov. He had recently been appointed Governor of Orenburg by Kolchak, although Orenburg had been captured long before by the enemy. He very decently offered to let me have two of his carts, which I accepted *faute de mieux*, as I saw no chance of getting any for myself.

Moss and I had spent weary hours tramping the town in search of transport, so I was delighted to be able to join forces with such a man as the Baron. We had been living all the time in the railway coach belonging to the mission, and what with constant shunting and the disappointment at not getting the carts we needed, our nerves were pretty much on edge.

Finally, just before leaving, I met Captain Gillespie, attached to the staff of the Third Army under General Sakharov. He had arrived from the front the night before, and took me along to see the officer in charge of operations of the Army. From him I learnt that Dutov was at Kokchetav, only 180 versts to the south, thus lessening my journey by half, and also that the Orenburg Army was now included in Sakharov's command.

The two *telegas* lent to us by the Baron were quite inadequate for all our kit, so we distributed some of it on his remaining seven carts, and left behind a quantity of forage which it was impossible to carry.

Soon after two on the afternoon of the 26th of October, all was ready, and followed by the cheers of the Railway Mission we moved off. Ahead in an old troika, rode the Baron and his wife, followed by nine *telegás* drawn by wiry steppe ponies. On the carts rode two Russian officers (the Baron's staff), a dozen militiamen, our three servants and the peasant drivers. Moss and I were mounted on our Canadian horses.

It was fine to be in the saddle again, and I cantered around the little convoy, full of joy at the feel of a good horse between my knees and the prospect of adventure before me.

Turning south across the railway, we marched leisurely,

for the carts were heavily laden, and our progress was necessarily slow. The scene was peaceful enough. Peasants passed us sitting sideways on their rough *tarantass* or walking clumsily in their big boots beside the straining teams. Overhead the sun shone brightly in the frosty air, bathing the rolling steppe and its scattered clumps of trees in a flood of soft light. No rumble of distant gun fire or the sharp rat-tat-tat of a machine gun as yet disturbed the silence, but only the creak of the wheels and the drum of the horses' hoofs on the hard ground.

On we rode through the quiet afternoon into the dusk and far into the night. The Baron, who had taken the guide with him, had long since trotted ahead into the darkness, leaving Moss and myself to bring the lagging convoy on as best we could. Some of the carts were more heavily laden than others, and thus tended to string out, so we had the devil's own job keeping them together. Although there were telegraph poles along the so-called road, it was easy to lose them in the pitch dark, for the track which we followed was but a worn ribbon across the steppe, and it was easy to wander from it.

At midnight, thoroughly tired after ten hours in the saddle, we reached the tiny village of Tolmach, having covered only thirty odd versts, and there found von Tiesenhausen and his wife, nicely rested and ready for us with a glass of steaming tea and some boiled fish. The hut was too dirty for Moss and myself, so we slept outside in a *telega*.

Next morning we were up at six, and I soon found out that the Baroness, a young and reasonably attractive woman, had a bee in her bonnet. The night before, she had heard a rifle shot somewhere in the distance, and would have it that the Bolsheviks were after us. Although her belief was palpably absurd, she drove us on with undiminished energy, giving us hardly time to snatch a mouthful of bread and to change horses, until we reached Kokchetav, 150 versts away. All through the 27th we rode on, past Karatamarsky; over pleasant rolling prairie land, where clumps of birch and alder, small lakes and scattered villages relieved the monotony, and where vast herds of cattle and horses browsed contentedly in the distance; through Kamishlovsky, where we secured fresh horses for the carts and swallowed a cup of tea; to Djamantusky which we reached an hour after midnight. All that day we had ridden slowly across sixty versts of steppe, while the Baron's carriage trotted swiftly ahead, covering the distance in a quarter of the time. At each halting place, the Baroness, nicely rested and well fed, awaited us, and we had no sooner dismounted that she drove her harried husband out to supervise our immediate departure.

Bitterly I rued ever having joined these Russians, but I was helpless. I could not unload my kit in the steppe, nor could I demand my own carts, for they were the Baron's. My protests were received silently by the Baron, who shrugged his shoulders helplessly, while his good lady merely laughed at me, and drove us all before her.

At Kamishlovsky, I had set Peter Rigo to boil a stew, as I was half famished, but before it was half ready, the carts moved off, Peter, Albert and Alexei raced after them to get a seat, and I went hungry till after midnight. I was pretty tired by then, but there was to be no rest. As Moss and I entered the dirty post-house, the Baroness met us with a fresh batch of alarming tales, and urged an immediate resumption of the march. Disregarding her I glanced mournfully at the table where glasses of pale, sugarless tea and hunks of grey bread gave little promise of a hearty supper.

'All right,' I said. 'We'll go on if you want to, although it's perfectly safe here. But I'm hungry, and I want meat.'

I pronounced the word meat, very loudly and angrily. I felt like a small boy, who is sent supperless to bed.

For once the Baroness forgot her cares, but only for a moment.

'Poor Kapitan,' she cried, shrieking with laughter. 'He wants meat. Well, he shall have it, but not now. We haven't time. At the next village perhaps.'

Once more we mounted our jaded horses, and moved southwards. The troika, with its jingling bells, moved swiftly ahead, and our convoy followed at a snail's pace. The night was dark, the guide had gone ahead with the Baron, and with difficulty Moss and I kept the straggling carts together. Once we wandered off the track, completely lost on the open steppe, which was destitute of landmarks, as with the last village the trees had disappeared. Not until dawn, did we find the telegraph line again, and soon after eight reached Mizgilsky, also called Kelorovka. This was rather an interesting little place, as the inhabitants came from East Prussia, and spoke German for the most part. Their houses were better built than those in the Russian villages, the horses better cared for, and the whole aspect of the place cleaner and more prosperous looking. The starosta, or headman, was delighted at my few words of German, and did everything to help us on our way. My hopes of a rest were soon dashed, however, for although we had covered seventy-eight versts in the last twenty-four hours, and had been constantly in the saddle, that insatiable woman knew no pity.

Again we pushed on, this time with better ponies and carts. I was so exhausted that I climbed on to one of the latter and slept as best I could in uncomfortable attitudes. I little dreamt that I should spend the next seven months doing much the same thing. The ponies trudged on slowly, sometimes breaking into a shambling trot, and by dusk we drew up in the village of Alexeyevka, having covered thirty-eight versts since the morning. One hundred and sixteen versts in thirty-six hours, almost without a halt, was all I could stand for, and I refused to move a step further. Moss and I were so stiff we could scarcely move, both our horses were lame, and we had not had a square meal since leaving Petropavlovsk. The Baroness relented, and we slept like logs.

Next morning, the 29th, Moss and the Baron set off immediately after breakfast for Kokchetav, while I followed with the carts, reaching the small steppe town early in the afternoon. As we topped a rise and came down a long gentle slope, I saw before me the half-frozen waters of Lake Kopa, some three versts long by two wide. At its south-eastern end stood the wooden houses of the town, and to their south-west rose a range of steep, rugged hills, which protected the place from the fierce winter winds. By the edge of the lake, a soldier examined our papers, and we then drove through the wide streets to the office of the Town Commandant. Moss led us to our billet, where we unloaded our kit and prepared for hot baths and other luxuries. The total cost of the transport from Petropavlovsk to Kokchetav, a distance of 175 versts, amounted to 1200 Omsk roubles, or about thirty shillings. Not very expensive!

CHAPTER 11

WITH THE ORENBURG COSSACKS

KOKCHETAV was then the Headquarters of Ataman Dutov, commanding the Orenburg Army. This force had been severely defeated in August in the vicinity of Orenburg, when under General Belov.

At that time it had consisted of about 13,000 cavalry, 10,000 infantry and 65 guns. This included the 11th Siberian Division, to which I had been attached in Barnaul in the spring, but its life was of short duration, for it was disbanded shortly after its arrival at the front, those units which had not deserted to the enemy being grouped with other brigades. I have already mentioned the disastrous retreat along the Tashkent Railway and the flight to Atbasar, which lay 150 versts or so south of us.

The Army was now arriving piecemeal in the Kokchetav-Atbasar area, where it was to be reorganised, rested and re-equiped as far as possible, with a view to operating on the left of General Sakharov's Third Army which was further to the north astride the Trans-Siberian Railway.

Before leaving Omsk, I had been given a copy of the Orenburg Army's 'Order of Battle' dated 15th October, which showed a strength of 8200 cavalry, 3600 infantry, and 22 guns. Of this total of 11,800 men, fully 9300 belonged to General Bakich's Second (late Fourth) Corps, which had not taken part in the retreat along the railway, but had retired south-east through Kustanai. Only 2500 men, therefore, remained of those who had begun the retirement on Tashkent, the remnant of three Corps, whose regiments were mere skeletons of fifty or a hundred disorganised men, often without arms.

The Orenburg Army had, therefore, lost half of its effectives and two-thirds of its artillery in two months, and could not be counted on unless a thorough rest and reorganisation could be obtained.

In France, during the costly offensives which the British Army had conducted from 1915 to 1918, it was no uncommon thing for a battalion to be withdrawn from the line after having lost four-fifths of its men and all but one or two of its officers. The arrival of drafts from England, however, soon brought the regiment up to strength, a month's rest in a quiet area restored its efficiency, and the nucleus of old officers and N.C.O.'s with their fine feeling of regimental history and tradition revived its morale. No matter how great the losses, or how severe the trials recently undergone, there was always the consciousness of unlimited support in arms, men, and money, the belief in ultimate victory, and the feeling of personal superiority over the Germans.

In the case of the Orenburg Army in 1919, the losses were not as heavy as those suffered by many formations during the Great War, but the other factors which entered into the situation were far different. Only a small percentage of the casualties were caused in battle, most were due to desertion and some to sickness; there were practically no drafts to fill the ranks of depleted units; there was a great shortage in all the necessary war material, rifles, guns, ammunition, clothing, equipment, and medical supplies; there were no safe back areas for rest and reorganisation; and worst of all there was no heart in the task, no trust in one's comrades, no faith in the cause, and no hope of victory. Added to this the mass of refugees and women hangers-on, who preceded, accompanied, and followed the Army, demoralised it as no other factor could have done. Every man was out to save his own skin, or that of his mistress or his family, and no troops can fight like that.

Given a cause in which they had faith, this remnant of an army could still have played an important rôle in the coming campaign, for the Bolshevik forces were in little better shape, and a determined force of twelve thousand men acting on the enemy's right flank might have saved the day. But this was not to be.

The day after our arrival, Moss and I called on Ataman Dutov. He was a short, round little man, with soft brown eyes and hair cut *en brosse*. Like most Russians he did not shave until evening, so he had a rather unkempt appearance. Clad in a brown Russian shirt, and dark breeches with the light blue stripe of the Orenburg Cossacks, he looked anything but the beau ideal of a cavalry leader.

He welcomed us warmly, and invited us to meet him every morning at eleven, when the *communiqués* were read by the Operations Officer, Captain Troitsky, and the general situation discussed. With the Army were already two French officers, one of whom, Colonel Pichon, we met next day. He was a tall, handsome man, who wore an enormous fur cap, and told us that he had been made an honorary Cossack by one of the regiments.

The news from the main front was bad. On the 30th,

four days after we had ridden south across the steppe, Petropavlovsk was reported under the fire of the enemy's guns, and next day they entered the town. The telegraph being cut, our wires went along another line *via* Pavlodar to Omsk. Kolchak's forces continued to retire 'according to plan,' and we now found ourselves practically out of touch with his left wing, and opposite, though at some distance from the Bolshevik flank. If the main Army continued to retreat, it was difficult to foresee what would happen to us.

The main body of Dutov's force was composed of Orenburg Cossacks, and the Ataman knew only too well that the further they marched from their own country, the less reliable they would be. I believe that he expected to be left in peace by the enemy, at any rate for a time, as they would be concentrating on the capture of Omsk. Given a couple of months, he could collect his scattered troops, reorganise them, and hold the area Atbasar-Kokchetav-Akmolinsk, which as yet had been little disturbed by the war, and could provide him with food, forage, horses, felt, sheepskins, and possibly recruits. With winter coming on, he might hold out until the spring, and then march back on Orenburg with fire and sword.

Dutov, however, was under Sakharov's orders, which he resented bitterly, as he desired an independent command. On 5th November, he called Colonel Pichon and myself to his office and told us that he had been ordered to place himself on the flank of the Third Army and conform with its movements. This meant his abandoning the important Atbasar area, marching his already weary men across an almost uninhabited region, and giving up all hope of reorganising the troops. Much as he regretted disobeying orders, he informed us that he could not carry out these instructions, and asked us to use our influence with Generals Janin and Knox to have them modified. Meanwhile, he would send out a detachment to keep in touch with Sakharov, remove his H.Q. to Shchuchinskaia some sixty versts to the east, and concentrate his troops there and at Kokchetav.

Not until afterwards did I learn that his forces were far more scattered and demoralised than his Staff had led me to suppose, and that it was physically impossible for him to obey the orders he had received.

I, however, immediately drew up a report for General Knox, and entrusted it to Colonel Pichon, who was proceeding to Omsk by motor car the next day.

The von Tiesenhausens, or perhaps the Baroness alone, had decided that the situation was too precarious to remain with the Army, and already began preparations for the return to Omsk. I dined with them the night before they left. Already I was 'Sasha' to them, Sasha being the dimunitive for Alexander, one of my unused names, and already I had forgiven the Baroness for the discomforts of our recent journey. She, her black eyes sparkling and her cheeks glowing, chattered incessantly and seemed overjoyed at the thought of returning to Omsk. He, grey-haired, erect, and handsome, drank with us all in a most courtly manner, and seemed to forget that he had only just arrived with the Army as Governor of distant Orenburg. Both their thoughts were concerned with Omsk and safety, but it was already too late. The road to Omsk was cut.

On the eve of evacuating the town, the Army staff

ordered the destruction of the local vodka factory, which led to a night of debauch on the part of the town militia and some of the Cossacks. As Moss and I walked back to our billet from the operations office, the flames of the burning factory lit the sky, rifle shots rang out across the sleeping town, there were sounds of crashing doors, shouts and screams. A Cossack patrol galloped past, and drunken groups staggered through the streets roaring snatches of song. Next morning the militia was disarmed.

At the same time, news reached the Staff that an enemy force, estimated at five hundred men, had taken Mizgilski, the German village at which we had stopped a few days before, so the Bolsheviks were apparently sending a force in our direction.

As I had seen nothing of the combatant troops, there being only the Staff and a couple of hundred Cossacks in Kokchetav, I decided to send off the servants with our kit to Shchuchinskaia – whither the Army Staff was going – and remain behind with Moss for a day or two. I would then have an opportunity of seeing General Shilnikov's First Corps, which was due to arrive at any moment and take over the defence of the place.

The three servants departed at midday leaving Moss and myself with the two horses. We were therefore free to ride around as we wished, without encumbrances.

All that afternoon, long lines of carts moved eastwards, carrying stores, barrels of vodka, and many sick, principally typhus cases, and guarded by small detachments of Cossacks. Other carts carrying refugees also left the town, among the latter being many local Cossacks, who, during the last few days, had been the loudest to proclaim that the hated Bolsheviks would only enter the place over their dead bodies. Words, words, lies, false information. How sick I was of it all.

By evening the town was almost empty of troops, as most of the Staff, headquarters troops, and hospital cases had already gone, and the First Corps had not arrived. By nightfall all shutters were barred, and hardly a soul was to be seen in the streets, for the looting of the vodka factory had placed no small number of buckets of spirits in the hands of the disorderly element, and further excesses were feared. However, beyond occasional shots and the sound of drunken voices, there was no disturbance. Much vodka, luckily, paralyses the limbs, so that sustained movement is impossible.

Until midday, Moss and I waited for the expected troops, but as they did not appear, we decided to follow the Staff, especially as the market had closed and it was impossible to buy food. I was also anxious about our kit, and had just heard that Shilnikov would not arrive until the following morning.

As we saddled our horses and munched some dry bread, I overheard our landlady and an old crony of hers chattering in the next room, trying to keep up each other's spirits. Both had decided to fly to Shchuchinskaia the day before, but could not summon up sufficient courage to take the fatal step.

The old dame kept repeating, 'I'm not afraid of the Bolsheviks. Let them come, and if they try any of their dirty tricks on me – !' But her quavering voice betrayed her stout words.

Mounting our horses, we trotted through the deserted streets, waved farewell to Kokchetav, and rode into the open steppe.

CHAPTER 12

RETREAT

THERE is nothing like riding off into the open country, astride a good horse, to raise one's spirits and to forget one's cares. As we trotted gaily across the steppe, our eyes delighting in the play of sunlight and shadow on the undulating plain, and our bodies tingling with the motion and the hint of frost in the air, I was carried back to the early days of 1915, when, after two months of strenuous work in the line, I had ridden away at the head of a party of signallers for a couple of weeks' rest. My own battery had already marched, and I had been left to hand over to a relieving battery of French 75's for a day or so. Riding away across the fair fields of France at the head of my half-dozen gunners, I had felt like a knight of old, pricking forward with his clattering men-at-arms behind him.

Late at night, after riding hard for sixty-five versts, we reached Shchuchinskaia, failed to find our servants, and spent three weary hours in search of a billet. In the end the Town Commandant put us up in his quarters.

Next day, I moved to the Posthouse, where we were fairly comfortable, but no one had seen our three men, and I had a sinking feeling that they had deserted. Not until two days later did I find them, when quite by accident I ran across Albert in the street. We almost fell on each other's necks.

He had been to the Commandant's office three or four times a day to get news of me, and so had I to find out where he was, but the fools had denied all knowledge of either of us. I was ready to shoot up the place.

Telling him to bring our kit round to the Posthouse, I returned there and sat down to lunch. Moss was there and also Colonel Kortashevsky, whom I had met in Omsk, when he was attached to the British Mission. We had nearly finished when the landlord came in. He was a powerful, black-bearded Cossack, considerably the worse for drink, and he sat down opposite to us, inclined for conversation. Leaning his elbows on the table, he became rather too familiar for the Colonel, whose feelings of caste were quickly outraged.

The latter became more and more infuriated, and finally rose, pointed to the door and shouted, 'Get out of here, you – ' The man's wife came in just then to persuade him to leave, but he was obstinate, and insisted on staying where he was. Kortashevsky then really lost his temper, jumped across the room to where our two rifles were leaning against the wall, seized one and struck the Cossack a heavy blow with the butt. His wife uttered a cry, and almost immediately the room was full of drunken Cossacks headed by the inn-keeper's father, an enormous old man with white hair and beard, who seemed intent on tearing us to pieces. I hadn't felt so near to death since the war. Around us swarmed the furious mob intent on our blood, each man roaring with the full force of his powerful lungs, accusing us of intent to murder their brother, of being Bolshevik spies, and of any crime that came into their befuddled heads. Shouting and screaming, eyes glaring, and beards bristling they edged closer, each waiting for the next man to make the first rush. It was impossible to argue or explain, impossible to get out, for they were between us and the door. It was bedlam let loose, above which rose the wails of the woman, who sat, apron over her head, rocking to and fro in an ecstasy of fear.

We stood white-faced and watchful, and I think it was that that saved us – our standing perfectly still and showing no fear, but it was touch and go for a few minutes. To me it seemed an hour.

Suddenly, half a dozen militiamen burst into the room, having heard the fracas from outside, and in a moment it was cleared. Kortashevsky certainly knew my opinion of him before another five minutes had passed.

News from Omsk was bad. General Dietrichs had been relieved of the chief command, and was now at Novo Nikolaevsk forming an Army Reserve. Sakharov had replaced him, with the Cossack General Ivanov-Rinov as Chief of Staff. Belov, lately in command of the Orenburg Army, was in charge of the evacuation of Omsk. This last piece of news staggered me.

We had left Omsk on 20th October, passed through Petropavlovsk, and reached Kokchetav on the 29th. It was now 8th November. Petropavlovsk had been taken by the enemy on the 1st, and here was the capital of Siberia one hundred and fifty odd miles to the east being evacuated as if it were the most natural thing in the world. No word of defence, or even of a serious attempt to delay the enemy! Meanwhile Dutov had had his wish, and was now independent, but his troubles were just beginning, for there were indications that the Bolsheviks had no intention of leaving him in peace.

Our friends, the von Tiesenhausens, had reached Shchuchinskaia safely before us, but the Baroness had been afraid to try and reach Omsk, so they were heading for Akmolinsk further to the south. After saying good-bye to them once more, I returned to the Posthouse and supped with Kortashevsky, who proceeded to give me a perfect example of the average Russian officer's point of view.

He complained in a pained voice that the Bolsheviks were conscripting and arming peasants, and sending them straight into action without any training at all. It seemed to him most unsportsmanlike, but it apparently did not occur to him that to retire hastily, without firing a shot, before an undisciplined mob of unwilling conscripts was the most damning proof of his own side's cowardice and incompetence. I felt like advising him and his companions for the sake of their own honour, to draw their oft-rattled sabres and commit *hara-kiri* on the spot.

It was too discouraging to think of England pouring out arms and money to these men, who did nothing but boast loudly until an enemy was heard of fifty versts away, and then retire hurriedly in the opposite direction. Here was this Army Staff, large enough for a force ten times its size, issuing lying *communiqués*, talking grandly in terms of brigades, divisions, counter-attacks, and retirements according to plan, and doing nothing to make the Army a fighting force. I was just beginning to realise that Dutov had no intention of fighting, and had it not been for the novelty of the experience, I would have wired Omsk for permission to return.

The Orenburg Army, I began to see, was but a small example of the majority of Kolchak's troops. The incompetence and arrogance of the Staff was amazing. I remember General Knox telling me that a certain Russian general had demanded that clothing, arms, and equipment for six hundred thousand men must be supplied immediately by the British Government, when Kolchak had not been able to use what we had already sent out, and had not one hundred thousand men under his command.

When paying a visit to the Staff Commandant, one Colonel Shaposhnikov, I met an old friend, Colonel Snegodsky, who had been in command of the 11th Siberian Artillery Division at Barnaul. His appearance shocked me. His cheeks were sunken, his eyes had a hunted look, and a straggling beard streaked with grey hung down over a tattered sheepskin coat. We were delighted to see each other and I dragged him off to our billet to dine and spend the night with us.

Next day the remnants of his four batteries arrived, now known as the 1st Turkestan Artillery Division! Two mud-splashed 15-prs., and two 5-inch howitzers were all that were left, together with about eight rounds of ammunition per gun. I was fond of guns, and felt a twinge of remorse, as if the Regiment had sold into degrading slavery these four dumb, trusty servants, who once upon a time had been the pride of limber gunners in spotless British gun parks. Perhaps they had seen action at Spion Kop, Ladysmith, or the Modder River, but their days were almost numbered. Their once bright breech blocks and spotless bores would soon be rusting, forgotten and forlorn, somewhere on the Kirghiz steppe. Here was justified, perhaps, our proud *Ubique*, but not the motto *Quo fas et gloria ducunt*.

Among the handful of men that still remained were

most of those that had been in my demonstration section, and our meeting was mutually joyful. Poor devils, they stood shivering in their ragged khaki, their broad peasant faces creased with smiles, and I could scarcely answer them. My heart was really full, for these men deserved a better fate than to serve such worthless leaders.

Colonel Snegodsky, the battery commander, one Captain Polonsky, and a couple of other officers known to me came to dine, and throughout the night I listened to tales of cowardice, jealousy, incompetence, and despair. Their bitterness was terrible, and their hatred of the Cossacks intense. I heard of the disastrous campaign, the retreat along the Tashkent Railway, the flight over the Hungry Steppe. They told of the apathy of the Cossacks, and how once Captain Cook had driven a troop of them into action with the flat of his sword. Came tales of intrigues and jealousies among the Staff and higher officers, of the preferential treatment shown to the Cossacks, and of all the hopeless mismanagement, cowardice, and treachery of the campaign. Although it was already mid-November, their men had been refused winter clothing, in spite of the fact that it was available and the Cossacks had received their share. Even the vodka ration had been refused in Kokchetav, while the Staff carried off great drums of it.

Knowing these men, and believing them to be above the average, I think that most of what they said was true, and it was as damning an indictment as one could find against the Russian leaders.

These men were worn out, dispirited, enraged at the treatment they had received, but helpless, borne along in the irresistible current of disaster, unable to stem the tide, unable even to desert, for they would have been shot by the Bolsheviks. And so they existed from day to day, not knowing what fate held in store, sometimes hoping for some miracle to save them, but more often fatalistically bowing to the inevitable.

Meanwhile, the news from Omsk sounded a little more comforting. The city was not to be abandoned at once, for the First Army was to be withdrawn east of the town to reorganise, while the Second and Third retired slowly for two or three weeks and then give battle west of the Irtish. I was told that the Red troops had been offered six months' pay if they took the city. This sounded very much like a capitalistic bribe, and I suggested that our side double the amount if they kept off. Roubles were easily printed, and a few million here or there wouldn't make much difference.

As regards our own Army, I now learnt that the troops were by no means in their allotted areas as I had been led to believe a week before. In fact Bakich's Second Corps, which included nearly three-quarters of the Army, had not yet assembled in Atbasar, and still had 180 versts to march across country before it could reach us. Meanwhile, the weak First Corps and Stepanov's Cossacks, (who had yet to reach Kokchetav) was the only force with which to oppose the Bolsheviks. At the most two thousand men.

The Staff, apparently, felt much too near the 'front,' so a new disposition of forces was decided on. The Army Staff was to leave immediately for Akmolinsk, 210 versts further south, leaving the defence of Kokchetav and Shchuchinskaia to the First Corps and Stepanov, while Bakich remained in Atbasar. By this arrangement, Army

H.Q. would be over 200 versts from the First Corps and more from the Second, the two corps would be 180 versts apart, and the First Corps and Stepanov's Cossacks would be split up, with 65 versts between the two halves. This with the enemy's advance guard reported not more than 40 versts from Kokchetav! A truly brilliant piece of staff work.

Five hundred of the enemy had been reported – not seen, mind you, by any responsible officer – but do you think any effort was made to find out their real strength or intentions? Not a bit of it. But the Staff retired another two hundred versts. That's why I have to laugh sometimes, when the Bolsheviks talk of their hard-won victories during the Civil War.

That there were thousands of brave Russians on both sides, I am the first to admit. I have met many and some are my friends, but that does not alter the fact that the White troops were badly led and there were far too many officers behind the lines. Serious fighting in our sense of the word was unknown, except perhaps in very isolated cases, and I would be wrong if I pretended that the conduct of these particular operations were anything but disgraceful. I have seen something of war, and I know what a handful of Czechs could do in Siberia against tremendous odds. It was not numbers that the Whites lacked, but leaders and fighting men.

We were to leave for the south on the 11th, and as it was too cold to think of riding those two hundred versts to Akmolinsk, I started out in search of transport. Luckily, the Staff Commandant, Colonel Shaposhnikov, who was a genial and kind-hearted soul, invited Moss and myself to travel with him, which we accepted gladly, as he was all-powerful as regards the supply of horses and carts, and we could not have had a better companion.

Accordingly, we packed our valises once more, said farewell to our now repentant and grovelling landlord, and set our faces to the south.

CHAPTER 13

RETREAT (*continued*)

THAT week-long journey from Shchuchinskaia to Akmolinsk, although sadly lacking in spectacular events, was perhaps the most interesting I had yet spent in Siberia. For the first time I really lived with the Russians, drove with them by day, ate with them, slept beside them, and talked for long hours with them. For the first time, I came in close contact with the sullen peasants, slept in their houses, ate their food, and heard something of their simple views.

My previous contacts had always been momentary, fleeting, broken by a return to the British Mission or to my own Mess each night, but now, as we travelled leisurely across the steppe I lived their life, withdrawn from all contact with the outer world, and came perhaps to a better understanding of them than I had done in all the previous months.

Educated in a great public school and at the Royal Military Academy, Woolwich, brought up with very definite ideas as to what is 'done' or 'not done,' and used to the high standard of discipline and morale of the British Army, it was hard for me to forgive the Russians many things. Their unpunctuality, lack of personal cleanliness, uncouth table manners, boastfulness, incompetence, and apparent cowardice had often disgusted me.

My intolerance was greater than it is now, for I was only twenty-five, and there were many things hidden from me at that time that I see now. All these faults the majority of them had, and often acknowledged, but I do not mean to brand them with the stigma of personal cowardice. Many of them were brave enough, but collectively they acted like a flock of frightened sheep, were too easily depressed, and seemed incapable of sustained or intelligent work.

My companions were typical Russian officers of the period. Colonel S., dark, jovial, easy-going, proud of being a Cossack and melancholy when in his cups. He had an endless supply of stories dealing with his own amorous adventures, and was cynically humorous on the fighting qualities of the troops. Captain B., and Lieutenant G., similar in many ways, ignorant, superstitious, credulous, easily depressed or elated, frankly disinclined to do any fighting. All three were almost destitute, for their small pay was worth but little, and they had almost nothing in the way of clothing except what they stood up in.

While they often let me pay for what we had to eat or drink, they never tried to borrow money or asked for clothes or other articles, which I might have been able to spare. I'm glad they didn't, because at a later date we needed everything we had.

Moss, who was two or three years my junior, was a stout-hearted fellow, and of tremendous help to me. Although I had made great strides in the language in my seven odd months in the country, and could understand practically everything that was said, I spoke badly, and would have been in a much worse position without Moss.

He was a big, fair-haired youth, who had played soccer for Petrograd at one time, and on his broad shoulders rested most of the dirty work of the Mission, and in addition he put up with my impatience and anger at the situation with imperturbable good-humour. He must have found me trying at times, but his slow smile and amusing remarks on the situation often restored me to a more normal frame of mind.

It was very cold, and I was glad not to have attempted the journey on horseback. Each day our programme was much the same. Our servants with the kit and horses set out early in a couple of heavy carts, while we followed later in a troika and a *telega* drawn by Colonel Shaposhnikov's own fine horses. We were seldom more than six or seven hours on the road and usually less.

On our arrival at a village, the local Commandant would allot us billets, sometimes already crowded, in a peasant's hut. Usually the hut contained only one or two rooms, so that Moss and I washed and shaved under the ever-astonished eyes of our companions and the curious stare of the peasant's family who never ceased to wonder at the trouble we took to shave and wash each day. Feeling almost clean, we would sit down to a meal of kasha, boiled lake fish (mostly bones), *pilmenie* (mince meat wrapped in dough and dropped into boiling water), grey bread, and weak sugarless tea. All evening the Russians, after a very perfunctory wash, would sit talking, cracking sunflower seeds between their teeth, and spitting the husks all over the room. In one corner the peasant and his entire family slept fully clothed upon the great earthen stove, their unwashed bodies giving off a none too pleasant odour.

IN THE CENTRE, ALEXEI AND ALBERT

The Retreat to Akmolinsk, November 1919

Facing p. 1..

Our companions never ceased to marvel at our clothing, arms, and equipment, and to ask endless questions about England and her part in the war. Till then they had no idea that we had made any serious effort, for German propaganda had cleverly worked upon them, until they believed that Russia alone was bearing the whole burden of the war. When we told them of the battles on the western front, of the number of enemy Divisions employed there, and of our campaigns in Mesopotamia, Palestine, and Macedonia, they could scarcely believe their ears. Nor could they understand how the invincible Germans had been beaten, after the withdrawal of Russia in 1917.

Their attitude towards Germany was surprising. German efficiency, industry, and power had so impressed them before the war, that, according to Shaposhnikov and his two companions, the majority of Russian officers went to the front with no hope of victory. He told us that on one occasion, so great was their awe of the enemy, when his regiment had taken two or three German officers prisoner, the latter refused to march back under guard, but demanded horses. Several Russian cavalrymen were then ordered to dismount, and the Germans rode off haughtily surveying their escort, which plodded through the mud on foot.

One evening, Shaposhnikov called in three of his Cossacks, and they entertained us for two or three hours with their sad, wild songs. One of them, a weather-beaten black-bearded giant whose natural voice was bass, sang the high tenor parts until I thought the veins in his forehead would burst, as the tears streamed from his eyes and his face grew scarlet with exertion. After each song, the Colonel gave each a glass of vodka, but before drinking they swallowed a piece of bread, crossed themselves, and bowed low to the gilded ikon in the corner. When I fell asleep, one of the singers and Shaposhnikov, with arms about each other's neck, were crooning drunkenly and weeping maudlin tears.

For about half the journey the country was fairly hilly, dotted here and there with copses of poor-looking fir, and brackish lakes. The villages were thirty to forty versts apart – Makinskaia, where we lodged with the local priest; and Elizabetskaia. All fair-sized, each built beside a lake, which supplied water and a quantity of bony tasteless fish. The last hundred versts the country was flatter, trees gradually disappeared, and we journeyed silently, heads bent against the icy wind. One day, a fine driving snow blew steadily in our faces, sifting through every opening in our sheepskin coats, and freezing our eyelashes together, so that we must stop frequently to thaw our eyes open again.

As we approached Akmolinsk, the barren steppe stretched in all directions, covered with a light blanket of snow which swirled and eddied, half obliterating the road we followed. The scene was bleak and desolate in the extreme. Nothing but grey sky, iron-bound earth, dead grass and the howling of the wind. Only once did we pass a human being, when from out the falling snow appeared a dejected-looking horseman on a diminutive pony. Behind him paced a string of melancholy camels, each with a wooden plug through the nose, roped to the beast in front. Their mangy, shaggy coats were stiff with ice, and here and there a frozen, scarlet muzzle showed, where a nose-pin had torn the flesh. Supercilious even in their misery, they paced slowly on and disappeared.

Early on the afternoon of the 17th, Akmolinsk appeared in the distance, a grey treeless town, standing unprotected on the open steppe. However, it meant houses, warmth, and a bed of sorts, and, we hoped, a long rest until fighting commenced again in the spring.

CHAPTER 14

AKMOLINSK

Akmolinsk was a typical overgrown Siberian settlement, containing a few brick buildings in addition to the usual one-storey wooden houses of the Russian colonists and Cossacks, and standing unprotected from the fierce winter storms, or burans, which rage in this part of the country. Having secured a comfortable billet, Moss and I repaired to the operations office to see Captain Troitsky of the Army Staff to get the latest news. To our consternation, Omsk had fallen on the 13th of November, four days after it had been announced that Kolchak's main forces would retire slowly from Petropavlovsk and then offer battle west of the town about the first week in December. I shuddered at the scenes of horror which must have taken place during the evacuation, and hoped that none of the British Mission had been captured or killed. Later I heard that several had been taken and sent to Moscow, but as far as I know none lost their lives.

Kokchetav had fallen two days before, on the 15th. It was reported that General Shilnikov had retired without fighting, saying it was too cold to defend the town! To offset the depressing effect of this news, the Staff issued communiqués with the usual claptrap about the low morale of the Reds, their lack of winter clothing, rumours of anti-Bolshevik risings in Samara, Orenburg, and other cities, and the receipt of a mutilated radio from Denikin in South Russia announcing the fall of Moscow. We saw Dutov later in the day, but got nothing out of him except that he expected to remain where he was for some time and rest his troops. In case of further retreat he depended on joining forces with the Second Steppe Corps of fifteen thousand men at Semipalatinsk, an important town on the upper Irtish, connected by rail with the main Trans-Siberian line by the branch running south from Novo Nikolaevsk through Barnaul. In Semiryechie, south of Semipalatinsk, at about the same distance from us, that is, seven to eight hundred versts, was a force under Ataman Annenkov reported to be nine thousand strong. These two formations secured Dutov from any immediate anxiety as to his line of retreat, but he seemed confident that he would be able to maintain his present position for some months.

Our billet was on the southern outskirts of the town, and consisted of a fairly comfortable one-storey house with the usual yard and outhouses. The landlord was an old colonist, who could remember the days not so long ago when a fort stood on the site of the house, and the first man to build a hut outside the walls had been considered mad. In those days the Kirghiz tribes had not been subdued and frequently attacked the Russian colonies and Cossack stanitsas, carrying off prisoners and cattle whenever they could cut them off outside the stockade which surrounded every settlement, fort or cluster of huts. I shall have more to say of the Kirghiz later on, when I travelled among them, and learnt something of their language and customs.

It is interesting to note that one of the most tragic

events in history occurred not far from Akmolinsk. Those who have read De Quincey's *Flight of a Tatar Tribe* will remember it. The story is this. A Mongol clan, the Turguts, who had settled on the banks of the Volga, heard of the new era of peace and prosperity in China under Ch'ien Lung, and being harrassed by local raids and extortions, the tribe decided to return secretly to their ancient lands. In January 1771 they set out, a vast multitude of three hundred thousand souls, and were immediately pursued by the Cossacks who attacked and butchered them ceaselessly for eight months! Tortured by thirst, harried and worn they struggled on, strengthened by the news that Ch'ien Lung's cavalry was coming to their aid. Pushing on across the Hungry Steppe, they were again attacked by Bashkirs and Kirghiz. Pursuers and pursued almost dying of thirst they came at last to Lake Tengis or Tengris, S.W. of Akmolinsk where both, mingling in one great body rushed to the water, which was soon dyed with their blood. When the Turguts had almost given up hope, down swooped the Chinese cavalry and slaughtered the Bashkirs. Only a fragment of the original Turgut tribe reached the promised land.

On the 18th, we saw Dutov as usual in the morning, but there was little news, except that the Bolsheviks were already twenty-five versts east of Omsk, and that our connecting link with Kolchak's main forces, a small detachment known as the Steppe Group was 'somewhere' on the Irtish. A visit to our good friend Colonel Shaposhnikov brought us the unofficial news that Dutov had no intention of staying where he was, but was planning to retreat still further in a few days. This depressing information was forgotten on receipt of two slightly overdue telegrams from Omsk. One from the British Mission, and the second from General Burlin, Chief of Staff of the main armies, both dated more than two weeks earlier, ordered Moss and myself to return to the Mission with all possible speed. This was bad news for both of us, for in spite of the retreat and the doubtful chances of success, we were enjoying life to the full, and had no desire just yet: rejoin our companions and return to England.

However, orders had to be obeyed and we began to make preparations for our journey. Not only were we absolutely ignorant of the country to be traversed, but no one else seemed to have any very definite information. There were, apparently, two ways of reaching Semipalatinsk, whence we could proceed by rail to Novo Nikolaevsk, where the British Mission was supposed to be. One, almost due east for about five hundred versts to Pavlodar on the Irtish, and thence south-eastwards along the river for over three hundred versts to the railway, and the other, south-eastwards to Karkaralinsk, and then north-eastwards to Semipalatinsk, the total distance being over eight hundred versts. As far as travelling was concerned there was little to choose between the two, except that in the first case the second half of the journey would be easier, and in the second case the first half would be. With the military and political situation as it was, the Pavlodar route was very dangerous, as it was likely that the Bolsheviks would descend the Irtish and reach the town before we did, and we should then have found ourselves in a wild, desolate and practically uninhabited country, with winter already freezing everything it touched, and with the prospect of encountering fierce blizzards, which would have left us stiff and cold upon the steppe for ever.

The road to Karkaralinsk was safer both from Bolshevik and weather, and once arrived there we might find means to reach Semipalatinsk without any trouble. Meanwhile, special letters and passports to help us on the way had to be obtained from Dutov, money drawn from the Intendant's office, extra winter clothing purchased for all of us, and horses and carts arranged for the transport of ourselves and kit. Our journey was going to be long and difficult and I was determined to make preparations against every eventuality, and not to rush off in a hurry without having everything we required, although it was necessary to make as much speed as possible. Reluctantly I decided that our two Canadian chargers could not be taken with us, as we would travel as rapidly as changing horses would permit, and they could not have kept up. I, therefore, made a present of them to the Ataman, who was delighted with the horses and also the two sets of saddlery.

The next few days were very busy ones, and I shall describe them as the events occurred which led to our hurried departure.

On the day we received orders to rejoin the Mission, I met Captain de Kerangat, an officer of the French Mission, who had been with the Army since the late spring, and was now in Akmolinsk with two French Colonial soldiers, an interpreter, and a Cadillac car. He was a man in his early thirties, small, and active, with a handsome clean-shaven face and large nose, who had had the misfortune to be captured by the Germans early in 1914. He had spent over four years in prison camps, often in solitary confinement for attempts to escape, and was now seeking some of the glory he had missed during the battles on the western front. We had him to dine that night, produced some of our mess claret, and spent an amusing evening, for his experiences with the Army were worth listening to.

That day I had also been shown the strength of Bakich's Second Corps which was as follows:

Bayonets . . .	1043	Machine guns .	93
Sabres . . .	2480		
Soldiers without arms .	1379	3-in. guns . .	13
Recruits without arms.	2000		
Regular officers . .	23		
Temporary officers .	290		
	7215		

This remarkable admission that half the corps was without arms was almost unbelievable as at that time most of the peasants and the local militias were armed with rifles, or had them hidden away, and a vigorous search in Atbasar and the surrounding villages should have resulted in the rearming of all the troops. It was a lamentable admission of demoralisation and lack of effort on the part of the Staff.

Next day news was received that the Reds were advancing slowly on Shchuchinskaia, and that a small body of 250 men had taken a village eighty versts south-west of Kokchetav, and just off the main road from that town to Atbasar, where Bakich's Corps were supposed to be concentrating. A great deal of the intelligence received by the Staff was from Kirghiz, who rode about the country by little-known paths, and were said to do as much as one hundred versts a day on their wiry little ponies. Their information was quite reliable and they worked willingly for small presents of sugar and tobacco, if well treated.

Our friends, the von Tiesenhausens, being in town and preparing for another journey, I asked them, Colonel Shaposhnikov, and two other Russians to dine, and managed to procure the only band in the Army to play for us during and after the meal. There was nowhere else for the musicians except in the room where we dined, and as most of the instruments were of brass the noise was deafening. However, every one seemed to enjoy it, and even the landlady rose from her bed, put on a skirt and came down to beam on the company and get closer to the music. The dinner was a great success, every one got comfortably tight and went home swearing eternal love for England, that is, every one except the bandmaster, who, in one of the intervals, had discovered our bottle of chutney in the kitchen, swallowed its entire contents and became deathly ill soon after!

On the 21st, Dutov held a parade of the Atamansky Regiment, Convoy Sotnia, and a newly-raised company of Religious Volunteers of the 'White Cross and Green Banner.' The banner, of green silk fringed with gold, had been made by the ladies of the Army, and was presented to the Volunteers with due ceremony, after which a service was held in the Cathedral where they took the oath to defend the town to the last man against the Bolsheviks.

Meanwhile orders were issued to the First Corps to retire southwards and halt about eighty versts north of Akmolinsk, while Bakich was ordered to a village some 150 versts west of us. Stepanov's Cossacks were to fill in the space between the two corps. It was reported, however, that on the evening of the 19th, the enemy force which had already advanced south-west from Kokchetav had suddenly seized the village of Vladimirskaia on the main Atbasar road, this cutting Bakich's Corps in two. This looked serious because if this Corps didn't fight any better than the First Corps under Shilnikov we should soon be on the run.

We called on Dutov that evening and he promised to give us a letter to the Cossack Ataman at Karkaralinsk, (said to be the birthplace of the famous General Kornilov) asking the latter to provide guides and transport on our further journey to Semipalatinsk. We heard that the French Mission was also leaving shortly to rejoin their Headquarters.

On the 22nd, we learnt that the Reds had taken the village of Vasilevskoe, north-east of Atbasar, and were advancing south-east so as to cut off Bakich from us, but Captain Troitsky apparently did not believe this, as the Staff remained unperturbed.

Next morning, Moss and I went to the Operations Office as usual, but could get no news, although every one looked very worried. We then went to the Intendant's Office, borrowed 10,000 roubles for the expenses of our journey, and continued our attempt to secure warm clothing, which was very difficult to obtain. While returning to my billet, I was accosted in English by a Mr. Riabzov, a Russian, who told me that he was the Manager of the Spassky Copper Mine, some 230 versts south of Akmolinsk, where two English engineers, Smith and Morgan, were still working. In view of the situation I immediately telegraphed them to meet me at Karkaralinsk. Mr. Riabzov was on his way to the mine and would confirm my wire. At 3 p.m. General Zaitsev, Chief of Staff, called us to his office, and advised us to leave the town as soon as possible, giving as excuse that Dutov had been ordered to join the Second Steppe Corps at Semipalatinsk, whither Annenkov was also to move from further south. We expressed our willingness to go, but told him we had no carts, horses, sufficient winter clothing, or passports, and he promised to help us as much as possible to obtain what we required. At six, a Staff Colonel came to our billet with the passports and told us that the situation was extremely critical. The Red force had cut the road to Atbasar about one hundred versts from us, Bakich's whereabouts were unknown, and his Corps was reported to have almost ceased to exist through desertion and the murder of its officers. I was too disillusioned already to be much surprised, but this sudden elimination of our main force from the picture was rather a shock. Nothing now remained between us and the enemy on the west except Dutov's own Atamansky Regiment, the Convoy Sotnia, and the Religious Volunteers.

We dined that night with Captain de Kerangat, decided we could not leave before the 25th, as we were not ready, and went on to a Concert Ball, given to raise funds for the Religious Volunteers, where we had supper with General and Mrs. Zaitsev, Baron von Tiesenhausen and his lady, and a Russian engineer with his wife, a singer of really great beauty, both as regards voice and form. We were to see more of these people later on. The concert was the usual drunken affair, and Moss and I excited a great deal of interest, especially as several of my Barnaul friends were there and kept introducing us as very fine fellows to every one who would listen to them. Most of them were leaving at once for Semipalatinsk, as they were 'surplus to their regimental establishment'! By this time I was so disgusted with the conduct of most of the Russian officers that it was difficult for me to speak to any of them with any semblance of politeness or consideration, and this drunken concert, taking place as it did when every available man should have been under arms preparing for battle, almost destroyed the last vestiges of sympathy, which I felt for some of the more helpless and unfortunate of the men and women.

On the 24th there was still no news of Bakich, but reports came in from the First Corps and Stepanov, showing that they were retiring rapidly on Akmolinsk, Shchuchinskaia having been evacuated on the 21st. News was also received of a Red force moving down the Irtish towards Semipalatinsk, so things did not look too promising. The von Tisenhausens went off in the afternoon, and I had a note from Mr. Riabzov saying he was ill and could not leave Spassky. I therefore asked him to send a messenger to the English engineers confirming my wire. Also the Staff promised us four carts for the next morning, so we were all ready to move.

After dinner, I went to see Colonel Shaposhnikov, and found every one in a state of panic. One of his officers had come in and said that orders had been issued for the town to be evacuated by midnight. To confirm this the Colonel sent him back to the Operations Office with some other officers, and they soon returned saying that every one must be away by dawn at latest. If we had stayed in our billet we should have received no inkling of this, and I was furious for not having been warned. We left the Colonel's, set off to see Captain Troitsky, and on the way ran into a Russian friend on the Staff, who advised us to clear out at once, and if we couldn't get carts or horses, we must go on foot! Hearing that Dutov had just entered his office, I went in and asked him if there was any truth in the rumours that the town was to be evacuated at once, and if so, why I had not been informed. He replied that he had no intention of leaving the town for at least two days, that the reports of evacuation were untrue, and that I should know better than to listen to idle gossip. This made me angry as I knew he was lying, though why he should have done so at that critical time I don't know. Furious at Dutov's snub, I returned to Shaposhnikov's billet where I told him what had occurred, but he laughed and said that the Ataman would not stay in the town for twelve hours. All the Russian officers then returned to their vodka and the retailing of the latest alarmist rumours, but I had had enough of them for one night, and pleading a headache returned to my quarters with Moss.

As we had no means of transport, we retired to bed and were aroused at 4 a.m. by an officer from Dutov, who had brought us two miserable little carts. I pointed out that two carts were worse than useless and so we went back to sleep again! About seven, one of Colonel Shaposhnikov's officers arrived with three *telegas* and the information that at 2 a.m. the Bolsheviks had taken a village only thirty versts away on the Atbasar road. He advised us to leave at once, as every moment of delay meant certain capture and probably a painful death!

We breakfasted, loaded our kit, and after waiting for

half an hour for one of the drivers, who had disappeared, we set out with four carts, Moss driving the one in which he and I sat, and one of the servants sitting in each of the others.

That evening a weak body of Reds, riding on *telegas*, drove slowly into the market square, and proceeded to billet themselves on the town, without a shot being fired. Where were the noble volunteers of the White Cross and Green Banner, who had sworn so solemnly to defend the town to the last, and had been presented with the silken, gold-fringed banner in token of their high intent? Probably in their homes preparing welcoming speeches to the commissars, or already in full flight many versts to the south, seeking safety in the scattered settlements of the Kirghiz steppe.

CHAPTER 15

FLIGHT

THE few streets to the edge of the town were deserted, and the shutters and doors of every house shut and barred. No movement, except for a few hurrying *telegas* and an occasional Cossack, could be seen, but on emerging from the town a strange sight met our eyes. In the brilliant sunlight of the clear November morning, the steppe to the south appeared alive with slowly moving lines of vehicles of all descriptions. Standing out against the dazzling whiteness of the snow, an army of sleighs, *telegas*, *tarantass*, Red Cross carts, large farm wagons, and light travelling carriages covered the plain as far as the eye could see, spreading out on both sides of the road for two hundred yards or more, and moving at varying speeds according to the heaviness of the load and the quality of the horses. We were astounded at the number of refugees who must have been living in Akmolinsk for some time before our arrival there, and who had not shown themselves often in public. Here were literally thousands of people of all classes plunging blindly into the inhospitable steppe, with no conception of the difficulties and dangers that lay before them. Fearing the Bolsheviks as they did, and some with reason, perhaps, their only hope of safety lay in keeping the Army between them and the enemy. This time the Army was almost non-existent, and the suddeness of the catastrophe saw this great number of men and women break cover almost at the same hour, and head for the south.

Having four lightly-laden carts, as most of our stores had been consumed by now, we pushed on at a steady trot when the going permitted, and gradually gained on the majority, which were piled high with personal belongings, military stores, sick or other human cargo. Men, women, and children stared at us silently as we went slowly by, and I was told afterwards that they were surprised at our lack of warm clothing, and thought we should suffer severely from the cold. The truth was that I had not been able to get very much, and what I did get, went to the servants, who were worse off than we were. I had purchased several yards of felt, however, and this kept us fairly warm in the carts.

The steppe was covered with a thin layer of dry snow, scarcely enough to bear a sleigh, and stretched away on either hand in long undulating waves like those of the sea, broken here and there on the south-west by frozen marsh land and the steep banks of a water-course. Our first stop was at the little village of Alexandrovsky, about thirty versts from Akmolinsk. It was crowded with carts of all kinds, every available hut was filled to overflowing, and so, realising that it would be impossible to obtain shelter or change horses, I rested ours, managed to get some hot tea, and then pushed on another forty versts to a fair-sized village called Borisovsky, which was reached long after dark.

Shaposhnikov had asked us to meet him there, but in the confusion he could not be found and we finally managed to crawl into a small room with Captain de

Kerangat, his interpreter, Colonel Kirchman (Inspector of Artillery), several other officers, and a peasant ill with typhus.

Next morning only two small sleighs were available, so we kept two of our carts of the previous day (one of the drivers, a boy, cried all the way at being taken so far from home), and pushed on slowly as there was but little snow, reaching Donetsky (thirty versts) just before dark. Here we met Shaposhnikov and had something to eat, but I decided not to lose time by halting for the night, as it was important to get ahead of the main body of the Army and refugees, or we should be unable to secure changes of horses, and be delayed at every turn. Having obtained fresh carts and animals I set out again and did eighteen versts in the dark, reaching a small place called Akserovka about 10 p.m., where with the greatest difficulty we found sleeping space in a room already containing thirty people. Next day, we started off early, but our leading driver took us the wrong road, and after covering twenty-seven versts we reached a small village of about fifty houses, where the headman or starosta, was unable to read our passports, and was so slow at getting fresh horses, that we had to spend the night there. Again the only room available was full to overflowing, over two dozen people being crowded together in a small space, eating, drinking, sleeping, and stumbling over one another. While I was making myself as comfortable as possible on the floor near the stove, two little girls of about seven and ten years of age, refugees from Orenburg, sat and watched my every movement with an unblinking stare of fascinated interest. Poor little devils, I often wonder what their fate was.

Next day, the 28th of November, we left early and

pushed on, crossing the main road and covering the fifteen versts to Shokai, a village of a couple of hundred houses inhabited by colonists from Esthonia, who spoke little or no Russian. Our billet was clean and we had our first wash, shave, and decent meal since leaving Akmolinsk three days before. Fresh horses were again available and soon after midday we were once more on the road, feeling much refreshed. After leaving the village, we crossed a frozen stream, turned eastwards and eventually gained the post road. There was more snow here, and several sleighs passed us going at a much better pace than we were. The weather had been rather misty and now became still more so, and Moss and I in the leading cart had gone ahead faster than the rest of the party, when suddenly we saw some sleighs returning at full gallop towards us. As they passed, the people shouted and waved their arms at us, but their words were lost in the noise of the runners and the pounding of the horses' hoofs, and they quickly vanished around a bend in the road. Hoping that nothing was wrong in front, we continued on our way, when close at hand a number of horsemen appeared in the mist galloping towards us at full speed, and we reached for our arms, with every intention of defending our lives dearly, if these were Red Cavalry or mutineers. Just as I was about to haul out my revolver, the leader raised his arm in salute and we recognised some men of the Convoy Sotnia who had lost their way and had, by approaching the first party they saw, frightened it into headlong flight! I was distinctly relieved that no glorious fight to the death was needed that day, as I did not want to die in the least, and certainly not in that desolate country.

Colonel Shaposhnikov now overtook us, and together we reached Sergiopolsky, sometimes called Doshai (thirty versts), and were billeted with General Kornauhov, who had been commanding a detachment of Cossacks when the Bolsheviks crossed the Kokchetav-Atbasar road, and cut the Second Corps in two. He told us that, forced to retreat, he had somehow become separated from his command and alone reached a village and found lodging for the night. In the small hours of the morning, he awoke to find a Red soldier on each side of his bed. One of them handed him a letter, which proved to be from an old friend of his, Prince Havansky, now in command of the Red forces opposed to him, thanking the General for his abandoned kit and stores and offering him the command of a Red brigade! General Kornauhov declined, and managed to make his escape. He also told us that 250 Bolsheviks on carts had entered Akmolinsk on the evening of the 25th, the day we had escaped from the town.

The last two days had been better for sleighs than wheeled carts, so we obtained four of the former from the Commandant and set out for our next stopping-place, a little village thirty-eight versts away, called Sanikovsky. One of the worst features of this kind of travelling was the discomfort caused by the lack of room and the absence of any back-rest. Some of the carts would have a side rail of sorts, but on the majority one sat sideways with legs swinging just clear of the ground, and balanced precariously on a valise or box of stores. Sometimes, when the cart was narrow enough, Moss and I would sit back to back and feel more comfortable, but on the sleighs matters were much worse. As they consisted of two rough wooden runners about eight inches high, joined together at the top by about one-inch planking, one could not dangle one's legs over the side and had to sit cross-legged for hours, with aching back and benumbed feet. Our kit was placed flat on the sleigh, and then covered with a wide strip of felt, on which we sat. Wrapped in as many coats as I could put on, I felt like a fat, rather sulky Buddha, who has difficulty in getting his legs under him, on account of an over-developed paunch. This uncomfortable position, the bitter cold, and the monotony of the treeless, slightly rolling country, made our hours on the road hard to bear without a good deal of grumbling. Our arrival in Sanikovsky, however, was gladdened by the sight of our old friends, the von Tiesenhausens, who were driving in a sleigh along the one street of the village. Theirs had a box for the driver and a seat for themselves behind, which caused us great envy, and both the Baron and his wife looked so cheerful and bright that I asked them if they had had good news. Their rosy shining faces beamed at me, and they said perfectly seriously, 'Oh, no! We've just had a bath together in the village bath-house!'

We dined with them, and they did us very well, excellent vodka included. As usual he was full of wild schemes, and had decided not to go to Karkaralinsk, but to cut straight across country to Semipalatinsk, as he had managed to hire a Kirghiz guide and half a dozen others as an escort. He wanted us to join him and was very pressing, but as we had told the two English mining engineers to meet us at the former place, we could not now alter our plans.

However, it was arranged that one of the Kirghiz should leave at once for the Spassky Copper Mine with a note asking the engineers to hurry, while another was to accompany us next morning to Karkaralinsk, wait for us there, and then guide the whole of our party to wherever the Baron was in the steppe south-west of Semipalatinsk. Much refreshed by this excellent arrangement, and also by several helpings of *kulibyaka* (a magnificent baked fish) and many little glasses of vodka, Moss and I returned to our billet.

Next day we waited in vain for our Kirghiz guide and then set off with three carts and a sleigh, reaching the small village of Novo Nikolaevsk (twenty-five versts) after a bitter cold journey. This was the last village on the road to Karkaralinsk, which was still nearly 150 versts away. No fresh horses were available, so our leading driver, an old peasant, advised us to make for Horoshevskaia, fifteen versts away to the east, where we would be able to get transport for the next day. This village proved to be quite large, having perhaps four hundred houses, and we got a good billet, next door to a General X, who, on hearing of our arrival, asked us over to drink tea. We found him surrounded by about a dozen officers, and sitting next to him was a woman, supposed to be his mistress, who spoke French quite fluently and smoked innumerable cigarettes. To illustrate the disastrous effect that the presence of women with the troops had on the course of the fighting, this woman had such an influence on the General that in the summer of 1919, she persuaded him to evacuate the important town of Orsk, withdraw their special train over the river, and demolish the railway bridge before the stores and munitions on the other bank could be brought over, although the Bolsheviks did not reach the town for another three days, so that irreplaceable military supplies were needlessly sacrificed. This was told me by a foreign officer, who was with the Army at the time this happened.

General X was in command of the 4th Cadre Brigade, supposed to be a training unit, which consisted roughly of two hundred officers and four hundred men. When I saw them on the move next day, each officer seemed to have a cart, on which, in addition to himself were perched one soldier servant, one soldier driver, and one woman ('officers, for the use of,' as we should have expressed it during the war!). Thus the entire 4th Cadre Brigade was accounted for!

As X was not a Cossack, and continued to curse them throughout the evening, I realised that it was not only they who were responsible for the disasters of the campaign, if it can be called such, but also men of his stamp, who had no qualifications whatever for the command of troops in the field.

The next day was 1st December, and we set out soon after nine with three fair-sized carts, which Moss had obtained with some difficulty. X's Brigade was already on the move, and we were delayed at an awkward river crossing, where the frozen surface and steep banks made careful going very necessary. There were two or three more of these water-courses to be negotiated, and then being lighter laden we managed to push ahead and not long afterwards regained the main road. The snow had almost disappeared hereabouts, and those unfortunates with sleighs had a hard time of it. The country was, if possible, more bleak and desolate than before, rougher and more hilly. It was also very cold.

Soon after midday, we reached a Kirghiz *aul* (encampment) of *yurtas*, large round felt tents, which was full of

Red Cross carts, nurses, doctors, and typhus cases. The tents were laid out in long, orderly rows, and while our horses were resting, we munched some bread and sausage, and wandered around to look at the camp.

The Kirghiz are a short, stocky race of Turkic origin, with dark slanting eyes, flat noses, and high cheekbones. Their complexion is a yellowish-brown, and they have black hair, and almost hairless faces. Although short and inclined to be stout they are very strong and are excellent horsemen, leading a nomadic life, which keeps them constantly in the saddle, almost from the time they can walk. In summer, they live in these felt tents, which are quickly erected, as the felt and the semi-circular wooden hoops of the framework are carried on two camels, and can be rapidly unpacked and placed in position. The tents have an opening at the top, and as there is no tent-pole, a fire for cooking is kept going in the centre. Their food is almost exclusively flesh, mostly mutton, although they have a kind of flour made of barley which is made into primitive bread. The famous koumis, or mare's milk, is their favourite drink. However, if you have ever been offered a bowl of this nectar, and seen it poured out of a dirty sheepskin bag, with the wool inside, you probably declined it, as I did! In the winter, they usually retire to other pastures where their winter houses, or *zimovkas*, are to be found. These are mud huts of elementary design and construction, which keep them warm and safe during the howling storms of the winter months.

The men wear sheep or goatskin caps, coats, breeches, and boots, which are far from clean, as their domestic animals, especially the goats, wander in and out of the tents, like any other member of the family. I once saw a

Kirghiz riding through Omsk clad in furs from head to foot although it was a very hot day in July. My Russian droshky driver told me they believe that the skins keep out the heat as well as the cold, but the Kirghiz's face under his sheepskin cap looked anything from cool. The women wear large white head-dresses, and are usually as ugly as sin.

There was no room for us in this place, so we set out once more, and after another forty versts, reached a small encampment of half a dozen *yurtas* and a mud-hut. Here also there was not an inch to spare, for every available corner was full of refugees, and as we could not spend the night in the open, it was decided to push on a further twelve versts to a settlement of a few houses owned by colonists. When this place was reached late at night, we had done ninety versts, our horses were all in and we were completely exhausted and nearly frozen stiff. Refugees were already here too, and it was with great difficulty that we forced our way into a peasant's hut and found space on the floor near the stove. An oil lamp and several candles lighted this room, with its uneven whitewashed walls, rough table, and great clay stove. In every available corner, on and under the table, and on the stove, were people – sick and wounded, refugees with wives and children, officers and soldiers – thankful for this shelter from the piercing cold outside, and all talking, making tea, eating, trying to sleep, or snoring. The stench from many unwashed bodies, crawling with vermin, was almost unbearable, but the warmth was better than the freezing night, and we slept a little.

Leaving the foul air of the tightly-packed room early next morning, we travelled on over more rugged and hilly country, approached the steep pine-covered slopes of the Karkaraly range, skirted the eastern base of the mountain, and after covering forty-two versts, entered the town of Karkaralinsk, the last settlement on the Kirghiz steppe. Its wide streets, one-storey wooden houses, church, and a few stone or brick buildings, identical in character with a hundred other steppe towns, spread out on the flat ground at the base of the hills. On all sides except on that from which we had just come, stretched hundreds of versts of desolate steppe, uninhabited except for the nomadic Kirghiz, and it was with a feeling of almost tense excitement I rode through the town, for here was either the beginning of a fresh adventure over unknown wastes, or surrender to the pursuing enemy, for civilisation was behind us and the next few hours or days would determine our fate.

As our weary ponies dragged us through the streets, I noticed that there were more people abroad than was usual in such cold weather, and that they stood in groups, talking little and eyeing us curiously. Even at the windows, I could see faces peering through the frosted panes, and I realised that something must have happened.

Having discovered the office of the Town Commandant, we halted there, and climbed from our uncomfortable perches to the ground. A group of Cossacks, soldiers, and Kirghiz was standing nearby and they were edging closer to us to ask for news, when I saw de Kerangat's interpreter, Bielenky, come out of the house, and, seeing me, push his way through the crowd to speak to me. I could see he was bursting with importance, and that he must have news of some kind, but I was hardly prepared for what he told me.

Speaking quickly in French, he said, '*Mon capitaine*, I

suppose you have not heard the news? It is very grave. The Bolsheviks have taken Semipalatinsk.'

Such news, coming at the very moment of our arrival, and after an arduous and difficult journey of four hundred versts, was a bitter disappointment. Although such a possibility as the fall of Semipalatinsk had occurred to me, I could hardly believe that this goal of ours was already in enemy hands, and that our chances, not only of rejoining the Mission, but, of getting away at all were extremely small. Of one thing I was certain, however, that if there was any possible means of escape I would find it, and if it came to fighting our way through, my small party would put up a better show than the Orenburg Army had done in the last two months.

My remark to Moss, which appears in the first chapter, brought a happy smile to his face, and he replied so naturally and good-humouredly, 'All right,' that it quite cheered me up.

While he went in to see the Commandant about a billet for us, I questioned Bielenky about the situation. He knew very little except that on the previous evening the military telegraphist in Semipalatinsk had reported the outbreak of fighting in the town. Shortly afterwards communication was interrupted, and it was surmised that there had been a mutiny of the garrison, because the Bolsheviks from the main forces on the Trans-Siberian Railway could not have reached the place at this time. Information from the Kirghiz, who by some mysterious means seemed to be able to receive and send information at incredible speed, already reported that a rising had taken place and the town to be in the hands of mutineers. This was later confirmed.

While our line of escape was thus cut off in that direction, the local situation was apparently causing anxiety. The Cossacks of Karkaralinsk were evidently strong Red sympathisers, and the unfortunate refugees and the disorganised remains of the Army might receive a far from hospitable welcome. Crowded into this last small town, uncertain where to turn, followed by Red Guards from the north, and faced with a hostile population, I did not envy the oncoming tide from Akmolinsk.

When Moss came back, I told Bielenky to ask Captain de Kerangat to call at our billet at six that evening so that we could talk over the situation. Leaving him, we went off to our quarters, which turned out to be a small room in the house of a Tatar trader. Quite comfortable. We had scarcely unloaded the carts, when the two English engineers whom I had summoned by telegram came in. We must have made a curious picture in the little roughly-boarded room, with its tiled stove and double windows. Moss and I in travel-stained khaki, hair long uncut, several days' growth of beard, and tired out after the rigours of the last part of our journey; Smith and Morgan, two peaceable civilians, dressed in riding-breeches and boots, and huge fur coats, completely mystified at our arrival and the sudden danger threatened by the Orenburg Army's retreat. Mr. Gordon Smith, a Scotsman of about forty-five, was a short, rather stout, little man, with a beard, and hair getting rather thin on top, who had been mining in most parts of the globe at one time or another, and had lately been manager of the Spassky Copper Mine. Mr. Morgan was a short, wiry New Zealander of thirty-five, who had been nine years at Spassky, and proved to be an invaluable addition to our party as he knew a good deal about the Kirghiz, spoke their language well enough to be understood, and also proved himself an indefatigable worker and an excellent quartermaster.

I told them why I had wired to them, namely, because they were not safe where they were, and after a short explanation of the situation, I asked them to come back at six, when Captain de Kerangat would be present, and we would hold a council of war. When our washing and shaving were over, we hastened round to see the Chief of Staff, General Zaitsev, who confirmed the news about Semipalatinsk, and said that Ataman Annenkov was reported to be moving north from the southern border of Semiryechie, where he had been opposing the Bolsheviks of Russian Turkestan. He was said to command an efficient force of good men in the area between the Chinese-Mongolian border and Lake Balkhash, with Vyerni as the southern and Sergiopol as the northern extent of his operations. (*See* map, page 105). There were many rumours, of course, one being that Bakich had rallied his troops and retaken Akmolinsk, which I received with a cynical smile!

Promptly at six, our council of war was held. There were Captain de Kerangat, Bielenky, Gordon Smith, Morgan, Moss, and myself. Our position was not an enviable one when the situation had been summed up, but it was unanimously decided that every day's delay would increase our danger of capture, and that we should set out for Annenkov's headquarters at Sergiopol in two days' time. This was the only loophole by which we could hope to escape through the rapidly narrowing circle of our enemies, for Turkestan was in their hands to the south, they held the Orenburg-Tashkent Railway and the approaches to the Caspian Sea on the west, their pursuing forces were rapidly approaching from the north-west, and they already held Semipalatinsk and the railway to Novo Nikolaevsk to the north-east. Sergiopol was the only town, as far as we knew, that was still held by White troops, and which offered a means of escape into Mongolia or through southern Siberia by way of the Altai mountains to the far distant Trans-Siberian Railway.

Should Annenkov prove as weak as Dutov, it was possible and even probable that the energetic Bolsheviks from Semipalatinsk would reach Sergiopol before we could, for they were nearer by a hundred versts, and would have three or four days' start. Even if we reached the place in safety, after crossing some four or five hundred versts of almost uninhabited steppe, our difficulties were by no means over. It was easy to talk about crossing the border into Mongolia, but we were ignorant of the country and might be worse off there than in the hands of the Bolsheviks. No one knew whether there were towns or deserts, bandits or friendly troops. There was a rumour that an English consul was on the border, but it seemed unlikely, and to make the entry into a foreign country more difficult, we had no money but Omsk paper roubles, which eventually proved worthless. If China proved impossible, the only other means of escape was north-east towards Krasnoyarsk, which I judged to be fully 1500 versts, and an almost hopeless journey through hostile mountainous country in the depths of winter.

However, I don't think any of us were depressed, for our future journey would be one of hardship and adventure, such as few have the opportunity to experience, and as we were young and full of hope, we trusted in our good fortune to save the day.

Before turning in, I received a note by Kirghiz messenger from von Tiesenhausen saying he was waiting at an encampment on the steppe, and asking us to hurry and join him. I replied giving him the news, and saying we were making for Sergiopol, whither I advised him to go with all speed.

Next day was spent in making arrangements for the journey. The engineers had brought with them from Spassky a covered sleigh, a light carriage and a large farm wagon, five horses and a Kirghiz driver, so we arranged for four carts for ourselves to be ready that afternoon, in order that we could pack our kit and leave early the following morning. The carts did not arrive, of course, but were promised for the morrow at 11 a.m. Meanwhile from a Kirghiz I bought an ancient but serviceable goatskin *shuba*, which smelt to high heaven, and cost me 2900 roubles, and also made arrangements to procure a guide to take us across the waste spaces and to find shelter each night for us. Gordon Smith's Kirghiz driver was sent in search of one.

When all our preparations were completed, I went with Moss to say good-bye to General Zaitsev, and found him in the house of a well-to-do Tatar, where the drawing-room had a piano, and quite a company was assembled. The beautiful singer, whom I had met at supper at Akmolinsk, was there, now minus a husband, and also Mme. Zaitsev, Captain de Kerangat, Bielenky, and several Russian officers. We drank tea and talked while someone played, and Mme. Arseneva (the singer) sang to us.

Zaitsev informed us that the remains of the First and Second Corps were retreating towards us, one through Spassky and the other through Baianaul, while Dutov was expected to arrive on the seventh. The Bolsheviks were reported following close on the heels of the flying troops, and in order to put up some sort of defence all officers trying to escape to Sergiopol were being halted and formed into an Officers' Battalion. Owing to the number of refugees, the commandant was ordering many of them to go on to the Boguslavsky Copper Mine about eighty versts to the south-west, but Morgan told me that this place had long been deserted and the buildings demolished so that the poor devils either froze or returned to Karkaralinsk after doing 160 versts needlessly. I hope they shot the commandant. Officers were being sent out to establish post-stations across the steppe to Sergiopol, and to collect horses from the Kirghiz so that the troops and the refugees could cross the four hundred odd versts in safety. He wanted us to await Dutov's coming, but I told him that my orders were to rejoin the Mission without delay, and I could see no object in waiting for the Ataman. That night I had a bath, the last for many a long day.

The morning of the 4th all were up early making final arrangements. Moss and I were to ride in the engineers' carriage, which was something like a buggy, while they occupied the covered sleigh, which was placed on top of the farm wagon, as there was not enough snow to bear it, and it was too warm and comfortable to leave behind. To keep us warm, I obtained fourteen or fifteen yards of felt (*koshma*), for which I paid 2500 roubles, and this we cut up and used as rugs for our feet. For 6000 roubles, five thousand of which were payable in advance, I obtained as guide one of the dirtiest and most villainous-looking ruffians I've ever seen. He was a Kirghiz, shorter than the average, with wonderfully bowed legs, filthy, patched skin clothing, and a horrible split lip, which gave him a truly terrible appearance. For this sum he guaranteed to take us to Sergiopol and to find shelter for us each night on the road.

As I have already mentioned, Captain de Kerangat had a Cadillac motor car, and in this he proposed to cross the steppe in spite of our efforts to dissuade him. He insisted that he would be much more comfortable and do the journey in two days instead of two weeks, but being unable to carry more than four people, he asked us to look after his two French Colonial soldiers and his luggage, while he himself promised to leave Karkaralinsk the next day. The two Frenchmen, Sergeant Doumeng and Soldat Buffet, were a lazy and inefficient couple, and it was with little pleasure that I accepted their companionship.

I also drew 50,000 roubles from the Chief of the Garrison for expenses on the journey.

While away from the billet, making these arrangements, a letter arrived for me, brought by a mysterious Kirghiz messenger, who vanished as soon as it had been delivered. It proved to be from Major Steveni, our Intelligence Officer at Mission H.Q., and had apparently been brought by hand from Omsk, as it was written hastily in pencil and dated 8th November, nearly a month before, and just before the evacuation of the town by Kolchak's troops. It ran:–

Omsk, 8th November 1919.

CAPTAIN HODGES, R.F.A.

You have been instructed by telegrams of 2nd and 5th November to return to Omsk, or Novo Nikolaevsk, if former impossible. So far we have received no news from you whether you have received these messages.

All the remainder of Mission leaving Omsk early next week. You and Lieutenant Moss are to return by earliest, safest, and most convenient route to Novo Nikolaevsk where you are to rejoin us.

Please wire in Russian '*en claire*' confirming receipt of these instructions as none of your cipher wires have been decipherable.

Have sent a message to-day to you through General Dutov ordering you and Moss to return to Novo Nikolaevsk.

General K. [Knox] who left last night most anxious about you. Please wire immediately to me c/o Staff Eastern Front when and how you intend leaving to rejoin us.

(Signed) L. STEVENI,
Major.

The letter was addressed in Russian to Captain Hodges of the English Service, Staff of the Orenburg Army.

The news that all my telegrams had been undecipherable was most exasperating, for we had spent hours coding those messages and checking them over, so that the fault lay in the transmission or at the decoding end. I had a suspicion that the Russians jumbled the messages in order that the true situation could not be known at British Mission H.Q.

However there was no time to worry over the telegrams at it was already 3.30 p.m., the carts had just arrived, and I was determined to get away that afternoon, if only to gain a few hours. By the time everything was ready, the guide had disappeared and nearly two hours were wasted finding him, and collecting the two engineers and the

French Mission, who were late in getting ready. Finally at six, our little caravan of eleven carts was assembled outside the Tatar's house, where a crowd of Kirghiz and Cossacks had collected to watch us go off. I gave the order to get ready, climbed after Moss into the carriage the engineers had lent us, signed to our guide to climb on the box, and shouting, 'Walk – March' and waving my cap as a last farewell to Karkaralinsk, we moved slowly out of the town and, in the gathering darkness, plunged into the unknown steppe ahead.

CHAPTER 16

THE KIRGHIZ STEPPE

INSIDE the jolting carriage, Moss and I lay close together for warmth. Under us were two layers of felt and some straw; above – more felt. Fully clothed in sheepskins, fur caps and *pimies* with the carriage hood over us, and the squat figure of the Kirghiz guide in front, acting as a wind screen, we were not too cold. At least not to start with. But it was bitter cold for all that, and I pitied the guide on the box, as he swung his arms and swayed to and fro, and our servants and the two French soldiers on the open carts behind.

In spite of the tiring day we had been through, it was difficult to sleep. My newly-acquired goatskin *shuba* smelt as if every Kirghiz beggar for the last ten generations had lived his life in it in none too clean surroundings, and the squat figure that I could dimly see perched in front had an odour of his own, which was hardly pleasing.

Our horses' hoofs drummed on the frosty ground, and the wheels crunched and scraped over frozen ruts and hummocks of dried grass. Immediately behind came the heavy farm wagon from Spassky, on which was perched the covered sleigh of the two engineers, and when we went at a walk, I could hear the snorting and breathing of the horses as they followed close in our wake.

The minutes and the hours seemed interminable, and

always as I dozed came that extra jolt that shook one awake again, the rattle of the wheels, the noise of hoofs, the snort or whinny of a horse and the rumble of the moving caravan.

This dash across the steppe was not going to be any too pleasant. I had realised that, of course, but now we had actually started and were in the hands of this villainous-looking fellow, who had promised to find us food and shelter each night and to lead us by as direct a route as possible to Annenkov's headquarters, I began to have qualms. Rather late for that, now that we had started, and rather foolish when there was nothing else to be done, but it was only at times like this when there was nothing else to do but lie still in the dark that I began to think how serious our position was. Difficult and dangerous as was this first part of the journey over some hundreds of versts of almost uninhabited country, I wondered what lay ahead of us, once we had crossed the steppe. If the Bolsheviks had forestalled us, or Annenkov's men had mutinied, there was little chance of our getting through the more difficult country near the Chinese frontier without being caught by enemies. Even if we escaped capture it would be almost suicidal to plunge into an unknown, mountainous district at the end of civilisation without the slightest idea of what we were doing or where we were going. Supposing Annenkov's men still held out, and we were able to get some information about possible routes through the Altai, Mongolia, Central China, or south over the Pamirs, we were still in no enviable position. God above knew how we were to get out of this mess. I didn't, because I didn't believe it possible to cross the whole of China. Without money and months of preparation it seemed out of the question even to consider such a journey, but try as I might I could see no other way out of our difficulties. In summer, several different routes to the Trans-Siberian Railway might have been possible, but in winter I could not think of a single one.

Toward midnight we halted with a jerk and I got out of the carriage. Half a dozen *yurtas* loomed squatly in the darkness, and seeing a light in one I pushed aside the felt curtain and went in. Before a small fire I found Morgan warming himself and talking to a tall thin Russian officer. Our guide hovered in the background. I asked what the place was.

'This is the first *étape* out of Karkaralinsk,' said Morgan. 'Dutov is starting a regular chain of them across the steppe, so that he can be sure of getting horses on the retreat. This fellow says he is the first, and he doesn't think there are any others established yet. Better give him your papers to stamp so that we can get started changing horses.'

I handed over my special pass, which was duly stamped and dated.

Morgan went on:

'He says we'll find a few Kirghiz *auls* where we can get fresh horses, if we're lucky, but that he's been having trouble collecting what he needs. The Kirghiz are all scared to death about this retreat. They think they are going to lose all their horses and cattle, and many of them are packing up and making for distant parts.'

'I don't blame them,' I said, crouching down by the fire. 'Do we sleep here?'

'No. There isn't anything to sleep in except these *yurtas*, and there isn't any fuel. This fellow here says we had better change horses and push on for another fifteen versts to a couple of huts called Kotusovsky. We can sleep there and get away before the mob starts arriving on our heels. He says we're the second party on the road, so we'd better try and keep ahead.'

'That'll make fifty versts since six this afternoon,' I said. 'Quite enough for me as a first night on the steppe. Tell that ugly Tatar of yours to come and warm himself for a minute and then get busy with the horses.'

It was after midnight when we set out again, and I remember little of the next stage until we drew up before a peasant's hut. Half a dozen of them formed this isolated outpost of Russian colonisation, and on closer inspection were none too clean inside. I was dog tired and I was cold, and I wanted sleep and warmth, free from unwelcome insects, so I got the faithful Albert to put up my camp bed in one of the huts, and retired to rest under the interested and admiring gaze of a bearded peasant, his wife, and two daughters, who all sat up on the top of the stove and stared at me with such intensity that I got quite confused.

We breakfasted hastily on bread and tea chiefly, in fact I don't remember eating much else for the next fortnight, with one or two notable exceptions. I was anxious to travel as fast and as far as possible each day so as to keep ahead of the mob of refugees and disorganised troops which would soon be on our heels, and I had every one packing and harnessing up by eight o'clock. I could see that Morgan was going to be a very useful companion as he not only spoke Russian and a rough and ready, but very effective, brand of the Kirghiz dialect (a form of Eastern Turki), but also had a way of getting things done without any fuss. Both he and Moss were hard workers, who didn't mind manual work or giving a hand to the servants when necessary, and for that I was thankful. We hadn't any place for people who wouldn't pull their weight.

Although we were ready to move off in good time, the French were slow and delayed us for nearly two hours. Captain de Kerangat had asked me to let his men join our party, and I had agreed thinking they would simply trail along behind. Far from this being the case, the two soldiers, Sergeant Doumeng and Private Buffet, having served in Indo-China for some years and expecting the 'natives' to do everything for them, became rather a nuisance. Travelling with them, under the protection of the French Mission, were two Lettish ensigns. Who they were or how they had persuaded de Kerangat to look after them, I never discovered, but they also were a responsibility which I would gladly have transferred elsewhere.

Gordon Smith aptly described the very leisurely and amateurish loading operations of the French Mission, when he asked solemnly, 'Have those lads lost anything?' He had a way of standing with both hands in the pockets of his fur-lined coat, his black fur cap set squarely on his head, and his ruddy, bearded face set in patient resignation, which made his occasional pithy remarks a constant joy, which his Scots accent tended to heighten.

By ten, we managed to get away, and our eleven miscellaneous vehicles strung out in single file. Again it was cold and clear, and we sat wrapped snugly in our felt coverings, as mile after mile of rolling prairie land dragged past. Early in the afternoon, having covered thirty-five versts, a small cluster of *yurtas* and one or two mud huts (*zimovkas*) came into view. Again we found one of Dutov's officers acting as commandant of the *étape*, and had no difficulty in getting fresh ponies. I thought they were a poor-looking lot and asked Morgan's opinion.

'They're poor, grass-fed brutes,' he said. 'No strength at all. I doubt if they can pull us twenty versts.'

They did eventually drag us twenty-six versts before our guide halted before a large *zimovka* in a little valley, but they were almost exhausted and the last hour had been painfully slow. The hut which we entered was really a long, low dwelling of sun-dried brick, divided into half a dozen rooms, and faced on one side by a walled yard, partially covered with light poles and brushwood, as shelter for horses and cattle. The owner was obviously a man of some importance. The hard earthen floors were covered with felt rugs of many colours and original design, and against some of the walls stood heavy wooden chests studded with brass nails, doubtless containing rich Bokharan carpets, silks from China, silver-mounted saddlery, and other attractive things.

Our host was a fine-looking old man with an impressive white beard and dressed in flowing silk robes and a black skull-cap. He conducted us personally to one of the rooms and made his house ours with true Oriental politeness. He also gave directions to one of his servants to look after our needs, and Morgan was able to buy half a sheep, which was soon transformed into as delicious a stew as I have ever tasted.

With outer coverings removed we sat cross-legged on the soft felt rugs, before a round table, whose legs could not have been six inches long, and ate until we felt at peace with the world.

With pipes alight we sat and talked, I recounting experiences in the war and in the past few months in

Siberia, Morgan and Smith taking their turns with tales of the Spassky Mines, and anecdotes about the Kirghiz.

I listened with interest, for although we had already passed through country which might be called part of the Kirghiz steppe, and where Kirghiz names of lakes, rivers, hills, and towns predominated, I had seen but few of these people, and had come across their *yurtas* only just before reaching Karkaralinsk, for the slow but steady colonisation of the country by Russian settlers from Esthonia, the Baltic States, and other areas had gradually pushed the nomad tribes further south into the uncivilised steppe. Here we were already travelling through one of the most desolate parts of their country, which winter made almost impassable, and where we were spending each night in a felt *yurta*, or a primitive mud hut, and each day in the midst of their *auls* and with their horsemen.

The two branches of the Kirghiz are known as the Kara or Black, and the Kazak or Riders, the former occupying the country south of Lake Balkhash, and the latter the country north of that lake and between the Caspian Sea and the upper waters of the Irtish and the Ob. Their language is a kind of Turkic, with many Mongolian, Arabic, and Persian words and their writing closely resembles Arabic, while they themselves are supposed to have come originally from Asia Minor. As regards numbers, there are said to be over two million of them, divided into four hordes, the Great, the Middle, the Little, and the Inner, only the first two of which we came across. Their headmen are called *beys*, and they seemed to have a great deal of authority, although since that time the Bolsheviks have altered things a great deal, and I believe there is a Kirghiz republic, which must be a joke.

One of the chief peculiarities of these people from what I saw of them, was their great fondness for boiled mutton, which they ate at all times, regarding the eyes and ears as special titbits. The sheep is usually placed whole into a large pot, boiled until tender, and then every one helps himself with his hands, and the bones are thrown to the fierce dogs that crouch expectantly around the circle of feasters. A little coarse bread or cake of barley is also eaten, but the Kirghiz are lazy and not given to tilling the soil, regarding green food as fit only for beasts. However, their meat diet generally leads to scurvy in the winter, and when spring comes they gather wild onions from the steppe and eat them in large quantities until they are all well again. Their women are strong and do most of the manual labour, which results in their ageing prematurely. The majority of them are ugly as sin, and only the young girls have any pretension to good looks, but there were few of these, for we travelled amongst the poorest of the tribes, and saw little of beauty in anything.

They seemed to be a hardy race, as they must be, living in that vigorous climate, but they suffer terribly from smallpox, eye diseases, syphilis, and dirt. Hardly a face was not pitted, and many were the sore eyes, and evidences of a more dreadful sickness. To distinguished visitors they are said to offer the choice of their women for the night, and to consider it an offence if their hospitality is refused, but it must be a hardy man to risk the terrible scourge of syphilis for one brief night with an unwashed Kirghiz girl.

To outward appearance they are a sullen, stubborn race, but a judicious mixture of firmness and kindness will do much, and we found them very honest and trustworthy, although stupid at times and not always truthful in small matters. It being winter when I was there, I missed seeing one of their race meetings, which must be great fun, as the excitement is intense, the course perhaps for fifty versts, calling for endurance as well as speed, and as the riders near the winning-post, their friends ride out and urge on the failing ponies with cries and blows, even using ropes to drag the unfortunate animals in should they collapse before the finish. There is no pari mutuel, but large flocks and herds change hands, as the *beys* and khans make bets on their favourite ponies, while the festivities after the races are carried on well into the small hours of the morning, and great is the consumption of boiled mutton and koumis.

I should liked to have stayed longer with these people, and waited until the spring when they desert their *zimovkas*, and move with their horses, camels, sheep, goats, and dogs to better grazing grounds. There they lead as simple and pastoral a life as one can imagine, passing the time watching their peaceful herds, drinking vast quantities of koumis, and hunting with the eagle or the falcon, which is still an art, and a sport of which they are extremely fond.

Their religion is a kind of Mohammedanism, but they seem very lax, and their women do not wear veils, while the few mullahs, or priests, that I came across were poor, ignorant men, and were treated with little respect, for even though they carried the Koran, I believe they understood very little of it, and could scarcely read.

Later in the evening, another party of travellers arrived. There were two Russian officers and a girl of twenty-one or so. They were placed in an adjacent room, and as there were no doors we could hear some sort of altercation going on. From time to time, the girl would appear in our doorway, look us over and then go back to her companions. Just before we began settling down for the night she came in and asked if she could have a cup of tea with us. We made room for her, and she sat talking and combing her hair which was very long and silky and of a really lovely golden tint. Being an attractive woman and knowing it, she soon had us all very much awake, pouring out tea, handing her some of our precious sugar, and warming up the remains of the stew. Then having made a good impression she told us how she disliked her travelling companions and hinted broadly that we take her with us.

None of us took the hint, except one of the Letts, who was most warm in his invitation, but the rest remained silent, and the girl soon rejoined her two protectors. When she had gone, I turned to Moss and said, 'Tell our Lettish friend in the most forcible terms you can think of that if he wishes to start a harem he may do so, but he will leave our party on the spot if he does. We have had one experience of travelling with a woman in the party and that was enough for me.'

Moss spoke firmly and to the point and the matter ended there. We did not see the girl again, and the Lett came with us.

This question having come up, I thought it a good time to have matters thoroughly understood, so I said to Morgan and Gordon Smith:

'I know you agree with me that we cannot allow women to be picked up here and there, and that any one of us who does so will have to shift for himself. We are foreigners travelling through a strange country, and you know as well as I do what sort of position we are in. Being foreigners we shall probably have plenty of opportunities to collect a harem, and in other circumstances I should like nothing better, but until we are out of this mess we must keep clear of entanglements. I consider that I am still on active service, that I have orders to rejoin my headquarters somehow with all speed and dispatch, and that I must do my utmost to bring my small party safely through whatever is ahead of us. Any philandering or increasing the size of our party without strengthening it will make things more difficult, and no matter how hard and unchivalrous it may seem, we must let the Russians get out of their troubles themselves.'

There was no argument, and fortunately for my strength of mind, I never had sufficient temptation to make me stray from the straight and narrow course, although opportunities were not lacking.

While on the road the next day, crossing a particularly bleak and hilly tract, we heard the unaccustomed honk of a motor horn, and de Kerangat's Cadillac car drew up alongside. He got out to talk to us and told us that he had left Karkaralinsk that morning and hoped to be in Sergiopol the following day. He had passed quite a number of refugees on the way, but had no particular news. Dutov was still expected when he left, but there was no thought of defending the town. He expected what was left of the Army to try and cross the steppe and join Annenkov.

With de Kerangat, were his interpreter, Bielenky, a chauffeur and a Russian officer, but the car was so full of oil and petrol tins and drums that there was very little room to sit and no place at all for kit or supplies. In spite of that, when he waved good-bye and the swiftly moving car disappeared in the distance, we sighed enviously and climbed back into our slow carts with their weedy ponies that lay down almost exhausted after twenty versts.

After another ten versts, we halted at what we thought was the third *étape*. The usual cluster of *yurtas*, twenty or thirty squat, skin-clad Kirghiz and a couple of ponies completed the picture. We climbed out of the carts and went in search of the Russian commandant.

'They say there isn't any commandant and they haven't any ponies,' Morgan reported after a few minutes of wandering in and out of the felt tents.

'What are they here for then?' I asked. 'This isn't one of their regular *auls*.'

Morgan turned to a group of half a dozen Kirghiz who stood sullenly near by. He spoke quietly at first, but gradually he grew angry. I could see that the men were getting uneasy, as they glanced furtively at each other, but they made no move to get us ponies.

'Here! Give me that,' said Morgan suddenly, and taking a hunting-crop from my hand he turned to the group in front of us and brandished it threateningly. Crack went the thong across the back of one of the nearest men, and crack again on a second. Slowly sheepish grins spread over their broad yellow faces, and they shuffled away with bent backs as our stout-hearted New Zealander followed them with choice oaths and a loud (but harmless) cracking of the whip.

In a few minutes fresh ponies began to appear, dragged forward by laughing little men who seemed to like the treatment they were getting.

It was an interesting scene. Under the pale blue sky,

a barren country of low hills and long shallow valleys, coarse grass, a sprinkle of snow on distant slopes, or a gleam of white where a drift caught the sunlight, the dome-shaped felt *yurtas* grey and primitive under the open sky, sheepskin-clad figures squat and bow-legged, with conical fur caps and swarthy slant-eyed faces. Morgan, Gordon Smith, Moss, and myself directing and lending a hand occasionally, Albert, Peter, and Alexei, the two Frenchmen and the two Letts, guarding the precious loads on the carts.

I thought the ponies looked fresher, and there was more difficulty in harnessing them than usual. Such plunging, rearing, backing, and kicking I had never seen before. It looked as if they had never been in draft. Two of those between the shafts were blindfolded and held firmly by four grinning stalwarts.

When everything was ready, and our men perched on top of the carts, I gave the signal to move off, and then the fun began. As soon as the ponies' heads were loosed they started at a mad gallop across the steppe, kicking and bucking. In a moment our carts were scattered in all directions, bouncing and bounding over the rough ground, and casting servants, kit, French soldiers, valises, and boxes in all directions. For five minutes, the whole encampment was helpless with laughter and then began the chasing of the runaway teams, and the collection of our scattered belongings. Luckily no carts were damaged, and apparently the first wild gallop had so subdued the ponies that we had no trouble with them again, except that they soon tired and finished the day with difficulty.

In fact, early in the afternoon, when we had only done twenty-five versts, I found it necessary to call a halt and rest the teams. We were then far from any human habitation, and the guide shook his head when we asked him what was the nearest shelter.

It grew bitterly cold as night came on, and we were almost despairing of reaching even the meanest *zimovka*, when we turned off into the hills, the jaded ponies quickened their shambling steps, and after having covered seventy versts, we drew up at a miserable hut, thankful to get in out of the cold, and too tired to do anything but swallow some tea and lie down on the straw to sleep.

One piece of information we gained here, was that only one party of refugees had preceded us, at which we were truly thankful.

Next morning, we got to an encampment three versts from our starting-point, and changed ponies. Again the scenes of the day before were enacted, Morgan plying his whip, stirring the Kirghiz to action by lash and voice; the harnessing of the unwilling ponies; their first wild stampede when their heads were loosed; and the highly diverting spectacle of servants, French soldiers, drivers, and luggage falling in all directions as the carts swayed and bumped over the steppe. So widely was the caravan scattered that the men took nearly two hours to assemble it again and to reload our kit, while we speculated on how long our transport would last if this performance were repeated each day.

By this time we were in a country where vehicles were little used, and we could not obtain fresh ones if accidents were to occur, so that even a broken wheel or axle would have forced us to leave the whole cart as there was no material for repairs.

Luckily, these travel-worn *telegas* had stood the strain

so far, and we started without any loss for the next *aul*, as the encampments are called by the Kirghiz, which was forty-two versts away. The weather was still cold, the track none too smooth, and our ponies, after their first wild dash, seemed hardly able to pull the loads behind them. As darkness was falling we reached the *aul*, which consisted of *yurtas*, there being no huts or any shelter better than these felt tents. The cold grew intense as the sun went down, and we crouched around a fire in the middle of one of the tents, endeavouring to forget our freezing backs in the warmth of the flames, which were kept alive by an old Kirghiz, who kept feeding the blaze with rough briquettes of horse and camel dung mixed with straw. In the flickering firelight, our tired and silent party, wrapped in furs and skins, slowly sipped the scalding tea, which Albert passed round in a couple of enamelled mugs. Blankets and felt were brought in, placed round the fire and we crawled under them, huddled close together for warmth, while the keeper of the flames squatted stolidly at our feet, slowly and economically feeding his fuel into the warm blaze, hour after hour, while we slept fitfully, waking often to wriggle deeper under the coarse felt. Each time that I opened my eyes the firelight flickered on the grey walls of the tent, the weird shapes of recumbent forms, and the figure of the old Kirghiz with his expressionless, weather-stained face.

As dawn came, we rose, stretched our numbed and aching limbs, gulped down the inevitable tea, and were soon on the road once again traversing still more bleak and hilly country. The ponies were poor, and although our march was without a break, only forty-two versts had been covered by five in the afternoon, when we decided to halt for the night in a deserted *zimovka*, as the guide did not know any other place for shelter within easy reach. Apparently our hut had not long been deserted, as the embers on the hearth were still warm, and we suspected that news of the retreat had already reached the various *auls*, and that every Kirghiz had fled or would soon fly to winter quarters elsewhere far from the line of march of the Orenburg Army. Everything of any value had already been removed from the hut, but there was fairly fresh straw on the floor, a little fuel for the fire, and we were soon thawing our frozen fingers before a cheerful blaze, while water boiled in a pot.

The routine of eating and sleeping was interrupted by the entrance of a Kirghiz, of miserable appearance, clad in patched sheepskin. He had a note for me, written on the back of a piece of paper torn from a map, and approaching it to the solitary candle, I read:

8th December, 6 h.p.m.

DEAR CAPTAIN,

Our motor-car is broken, fifty versts from here. We went back till this *aul* without eating and drinking, only snow. We are very tired! One Kirghize told me that *you are one verste from here*. Please, sir, come here *to-morrow morning*, and we will continue the trip with you.

Yours truly,

CAPTAIN DE KERANGAT.

When I read this out, every one roared with laughter, not at our unfortunate companions' hardships, but at the remembrance of his passing us so gaily nearly three days before, when he expected to be in Sergiopol in forty-eight hours. It was the old story of the hare and the tortoise, and secretly we could not help but feel pleased at the correctness of our prophecy, that his car would break down in the middle of the steppe, and leave him hard put to it to escape with his life.

On the following morning, soon after the caravan had started, the French Captain and Bielenky appeared from a deserted hut, and we took them into the carts, Moss giving up his place for the moment to de Kerangat. The motor car had broken down on the evening of the 6th, miles from anywhere, and not knowing how far they would have to go forward to get assistance and shelter, they spent the night in the car, and then, leaving the chauffeur and the Russian officer in charge, the interpreter and de Kerangat set out to retrace their steps in the hope of meeting us. In the car they had no food except tea tablets and some sugar, so that after trudging wearily all day and seeing no sign of human habitation, they were weak and hungry by nightfall and slept in an empty and ancient tomb, several of which were to be seen near the road during the journey. The following day was worse, as they were almost exhausted from cold and lack of food, and the few Kirghiz they saw in the distance galloped away at sight of them, thinking perhaps they were robbers. In the afternoon, some *zimovkas* were seen, and hopes of shelter and food arose, but the huts were deserted and not a scrap to eat was to be found in any of them. This disappointment almost made them give up hope, when a party of refugees (probably the ones we had been told about a couple of days before) passed by not far away, and de Kerangat managed to attract their attention. These people gave him some bread, and soon afterwards a hut was found with a solitary Kirghiz, who gave them shelter and told them of our arrival at a hut only half a mile away. However, they were too tired to join us that night, and de Kerangat sent me the note to pick him up in the morning.

Just as his story was ended, an *étape* of *yurtas* was reached, and we prepared to go through the morning excitement of fresh ponies. This time they were wilder than ever, and three carts were overturned and dragged for some distance before the teams could be stopped. One of the Frenchmen's *telegas* was smashed and their kit therefore distributed on the others.

The wilder the ponies, the weaker they seemed to be, for although we only did about forty-five versts, it was ten o'clock at night before the last of the carts reached the *aul* where we were to sleep. I had got there first and was anxious for the last arrival, as I had seen the tracks of wolves, clearly marked on the snow of the road, where the packs had crossed. I had also passed de Kerangat's car ten versts before reaching our *yurta* encampment, and the chauffeur and mechanic swore that wolves had attacked on the previous night and been driven off by a few shots from a revolver. At the *aul*, we managed to hire six camels and some men from the Kirghiz, and the car was dragged with difficulty into the camp to be overhauled. I tried to persuade de Kerangat to leave it behind for good and all, but he was too fond of it to do that and said he would try it once more.

Another incredibly cold night was spent in one of the tents, and as the motor was not yet ready de Kerangat decided to come with us, until it should overtake the party once more. In the stampede which followed the harnessing several carts were again upset, and one smashed to pieces, so that a further distribution of kit was necessary, and we moved on with heavier loads, doing thirty-five versts to an *étape* of *yurtas* on a small frozen stream called Bakanas. Here we secured fresh horses and proceeded for another twenty-five versts, where a deserted and very filthy *zimovka* was the only shelter to be found. By bringing in our lengths of felt, and some feather pillows belonging to Gordon Smith, the dirty little hut was made quite comfortable, and as we had managed to get some mutton at the previous *aul*, a savoury stew was soon cooking. The sheep in that part of the country have no tail but in its place very large and fat quarters, which make delicious eating, and on which the sheep lives in the winter or whenever food is scarce.

During the day, several small parties of refugees came up and passed us, among them being some officers I had met at various times during the last few months. They had no news, and were chiefly speculating as to whether our destination (Sergiopol) was still in the hands of Annenkov, or whether the Reds had seized it. According to one of them, the nearest town in Mongolia was Chuguchak, and the roads thither were good, once we passed Sergiopol, so I decided that in case the latter place was in hostile hands, I could avoid the town by cutting across country further south, and so strike the road to China beyond.

That night, our *zimovka* was warmer than usual, having a large rough earthen stove, dividing the hut into two small rooms, which worked well and made the night more bearable than the last when we had nearly frozen in a tent. We also talked later than we generally did, and I learnt that during the Great War, the Turks had done their best

'DURING THE DAY SEVERAL SMALL PARTIES OF REFUGEES CAME UP AND PASSED US'

On the Kirghiz Steppe, December 1919

to stir up the Kirghiz tribes to revolt against the Russians, while German agents and propaganda tried to prove to the indifferent and rather bewildered natives, that Germany was the leading Mohammedan Power and the chief protector of the faith.

Our small party squatting in various poses on the straw-covered floor, was as odd an assortment of human beings as one can imagine, but it was an interesting mixture for all that. At any rate we had one fixed purpose, although we had been thrown together for such a short period, and that was to save our skins by getting out of the country as fast as possible. Our few days on the steppe had already warned us of the hardships ahead, and each one must have wondered many times a day whether Annenkov's troops were still loyal or not, but that night we were gay and anecdotes poured out of fighting in Morocco, mining camps in Venezuela, battles in France, and sheep-farming in New Zealand until a late hour.

The morning of the 11th saw us early astir, as nearly a week had passed since leaving Karkaralinsk, and a kind of routine was becoming noticeable, every one doing his own particular job, and not interfering where he was not wanted. We had already covered between 300 and 325 versts, and should have been only eighty versts from the post-road running north and south through Sergiopol, but our guide had turned too far south after passing the *étape* at Bakanas, and we eventually did more like 120 versts before reaching it.

As I was ignorant of the situation ahead, it was advisable to take precautions against riding into a village occupied by the Bolsheviks, should they have driven Annenkov away, so Morgan and I mounted a couple of steppe ponies and rode ahead of the caravan, in order to give warning in case of danger and also to keep an eye out for horses, as ours were very poor and needed changing at the earliest opportunity.

I had expected an *étape* ten versts away, but although we passed a fair number of *zimovkas*, they were all deserted, and it was not until twenty-five versts were behind us, that we caught sight of a group of huts off the track and on the banks of a frozen stream. The coarse grass was rather tall here, but there were several ponies feeding near the *aul*, so, with Morgan, I trotted out briskly to arrange for enough fresh animals to relieve our tired ones. When still a short distance away, a young boy dashed out of one of the huts, leapt on to a pony, and started driving the others away from us into the tall grass and towards the hills on the north. We tried to head them off, but he was too quick for us, and disappeared.

This was discouraging for our ponies were of very poor quality, and had scarcely been able to drag the now heavily-laden carts a short day's trek, while the Kirghiz drivers, who were in charge of them, were already two days away from their *aul*, and likely to make trouble if fresh teams could not be found. In addition, the cart with the French Sergeant failed to arrive, and we halted both to rest our animals and give him time to catch up. Just before dark a party of refugees under General Nikitin arrived, and joined us in the hut.

Our Kirghiz were so dissatisfied at the idea of another day's journey away from their *aul* that I ordered a guard with loaded rifle to stand over the ponies and carts all night, so that the men could not ride off and leave us stranded in the steppe. This precaution was justified, as when I was pacing up and down with my rifle much in evidence, three or four Kirghiz came round the corner of the *zimovka* towards the horses, saw me, hesitated for a moment, and then slunk back out of sight. About eight o'clock the unexpected sound of a motor car was heard, a pair of headlights lit up the hut, and de Kerangat's car drew up, much to his delight. Later in the evening, being anxious about the French Sergeant, I sent out a search party, which returned a couple of hours later without having found him.

In the morning a dispute arose among the guides as to whether we were on the right road, most of them claiming that we had come too far south and should return forty versts to regain the track that led to Sergiopol. General Nikitin was finally convinced and ordered his party to turn about, but I felt that most of the Kirghiz wanted to get back to Bakanas, and that their story was not true, so determined to push on in a general south-easterly direction and we would then be sure to strike the Sergiopol road.

Knowing that horses were to be had, for we had seen the boy drive off a number of them the day before, we attempted to get them from the Kirghiz whose *zimovka* we had occupied, but he stubbornly refused, and only the efforts of Morgan with his whip and string of oaths, finally frightened him somewhat and four ponies were produced. The remainder had to go on with us, and hearing that the French Sergeant was only five versts behind, we set out about ten o'clock, de Kerangat having left with Bielenky shortly before in the repaired Cadillac.

Soon after midday, the Sergeant rejoined us, his cart drawn by a supercilious-looking camel, for his ponies had given out the night before, and all he had been able to get was this mangy-looking animal. With our half-starved ponies we made slow time, and the track became so difficult to follow that I began to think we were going wrong after all. No sign of human habitation could be seen in that desolate waste with its high coarse grass, dried-up water-courses, and barren hills, forty or fifty versts south of which lay the sandy deserts surrounding Lake Balkhash. To make matters worse, snow began to fall, the track disappeared almost entirely, and our teams became more and more exhausted. Night came down, the cold increased, and I ordered a halt to consider whether it was better to stay the night in the open or to push on in the hope of finding shelter. The hanging heads and heaving flanks of our little steppe ponies showed that much further effort from them could not be expected, and yet if the snowfall turned into a blizzard we had little hope of getting out alive, should we stay where we were. The guide seemed completely lost, and I believed that in the snow and gathering darkness he had led us too much to the left, for we had not kept a straight course and seemed to be edging off to the north. We must have covered fully sixty versts since morning, and should have been fairly close to the post-road, but if our irregular course had been followed for some time, we might still be far away, and it was little use struggling on in the dark with no idea of direction.

As I stood shivering, talking to Morgan, I suddenly saw a faint light in the distance, and called his attention to it. The sight of this put new heart into every one, the ponies made a last effort, and in half an hour we halted at a tumble-down *zimovka*, where a familiar shape against the wall proved to be de Kerangat's Cadillac, the tyres of which had all punctured. His chauffeur and mechanic, however, were not to be defeated and were stuffing felt into the outer covers, to make them serviceable for another few days! This had been one of the most exhausting days so far, and even the extreme filth of this hut could not keep us from sleep. The French Sergeant had again been unfortunate, as his cart had broken down, and in the snow this had not been noticed by the rest of us. His Kirghiz driver did not desert him, but managed to obtain another camel somehow, and all the kit was loaded on to the two beasts. As they tried to overtake us they came across a grisly sight, according to the Frenchman, for a camel and a young Kirghiz boy lay on the plain where they had been killed and partly eaten by wolves, the night before. The camel was carrying the kit of a Russian officer, and this the Sergeant and his driver brought with them, finally reaching our *zimovka* after midnight.

The next day was the 13th, and we had been nine days on the Kirghiz steppe, but our nights in *yurtas* and *zimovkas* were almost over for the present as we found ourselves only ten versts from the post-road, which runs south from Semipalatinsk through Sergiopol to Russian Turkestan. The Kirghiz reported that no Bolsheviks had been heard of in the neighbourhood thus far, so Morgan and I mounted a couple of ponies and rode ahead of the caravan to the road, where we found a post-house and about twenty Kirghiz *zimovkas*, the whole known as Malo Ayagusky, from the River Ayagus that flows south alongside the road until it empties itself into Lake Balkhash. The picket, as post-stations are called there, we found to be 105 versts south of Sergiopol, which the local commandant reported to be in the hands of Ataman Annenkov's troops.

He also told us that Semipalatinsk and Barnaul had been taken by mutinies of the regiments of the garrison, and that Annenkov had sent soldiers towards the former town to prevent a Bolshevik advance to the south. The province of Semiryechie, or Seven Rivers Land, in which we now found ourselves seemed tranquil and well organised, for after having examined our passports, the commandant promised us horses for the next day, and issued us food at very moderate prices.

I have been brought up to distrust melodramatics and heroics, and in this story I write things as they occurred. Our nine days' journey, with its peaceful ending, sounds rather tame in the bald narration of facts, but in truth our uncertainty as to the nature of our reception at the journey's end, together with the hardships on the road made the whole period one of intense strain. Food was often short, and consisted of little more than bread and tea, the cold, especially in the tents, was often verging on the unbearable, and the long exhausting days took a lot out of us. It was a constant struggle to obtain ponies, keep the carts together, find shelter and food, and look after the various members of the party. Added to the physical hardships, was the constant dread that our journey would be in vain, that on arrival in Semiryechie we would find the country in the hands of the Reds, and the subconscious anxiety as to future means of escape.

The knowledge that Annenkov still held the reins was therefore a distinct relief, and it was arranged that, in order to lose no time, de Kerangat should set out in his re-resuscitated car for the next picket, Kizil-Kisky, where he could reach the Ataman by telephone, and obtain some news. He was to wait for me, as I was to set out the following morning by post-horse with Albert, while the remainder of the party followed as quickly as possible. We were to reassemble at Sergiopol, when I hoped to have definite plans ready for our future movements. The mere thought of talking to someone on a telephone, brought civilisation nearer, even though the barren hills and wastes about us proclaimed our present resting-place as still an unknown spot in the heart of Asia.

That night in an old disused barn, strewn with straw and piled high with luggage, we sat around on boxes and valises, eating a savoury stew, talking as we had seldom done before, with hope higher than it had ever been, that our perilous journey would be brought to a successful conclusion. But the road before us was long, and we had been travelling almost incessantly since 25th November when we left Akmolinsk nearly three weeks earlier, so that the sight of our blankets spread on clean bundles of straw was soon too much for us and we lay down in a long line against the wall and fell asleep.

CHAPTER 17

IN THE LAND OF SEVEN RIVERS

THE district between Semipalatinsk and Turkestan is a country of rivers, lakes, mountains, and sandy wastes, but with little of that wide and undulating steppe with which we had lately grown familiar.

Its inhabitants are mainly Kirghiz, the Russian colonists being comparatively few, especially at that time, when the revolution and its resulting robbery and murder had driven a great number of the latter to Semipalatinsk or even further in the hope of escaping the attention of marauding bands, which attacked and burned many of the isolated villages.

We were now in the midst of this country, and on reaching the post road, found ourselves at Malo Ayagusky, some 350 versts south of Semipalatinsk, sixty-five versts from the eastern end of Lake Balkhash, and 240 from the nearest point on the Chinese border, surrounded on three sides by the Bolsheviks, and ignorant of the country to the east, through which we must pass to reach safety. As the only road to the border lay through Sergiopol, it was necessary to make all speed to get there in order to acquire definite information and to obtain assistance, if possible, from Ataman Annenkov, who appeared to be the only man of importance in the district.

De Kerangat had already started in his car to get in

touch with the Ataman, and I decided to take our one carriage and travel after him with Albert as fast as possible, using post-horses and leaving the remainder of the party to follow with the luggage, which had to be drawn or carried by camels, as no ponies were available. Accordingly, on the morning of the 14th, my servant and I set off alone, well wrapped up in our carriage, with a Kirghiz *yamstchik*, or driver, who urged on the three ponies and made good time. As we got further north, the country became more rocky and uneven, and we plunged into ranges of low barren hills, which seemed even more inhospitable than the open steppe. The weather was bitterly cold, but the lack of wind helped us to bear the low temperature. The journey was uneventful, and we changed horses at Kizil-Kisky (twenty-six versts) and Taldy-Kuduk (twenty-four versts), finally reaching the picket of Ayagusky (twenty-seven versts) after dusk. In the post-house were de Kerangat, Bielenky, some Russian officers, and a few refugees, all drinking tea around a crowded table which was littered with scraps of food, dirty plates, glasses, and a *samovar*. The Frenchman had already spoken to Annenkov on the telephone, and the latter said that he expected to be in Sergiopol in a day or so, and feared the effect of Dutov's demoralised troops on his own forces.

The Russians in the post-house were much depressed as they were afraid of Annenkov, who had threatened to shoot any officers caught trying to escape into China. They were therefore planning to avoid Sergiopol and cut across country to the border, thereby hoping to elude the Ataman's posts.

De Kerangat decided to finish the last twenty-eight

versts to Sergiopol that night, and left me about eleven. I spent a thoroughly uncomfortable night on the floor which was covered with sunflower seeds, and much other refuse, packed tightly between two uneasy sleepers.

On the following morning I had a hard time to get horses, and then the kicking of the centre pony broke a shaft, which took some time to replace. The country was now very wild, our road running over rocky spurs or across the frozen bed of some small stream or the River Ayaguz, which we crossed several times during the trip. Just before midday, we emerged on a flat plain, intersected here and there by the steep banks of sunken water-courses, and covered with a coarse vegetation of scrub and stunted trees. A couple of versts away the straggling outskirts of Sergiopol were visible, showing a line of dirty grey huts on the desolate plain. The town proved to be small and of poor appearance, with a miserable market-place and squalid one-storey houses.

As usual the Town Commandant knew nothing and we tramped the streets disconsolately in search of the French Mission. It took us two hours to find de Kerangat, who was in a small, very cold but clean room, perfectly happy, and without any food. In the evening Annenkov arrived, and we went to call on him.

He was a slim handsome man of twenty-eight or thirty, probably a couple of inches under six feet, but very strong and full of vitality. In his dress, he was rather theatrical, with heavily embroidered calfskin breeches, and a great tuft of hair on the left temple, which stuck out from under his cap like an English soldier's overgrown 'quiff.' His personality was distinctly attractive, and though in conversation was rather given to boasting and over-confidence, he produced a good impression. He asked a good many questions about the Orenburg Army, informed us that he was going to inspect his southern front in the neighbourhood of Kopal (about 350 versts south of us) next morning and would return in three days, when he would personally take us across the border to Chuguchak, where a regiment of his was stationed, supply us with money for transport, and do everything in his power to assist us on our further journey. He was rather vague as to what we should do once we were in Mongolia, but his confidence that everything would turn out all right was so obvious that we returned to our billet much comforted.

Our information about China was still very sketchy, in fact all we knew was that Annenkov appeared to have great influence in the nearest town, Chuguchak, where there were Russian and Japanese Consuls. The most encouraging news was that the telegraph line connecting us with Chuguchak went on across the continent to Peking, and we hoped therefore to be able to get a message to Vladivostok, inform the British Mission of our plight, and also let our various families know we were still alive, as there had been no chance to send letters since Colonel Pichon left Kokchetav for Omsk at the beginning of November, and my last telegram to Britmis had been from Akmolinsk on 23rd November.[1] However, on my applying at the military telegraph station at Sergiopol to send a wire to Vladivostok, the officer in charge said it was impossible, and my hopes of immediate assistance from the coast, in the way of instructions and money, were disappointed.

[1] One of these letters was posted in Canada two years later, and eventually reached its destination. Who posted it, or what caused the delay, I never knew.

Meanwhile, the time passed slowly as there was nothing to be done, and the town was lifeless, as the uncertainty of the situation kept people indoors, and the lack of food and merchandise closed any shops there may have been in normal days. The market had little to sell, the streets were dirty and full of great holes and ruts, and as there was nothing to see, I stayed indoors most of the time, occasionally calling with de Kerangat on some of his refugee friends, and meeting again the Zaitsevs, the beautiful singer, and several other officers and their wives. Not a few of these women were anxious to attach themselves to us, as they were afraid of the future, and thought our protection would be more efficacious than that of their husbands or lovers. I must say that in each case where the woman showed her willingness to come with us, the man was ineffectual, weak, or selfish, and ready to save his own skin first. I do not blame the poor women in the least, as the danger of the situation, and the hopelessness of their cause were only too apparent. They had to choose either terrible hardships and privations without end in that God-forsaken part of the world in the company of men who had already proved themselves no good, and whom they probably did not love; or, the protection of foreign officers, who still had Governments to appeal to, and would probably receive assistance from Chinese officials and a safe-conduct to the coast. I am surprised they didn't make more of an effort to go with us, and think that if we had encouraged them at all, they would have done so, but I had had enough experience of travelling with even one woman in the party for so short a distance as from Petropavlovsk to Kokchetav, and I was determined that our band should be a bachelor one, no matter how great the temptation to make it otherwise.

On the 17th, the remainder of the two Missions arrived, looking dirty and cold, in fact we were all pretty sights for not one of us had shaved or bathed for a fortnight, and even our washing had been of the 'lick and promise' kind. When I saw my unkempt hair and stubbly beard in a mirror, I nearly had a fit and immediately set about shaving, while Gordon Smith trimmed my hair with a pair of nail-scissors. The newcomers crowded the room to suffocation, but it was not worth while searching for better quarters as Annenkov returned from the south next day, promised to supply us with a lorry for our kit, and to take de Kerangat and myself by car to his headquarters at Urdjar on the way to Chuguchak, and then hurried off to inspect the troops south of Semipalatinsk. De Kerangat had at last realised that his car could not safely carry him further, and therefore made a present of it to the Ataman, much to the latter's delight and my relief.

In view of the difficulties ahead, I called in the three batmen, told them a trying journey lay before us, with many months on the road ere we could hope to reach civilisation, and gave them the choice of going with us, or of being paid off and handed over to the local commandant, who would probably allow them to enlist in the White forces, or give them some kind of work to do. They held a hurried consultation, and Alexei elected to remain in Sergiopol, while Albert and Peter both decided to go with us. I was pleased at the result as Alexei was rather a surly individual and the other two got on much better without him. Our dreadful-looking Kirghiz guide was paid off, and so was Gordon Smith's driver from Spassky, who refused to go further.

On the 19th, the motor lorry promised by Annenkov arrived late in the afternoon, and we sent Peter and the French soldiers off in it with most of our kit, while Gordon Smith, Moss, Morgan, and Albert also set out for Urdjar in the carriage and farm wagon. De Kerangat, Bielenky, and I remained behind to wait for the Ataman.

That afternoon a message arrived for me from Baron von Tiesenhausen, who said he was twenty-five verstsa way in the steppe and asked what my plans were. I sent back a reply saying that we were going very shortly to Chuguchak. Soon after dark, he arrived himself, and spent the night with us, reviling Dutov, and asking me to come with him. The poor old man's mind was now fixed on a place called Lepsinsk some 260 versts due south of us, in the foothills of the Ala-Tau range, the summit of which forms the international boundary ten versts beyond. It was his last hope, and someone had told him that it was warm there and that grapes were grown, so that he kept on interminably asking me to accompany his party to this garden of Eden, where 'it was warm and there were beautiful vineyards.' He seemed incapable of understanding that I was under orders to rejoin my H.Q. with all possible speed, and what he thought we were going to do in that isolated mountain village, I haven't the slightest idea.

After a round of farewell calls next day, we went to see Annenkov, who had just returned, and he asked us to be ready by seven the following morning. We were up in good time and said good-bye to the Baron, who kissed me with emotion, much to my discomfiture! I wonder what happened to that rather handsome, grey-haired old man, so full of impossible schemes and alarmist rumours, and to his young red-cheeked and energetic wife, who had been so relentless in her determination to reach Kokchetav in good time. They must have fallen on evil times in captivity, or in still worse concentration camps across the Chinese border.

The Ataman soon drove up in one car, followed by another in which he asked us to ride and we set out towards the south-east over the snow-covered tracks, and through barren, hilly country, leaving the squalid streets of Sergiopol without regret, except for the fears we felt on behalf of the miserable refugees and soldiers whose unhappy fate would in all probability soon overtake them.

All went well until the picket of Narinsky, thirty-one versts out, when the tyres of our car began blowing out, and we reached Djaksy Djartasky, ninety-seven versts from Sergiopol, on the rims. Here Annenkov was waiting for us, and we had some food while the punctures were being repaired, but the Ataman could not stay until we were ready, and set out, saying he would see us in Urdjar that night. He drove his car himself, and in spite of the cold did not wear a fur coat, although I suspected him of being well padded underneath. His energy and strength were greatly admired by his followers, who pointed with pride to his physical strength, powers of endurance, and energy. Besides driving his own car, he showed remarkable industry, conducting his own correspondence, supervising everything himself, and dispensing almost entirely with a staff. While waiting in the Kirghiz hut, which, with two or three others, formed the picket, the people showed us several pieces of native workmanship, such as a beautifully embroidered leather jacket, Turkestan tapestry, and carpets, which I tried to buy but they would not sell. Our car being ready we took the road once more, de Kerangat suffering severely from the cold as he had lost his fur cap and only had a kepi to cover his bald head. The dazzling snow was also very hard on the eyes, and I am surprised we did not get snow blindness.

Our tyres were very old and many times repaired, so I was not surprised when they all blew out again, and we were forced to halt at the next picket, Karakolsky, some twelve versts further on. I sent a messenger off to Annenkov saying we could go on no further that night, asked him for assistance the next day, and then prepared to spend the night in an unusually dirty *zimovka*, where we ate a little bread and fell asleep on the floor. That day our eyes had been gladdened by the view of snowy mountains, for we were approaching the Tarbagatai range which runs east and west in places along the Mongolian border south of Lake Zaisan, and the sight of lofty peaks sparkling in the sunlight was wonderful after the flat country of the Kirghiz steppe.

We were now only fifty versts from Urdjar in a direct line but it took nearly twelve hours to get there. Our tyres blew out again, and the heavy snow on the road made the chauffeur travel in third most of the time, so that the water in the radiator kept boiling, and we had to stop frequently to let the engine cool although the temperature was well below zero. On reaching the picket of Ters Bakansky, about twenty versts out, the chauffeur tried to proceed by the usual road, which makes a detour at the south through Burgonsky picket, but an impassable sunken water-course, with a thin treacherous covering of ice, forced us to turn back and take the more direct track to Urdjar. On reaching the steep banks of the frozen River Terekty, we found the lorry with the luggage which had left Sergiopol two days before us, stuck on the opposite slope, and we too tried vainly to mount the slippery bank, although all gave a hand to shove the old car up. Finally, followed by the lorry, we backed down and drove upstream on the ice until a practical ramp was discovered, and the two motors managed to get out successfully. Although our destination was soon visible, it took some time to reach the place, as the plain south and west of the town was cut up by sunken river beds, and in the growing darkness it was difficult to pick our way across the rough country, up and down slopes, and across the ice. We were glad when the twinkling lights of the town were reached, and the car stopped at Annenkov's headquarters. In the clear starlit night, the village looked singularly beautiful, with wide, snow-covered streets bordered by trees, and solid, comfortable-looking houses of one or two storeys, through whose frost-encrusted panes the warm yellow light streamed forth to gladden the heart of each weary traveller. On three sides rose the protecting mountains, whose steep slopes, patterned in bold black and white, seemed extraordinarily near and comforting, while the deep silence of the winter night and the innumerable stars, whose brilliancy in the clear atmosphere was marvellous, gave a soft unearthly quality to the scene, which I have never forgotten. I stood out in the snow, lost in the quiet and beauty of this outpost nestling among the hills, until the approach of a sleigh, whose tinkling bells sounded fairylike in the stillness, forced me to move and broke the spell.

From the cold outdoors, we entered a two-storey building used by the Ataman as his headquarters, and went upstairs to the mess-room.

Having been asked to dine, we were curious as to the style of living of this young Cossack, whose vigour and determination seemed to single him out from the other Russian commanders we had seen, and our surprise was great at the comfort and even luxury of his headquarters. The furnishings were, of course, not handsome and there was an absence of many things which would be considered necessary in Europe or America, but the room was clean, with curtains at the windows, a fresh cloth on the table, a large carpet on the floor, and oil lamps. Vodka and *zakuskas* (a sort of *hors d'œuvre*), were served before dinner, as is the Russian custom, and the servants were cleaner and better trained than I had seen elsewhere. As we drank to each other, an orchestra in smart red shirts played selections in the next room, and we were soon sitting down to an excellent dinner to which we did full justice, our tongues looser after so many little glasses of vodka, and our ears delighted by the unaccustomed sound of pleasant music. The band was made up of prisoners of war, chiefly Germans, who played very well.

Annenkov was in good spirits, talking of his plans, which were to take the offensive against Turkestan on the south, while Dutov's forces held the Semipalatinsk front. I told him he would be lucky if he got six hundred good troops from the Orenburg Army, but he was optimistic, talked of making himself independent of the outside world, and showed us cloth, buttons, and chocolate, which he said were manufactured in Urdjar! His egotism and the amazing exploits of which he was the hero, were rather too much for me, but he still remained an interesting and forceful character for all that.

Just before returning to our billet, which was not far off, I received a telephone message from Moss, who reported that he expected to rejoin me next day, which he did about noon, together with Gordon Smith, Morgan, and Albert. They had come by a more direct route than I, following the same road from Sergiopol as far as Narinsky, and then taking the northern branch which is shorter, but more difficult than the southern. Although this track is marked on the Japanese Staff Map, the pickets are not shown, and for the information of prospective travellers the names and distances are as follows:

From Sergiopol:

Narinsky	31 versts
Aisky	22 "
Djaman Egenskoy . . .	18½ "

from here the road is very difficult and mountainous as far as:

Novi Troitskoy (or Aibuzu) . .	22 versts
Blagodatnoy Celo	12 "
Picket name unknown . . .	16 "
Urdjar	16 "
	137½ "

They had taken nearly four days to cover the distance, averaging about thirty-five versts a day, which was not bad going as the road was apparently quite mountainous, and impassable to motor traffic in the winter. There is a post-house at each picket, where relays can be obtained, and the telegraph line follows this route.

That afternoon de Kerangat and I were asked to inspect the Cuirassier Regiment, so we donned our best uniforms, buckled on our swords, and accompanied Annenkov and his A.D.C. to the main street, where about four hundred dismounted men were drawn up in line. They were dressed in long grey greatcoats with yellow facings, leather knee boots, and large fur caps, and seemed well fed and clothed. Every man was armed with a sabre, and the officers with revolvers in addition. At the head of each squadron, the Ataman halted, and as we stood at the salute, he shouted the Russian greeting, '*Zdorova, Molodtze*,' which is imposing in reality, but sounds ridiculous when translated as 'Good health, my lads!' As his shout died away, the entire lung power of the squadron answered in unison with a deep roar of '*Zdrayou Jelayou, Brat Ataman*' ('We wish you health, Brother Ataman,') for as a sop to democratic ideas, the old form of address had been changed from Mister Captain to Brother Captain, Brother not being so familiar as the Bolshevik word Comrade. After passing down the line, we stood at the saluting point while the troops marched past in sections, using the German parade (or goose) step, which was difficult on the slippery snow, and rather marred an otherwise commendable turnout.

We spent until the 28th in this attractive little village, which nestled so comfortably in the semicircle of mountains, but I believe we saw it at its best for a mantle of white snow covered the countryside and hid a multitude of

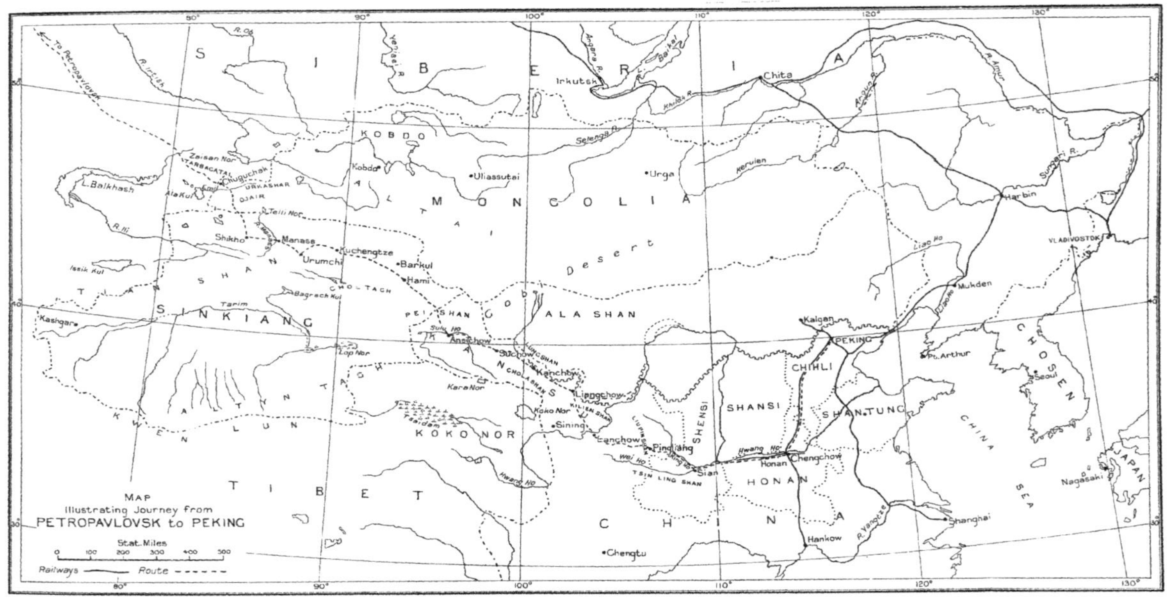
MAP
Illustrating Journey from
PETROPAVLOVSK to PEKING
Stat. Miles
0
100
200
300
400
500
Railways
Route
SIBERIA
MONGOLIA
KOBDO
ALTAI
Desert
GOBI
ALA SHAN
SINKIANG
TIAN SHAN
ALTYN TAGH
KWEN LUN
TIBET
KOKO NOR
NAN SHAN
CHINA
CHIHLI
SHANSI
SHENSI
HONAN
SHANTUNG
CHOSEN
CHINA SEA
JAPAN
To Petropavlovsk
R. Irtish
R. Ob
Yenisei R.
Angara R.
Baikal
Selenga R.
Khilok R.
Argun R.
R. Amur
Sungari R.
Kerulen
Liao Ho
L. Balkhash
R. Ili
Issik Kul
Zaisan Nor
TARBAGATAI
Chuguchak
URKASHAR
DJAIR
Ala Kul
Telli Nor
Shikho
Manass
Urumchi
Kuchengtze
Barkul
Hami
CHOL TAGH
Bagrach Kul
Tarim
Kashgar
Lop Nor
PEI SHAN
Sulu Ho
Anschow
Suchow
Kanchow
Liangchow
Kara Nor
Koko Nor
Sining
Tsaidam
Hwang Ho
Lanchow
Pingliang
Wei Ho
Sian
TSIN LING SHAN
Honan
Chengchow
Hankow
R. Yangtze
Shanghai
Chengtu
Kobdo
Uliassutai
Urga
Irkutsk
Chita
Harbin
VLADIVOSTOK
Mukden
Kalgan
PEKING
Pt. Arthur
Seoul
Nagasaki
80°
90°
100°
110°
120°
130°
50°
40°
30°

sins. In summer it must be hot and dusty, while in spring the melting snows rush in torrents through the many river beds, isolating the town, and emptying into Lake Ala Köl, or being lost in the sandy wastes of the plain.

Christmas Day was a memorable one, for Morgan succeeded in getting two geese for 500 roubles. Albert made pancakes, I produced a precious bottle of whisky, and someone else some cognac. This feast was spread out in the main room of the Tatar house where we were billeted, and every one set to with a will, forgetting the worn enamelled plates and cups, and the deficiencies in cutlery in honour of the occasion, and drinking 'Good Luck' to our further journey. I for one ate too much, and felt like one of these little black savages one sees in pictures of Central Africa, whose tummies are distended far beyond their natural size. I was beginning to sympathise with their belief in eating when the eating was good. Our square meals were sometimes far between, and the instincts of primitive man were reasserting themselves.

As regards our future, I had got in touch with the Russian Consul at Chuguchak through Annenkov, and learnt that there were two possible routes to Peking, which was the only place to make for, as all other roads were closed either by the enemy or by impassable mountains. The first was through Uliassutai and Urga in Mongolia, which necessitated leaving practically all our baggage behind as the mountainous country during the early part of the trip would only be passable to ponies with light loads. The second was through Urumchi and Hami (Qomul) further to the south, and was practical for carts at all times of the year. The Consul also said that ten thousand Romanov roubles, as the old Tsarist money was called, in notes of small denominations, were necessary to start the journey, and that we should telegraph to Peking for assistance.

Thinking that it would be difficult to receive word from our Ministry there for some time, and not knowing how they could assist me financially, I approached Annenkov and asked if he could advance me some money. This he promised to do, but no cash was produced in spite of further requests, although he renewed his assurances that everything would be arranged by the time we reached Chuguchak. I telegraphed to Britmis, Vladivostok, therefore, telling them that I expected to reach the border town at the beginning of January, would have to cross China to rejoin the Mission, and would wire my plans later on when I had more information. I do not believe that this wire ever reached its destination.

While endeavouring to secure all the data I could on the road before us, and to borrow money, I was also engaged in an attempt to buy horses, which were considered necessary, as we did not know what to expect once we had crossed the frontier. Also our Omsk roubles would be worth little in China but if we had even steppe ponies, we could exchange them for a certain number of silver taels. However, not only were very few to be had in Urdjar, but the prices were ridiculous, and I decided reluctantly that post-horses would have to carry us to Chuguchak, and we should then do the best we could to get some other form of transport there.

While our own troubles were being slowly thrashed out, the unfortunate arrivals from Dutov's retreating Army were immediately arrested on their reaching Annenkov's area, unless they carried *bonâ fide* papers of some sort ordering them to a definite destination on duty. Not only the junior officers, but even the generals, were treated in this fashion, for Annenkov was young and was not going to have any arguments about seniority, and he also thought it prudent to relieve each prisoner of all the cash in his possession over ten thousand Omsk roubles. Until the Ataman should decide on their fate, these first-comers remained under guard, and would have been shot should they have attempted to escape, and this firm action undoubtedly prevented an exodus over the border. I was interested to see how he would control the situation.

He was charming to us, had us to dine or drink tea until all hours of the night, and talked indefatigably about himself, his horses and his exploits, which should have done credit to Baron Munchausen. I have never heard such incredible deeds described with so much vigour and plausibility, while de Kerangat and I sat with perfectly straight faces, drinking in every word as though it were Gospel truth. He must have thought we were damn fools. For instance, he had often referred to his Regiment of Black Hussars in Chuguchak, which we found to consist of twenty-five Cossacks, and his boasted army of forty thousand men was in reality less than nine. Two or three of his horses were fine-looking animals, and he loved to talk of them and the feats of endurance and agility he had performed with this or that one. I believe he was a good horseman, and his physical strength was astonishing. One evening after dinner he showed us a spherical cast-iron weight, with a handle cut in the surface, and asked us to lift it. De Kerangat bent down, and grew very red in the face, but failed to budge it, and I moved it only a couple of inches from the floor with great effort. The Ataman then seized and slowly raised it above his head, holding it up at arm's length, and then returning it easily to the floor, while we looked on with admiration.

The day for our departure came too soon, as we liked Urdjar more than any other of our halting-places, and all were sorry to say good-bye to Annenkov, who had treated us very well. Though all his promises were not fulfilled, yet he did a great deal to help us on our way, even if an actual loan was not forthcoming, and for that he was not to blame for he didn't have the money. We said good-bye on the morning of 28th December, and he again assured us that the Consul in Chuguchak had had instructions to supply us with the necessary funds, and that our billets along the road had already been prepared. We thanked him for his hospitality and the trouble he had taken, and then returned to our billet, where our caravan was being loaded.

Gordon Smith and I were to ride in his sleigh, which had a cover and was quite comfortable, and was drawn by two post-horses. Moss and Morgan were to follow in the carriage, and the two servants in the farm wagon, both drawn by the five horses that the engineers had brought from Spassky. For the French Mission, I had hired four uncovered sleighs, which were the only practical transport available, and four teams, each of which cost 2000 Omsk roubles for the whole journey. Besides de Kerangat and Bielenky, there were Sergeant Doumeng, Private Buffet, Ensigns Ullman and Garno (the two Letts), and a prisoner of war called Samstag, who had acted as chauffeur.

As we filed out of the town, we passed Annenkov and a group of officers on their way to inspect the Cuirassier Regiment. He waved a farewell with his curved sword, and we with our fur caps, until the little knot of officers was lost to view, and we turned our faces to the east and the mysterious frontier.

The road was flat, with less snow than we had expected, and at times the horses had difficulty in dragging the sleighs over bare patches of earth. Before reaching the deserted picket of Barakpaisky (twenty-two versts), three sunken river beds, in two of which water was still flowing in a thin stream, had to be negotiated, but this was accomplished without much difficulty, and we pushed on to Makhanchy (twenty-six versts), reaching there about five. This little place had been half destroyed by the Bolsheviks in 1918, when they ravaged the country, but a few houses were still standing, and we found a billet ready and an excellent supper awaiting us, all prepared by wire from Urdjar. De Kerangat had had a bad time during the day, as he and his party sat on the open sleighs and were frequently tipped off into the snow, wherever the road was uneven, which was quite often! Moss and Morgan did not arrive until two hours after us, as the Spassky horses were in poor condition, and could not keep up with the others.

Next morning our landlord was very averse to taking Omsk roubles in payment for our night's lodging, but as we had nothing else he had to accept them. As we approached the frontier, the value of Russian paper currency depreciated rapidly, especially the Omsk roubles, which were all I had.

The road was again bad for sleighs, and two river beds with steep banks had to be crossed soon after leaving the picket. We passed the ruined huts of Ataghaisky, eighteen versts out, and a further deserted picket at the end of twelve more. Deeper snow now covered the road, and our leading teams reached Bakhty, the last picket on the Russian side of the border, about half-past four, after a day's trek of fifty-two versts. Moss and his two vehicles did not arrive until after nine, as the teams were almost exhausted.

Our billet was again ready for us, and I had just taken off my *shuba*, when an officer with two N.C.O.'s entered the room, and introduced himself as Lieutenant Vouitch of the Serbian Army. He explained that he had been detailed to take a convoy containing silver bars from Semipalatinsk to Chuguchak, with an escort of twenty-five men, and had successfully accomplished his task, when the mutiny at the former town had cut him off from the remainder of his regiment. Without funds, or any idea what to do, he had been offered a place in Annenkov's Partisan Division, but being a Serb, had no desire to enroll himself in a Russian unit, and considered it his duty to try and extract his men from the predicament they were in. I believe he had his Russian wife with him also. How he came to be escorting silver bars in that wild part of the world, I never found out, but he was in a desperate situation, having existed on charity for some days, and we tried to help him out. De Kerangat said he would wire to General Janin for instructions, as the French were supposed to look after the Serbs, Poles, Letts, and other nationalities who had troops in Siberia, and I suggested we lend Lieutenant Vouitch some money to live on until a reply was received, as we could not take the Serbs to China with us, not even having enough money to feed ourselves, while he and his men could live on in Bakhty with Omsk roubles, at any rate for three weeks or a month.

The Frenchman and I, therefore, each produced fifteen thousand roubles, which we handed over to the young Serb, much to his delight. He left us and we then turned to thinking of other things, chiefly food, which was soon ready and we sat down to our last square meal on Russian soil.

Behind lay over two months of almost continuous travel, during which we covered sixteen hundred versts and had gradually been forced into more and more desolate country, until in the last days of the old year we found ourselves in this little frontier post, north of which at no great distance stretched the lofty crest of the snow-covered Tarbagatai range, while to the south lay the sandy wastes around Lake Ala Köl, and the foothills of the Chaghan Oba. Our next step would be across the border into a land which promised to be more bleak and difficult than that already crossed, and where not one of us spoke a word of the language. In spite of Annenkov's promise, I had little hope of assistance from the Russian Consul in Chuguchak, and the difficulties in the way of reaching Peking, over more than two thousand miles of unknown country, were so great that I should never have attempted the journey had any other route been possible. To enter Mongolia was like taking a step into a strange dark room, for not one of us had any idea of what the country was like beyond the frontier, and it was with a feeling of great interest, not unmixed with anxiety, that we looked forward to the morrow.

CHAPTER 18

ACROSS THE BORDER

OWING to the exhausted condition of the Spassky ponies, I borrowed five from the Commandant at Bakhty to replace them, and was soon ready for the road. Smith and I led the way in the sleigh, to the side of which I had attached a small Union Jack in honour of the occasion, and after us came de Kerangat and Bielenky, also with a flag, the French tricolour. Just outside the picket, which seemed to have no fort although it is an important point on the frontier, we crossed over a small bridge, and had not gone very far when we were met by a very lean and wall-eyed Chinese, who rode up on a shaggy pony and solemnly handed me three bits of red paper, each covered with a number of black characters. We had no idea what these signified but took them to be the cards of the local governor or some other official who had sent his servant to welcome us. After responding awkwardly to his many bows and smiles, he motioned us to follow him and rode on as a guide, until after crossing six versts of scrub-covered plain, we reached the frontier post, passed it with cheers, and drew up in front of a small and dilapidated mud fort, with a crenellated gateway.

Twenty or thirty Chinese soldiers immediately surrounded us, and began talking simultaneously, until there was such a jabber going on that we could not help laughing.

They were clad in a motley array of dirty sheepskin coats, or faded jackets and breeches of blue cloth padded with cotton, and two or three wore the regulation military cap with its five-pointed multi-coloured star, the badge of the Republic. The men were a poor, underfed, and physically repulsive crowd, diseased, undisciplined, and miserably armed. They could have put up no resistance to the feeblest kind of attack, and I now understood why Annenkov was able to quarter some of his own troops on Chinese territory. My eye kept trying to pick out someone in authority and I eventually spied an individual whose dress was little different from the rest, but whose broken old bowler hat proclaimed him to be the local commander. He also presented each of us with his little red cards, and examined our papers, although they were in English and Russian, of which languages he was entirely ignorant.

Nearly an hour was wasted, while the officer endeavoured to speak to us, and the soldiers gibbered like monkeys, but luckily two Cossacks arrived from Chuguchak, said they were from Annenkov's Regiment of Black Hussars, showed a note to the Chinese commander from the Russian Consul, and told us we were at liberty to proceed. This we did, crossing another twelve versts of flat sandy plain, then covered with a thin layer of dirty snow. No more mournful scene can be imagined than the barren desolation of that frontier tract, with its windswept covering of snow and sand, the miserable clumps of vegetation, and the absence of any sign of human dwelling. To north and south rose the naked slopes of mountain ranges, their white-capped peaks glittering coldly in the brilliant sunlight, while somewhere in the distance lay the mysterious oriental city still hidden from our sight.

As our destination grew nearer, some stunted trees appeared, then a few mud farm-houses with crude attempts at Chinese architecture showing in the gateways and the roofs; more vegetation; and then crossing a little bridge we came in sight of the massive crenellated walls of the city, the ornamented gateways, the booths, and the shops of traders and merchants. Past us flowed the busy stream, soldiers, beggars, and hawkers; a solemn slowly-pacing caravan of camels carrying great bales of hides or chests of tea; familiar-looking Kirghiz in sheepskin; Tatars with round fur caps; and other Mongolian types of many kinds. It was like being transported suddenly to another world. Eighteen versts away across the border not a Chinaman was to be seen, trade was at a standstill, civil war and a debased currency had strangled the life of the country, while here was a comparatively prosperous town, its shops and booths full of goods, and inhabited by a population as different in appearance, speech, and customs as one could imagine. To the eyes of a traveller, arriving from the higher civilisation of Europe or America, the people, the streets, the merchandise for sale, would have seemed infinitely crude and miserably poor, but to our minds this sudden change to bustling life, where many things could actually be bought at reasonable prices, and where the normal existence of the inhabitants was going on, unaffected to all appearances by the great upheaval across the border, was little short of miraculous.

Led by our two Cossack guides, we kept outside the walls, and reached the small Russian colony, where the foreign traders and consuls were to be found. Our carts

AT THE RUSSO-CHINESE FRONTIER POST, 30TH DECEMBER 1919

Facing p. 214

and sleighs filed into the large courtyard of an imposing red brick house, and a fine looking Tatar of forty or forty-five, welcomed us in Russian. He was Ramazan Chaneshev, a rich merchant and friend of Annenkov, who had asked him to put us up during our stay in Chuguchak. The house, a long low structure, had been built at tremendous expense, of bricks brought by slow-moving wagon trains for hundreds of miles. We were led up a flight of outside steps into a hall, and shown a large high-ceilinged room with tall windows looking on the street, and furniture of Russian make. This was put at our disposal, as was another room for the French soldiers, Letts, and servants, while opening off ours, was a big salon also furnished expensively and tastelessly with modern Russian chairs, tables and curtains, which were obviously seldom enjoyed by their owner. Our host and his young son watched the unpacking of our kit with great interest, and brought us bowls of deliciously cooked rice mixed with raisins and meat, which we accepted thankfully. The magnificence of our new quarters was rather unexpected, but augured well for the future. Outside in the yard an inquisitive crowd of Tatars and Chinese had collected, and even penetrated into the house until ejected by Chaneshev, and finally pushed out of the yard and the gate shut to allow our people to work in peace.

As soon as we were presentable, de Kerangat and I went to the Russian Consulate nearby and met Mr. Dolbijev, the Consul for the old Imperial Government, told him of our predicament, and asked for information as to how best to reach the coast. He was very helpful and promised to do his best for us in every possible way, first explaining the necessity of our calling on all the principal Chinese officials, who were most suspicious as to the reasons for our visit, and finally sending a Cossack with our cards to the Governor and other important men. All of these people returned this courtesy at once, and it was arranged to pay a round of calls next day. He also explained that the telegraph service to Peking was most unreliable, that we might have to wait several weeks for a reply, and that he would arrange to lend us enough money for the first stage of our journey to Urumchi, about a fortnight on our road. If I wired at once for the British authorities to credit me with funds at the Russo-Asiatic Bank in that town, we could start very soon and find the money waiting for us on our arrival there. I therefore sent the following telegram next day:

To British Embassy,
Peking.

31st December. Captain A. P. Hodges, R.F.A., with five British officers and men arrived Chuguchak. Must travel Pekin-wards *via* Urumchi. Borrowed sufficient funds Russian Consul reach Urumchi and request Embassy open account there at Russo-Asiatic Bank in my name and arrange help along road through Chinese authorities. Inform Spassky Company Harbin Messrs. Gordon Smith and Morgan with me. Wire please to next-of-kin safe arrival. Repeat telegram Military Mission Vladivostok for necessary action. Expect reach Urumchi end of January.

HODGES.

De Kerangat also telegraphed to the French Minister. As previously stated the southern route to Peking *via*

Urumchi and Hami was the only practical one to follow at that time of the year, as the northern mountain passes were too difficult in winter. Feeling much relieved at the apparent ease with which our shortage of cash was to be overcome, we returned to our palatial billet, looking forward with curiosity to the next few days in this isolated frontier town, so different from the steppe settlements on the Russian side of the border.

On the following morning, with buttons polished, swords at our side, and escorted by a dozen mounted Cossacks, de Kerangat and I rode on shaggy ponies with Mr. Dolbijev to pay ceremonious calls on the local officials. There were Yan Po Tuan, the Military Governor, a man of about sixty from South China; Ma Tuan Lin, Commander of the Garrison, a fine-looking man of fifty and a Dungan or Chinese Mohammedan; Liu Yin Chu, the Civil Governor, also from South China; Tsi Lan, the so-called Foreign Representative, in charge of foreign relations; and the Japanese Consul, Mr. Ota.

We rode at a trot through the snow-covered streets of the Russian settlement, past the booths outside the walls, into the Chinese city, passing gaping groups of Russians, Chinese, Kirghiz, Tatars and Sarts. In each case the calls were very similar and to describe one is to describe all in the main details. Preceded by a Chinese servant of the Consulate with our cards, we would ride up to the main gateway of the official's yamen, wait for the gates to open, and then dismount. Drawn up in the first courtyard would be a guard of honour of the most decrepit and pitiful-looking soldiers, clad in tattered uniforms, who brought their ancient rifles to the present in a manner which would have made any self-respecting sergeant weep. After rapidly 'inspecting' the guard, we advanced through several gateways to the entrance of the yamen where the official and his staff were waiting to receive us. Here there was much saluting, bowing, and handshaking, after which we were asked into a bare, sparsely-furnished room, each one trying to bow the other in first as ceremony demanded. Seated around a small table on bamboo stools, or uncomfortable straight-backed chairs, complimentary conversation took place translated by Mr. Dolbijev. Tea was brought in, and on the table were Chinese sweets, raisins, and nuts, of which we ate a little and found them very good. Around us stood an admiring circle of smaller fry, and outside a heavily-breathing crowd of domestics and soldiers peered through the dilapidated paper windows, and even poked their fingers through to make holes for a better view.

In order to make as imposing an appearance as possible, both de Kerangat and I were dressed in our best uniforms, with boots and belts polished, and buttons shining, but minus our greatcoats, which would not have looked so smart. The officials were evidently impressed, but the extreme cold, especially indoors, made itself felt, and we were glad that the calls were short. The discomfort of those rooms was appalling. Even the high officials slept on a plank or earth bed, covered with matting and a few skins, and the shallow charcoal braziers were of little use as the doors and windows were ill-fitting and allowed the cold air to enter making the temperature lower than the sunny atmosphere outside. The majority of the officials wore long padded coats of silk, the sleeves of which came well below the wrists, and they sat with their hands joined and covered by the ends. All wore round fur caps.

On our return to the house of Chaneshev, our calls were all returned, and the rest of the day was spent in repeating the ceremonies of the morning.

The Commander of the Garrison arrived in a two-wheeled Peking cart drawn by a mule and driven by a servant who ran alongside. He was escorted by a mounted bodyguard of fierce-looking Dungans, dressed in sheep-skins and sleeveless red jackets ornamented with Chinese characters in black. They formed up in line in the yard and seemed to have some idea of drill, saluting smartly as their Commander descended the stairs after his visit, and climbed on a little step to enter his cart, in which he sat cross-legged.

The Japanese Consul, Mr. Ota, was a very nice little man, who was said to be an officer, but was posing as a dentist!

1st January saw the start of the New Year celebrations which lasted several days, and left us all practically *hors de combat*. The Military Governor's feast was the first, and about one o'clock, the whole party, less the servants, French soldiers, and Letts rode once more through the crowded streets to the yamen, and were ushered with much ceremony to the banquet hall, a long low room, unheated except for a small brazier, and so cold that we nearly froze. Besides ourselves were all the principal Chinese officials, and a few Russians. No women, of course, were present. The long narrow table was covered with a coarse white cloth, and heaped with little dishes of fruit and sweets, and at each place were crude favours of coloured paper. After some delay owing to the late arrival of a few of the guests, the feast started, and proved to be an endless procession of Chinese delicacies starting with sweets and going on to sea slugs, bamboo shoots, tulip bulbs, fish of various kinds, chicken chopped in small pieces, bones and all; strange vegetables, nuts, sunflower seeds, tasteless heavy pastry, frozen pears, dried raisins, submarine weeds, sharks' fins, birds'-nest soup, and weird concoctions of rice and flour. Some of it was good, but the strange chopsticks were hard to handle, especially as our fingers were blue with the cold, and there were so many toasts that little time was left for eating although the meal lasted about five hours.

We drank a fiery spirit in little cups; it was, I believe, a kind of rice brandy, and soon after the guests had seated themselves the toasts began. Every one drank to every one else and then various games started, each of which had the object of getting one's opponent as tight as possible. The first one, 'one, two,' was merely guessing whether the other person had one or two nuts in his hand. If one guessed right the other drank, if wrong, one drank oneself. Most of the Chinese were playing at finger guessing, where two opponents simultaneously open their clenched fist showing one or more fingers, each shouting a number. The winner is he whose number equals the fingers shown by both hands. It is a quick and lively game and they are extraordinarily good at it.

Our host, who was dressed in the ill-fitting uniform of a Chinese General to which was attached by an enormous safety-pin some Swedish decoration, began to get paralytic and was continually coming round to us to drink our health, while he stood swaying gently back and forth with great drops of brandy trickling down his straggly grey beard. Apparently people were not enjoying themselves enough, so he ordered one of the soldiers to bring a

THE AUTHOR AT THE RUSSO-CHINESE FRONTIER, 30TH DECEMBER 1919

Facing p.

drum, had it placed against the wall, and sat solemnly with his back to us. A rose was then given me, and as the Governor began beating the drum, I was told to pass the flower to my neighbour. It passed quickly round the table as the drum-beats grew now slow now faster, and then suddenly stopped. A roar of applause broke out, I held the rose, and had to swallow another cup of brandy. This game was repeated several times, I playing the drum once, and then our host 'passed out,' and was supported from the room by his soldiers. That was a signal for us to go, and we were damned glad to find ourselves back in the billet, with aching heads and unsteady legs. We had stood the first attack manfully, but a repetition of the same affair was looked forward to with dread!

Next day was much the same as the day before, except that the Russian Consul gave the feast this time and vodka was drunk instead of the native brandy. It was, too, a typically Russian meal with *zakuska* to start with, and many kinds of fish and meat. The Governor, who had been the life and soul of the party the previous day, was a very sorry sight and was forced to sit all the afternoon sipping a little gruel! The drinking was very heavy, and by half-past five Gordon Smith was counted out and taken home, but the show kept up for another hour as custom demanded. Leaving the Consulate, very happy, I suggested to Moss that we chuck Bielenky into a snowdrift, so we seized him, turned him upside down and threw him into a deep pile alongside the road. The Russian Vice-Consul, a large fat fellow, was convulsed at the sight, but in a second we'd stood him on his head and tossed him after the interpreter. De Kerangat was laughing so hard by this time that our combined attack took him unawares, and soon three hilarious figures were struggling in the snow. The amount of drink, the exertion and the extreme cold were then too much for me. My mind became a blank. I was apparently horribly sick and the next thing I knew was next morning when I found myself lying on my camp bed in the billet.

Gordon Smith was still prostrated, and my fat head prevented my lunching with Mr. Ota, although I managed to stroll round the town and look at the bazaar. Cheap cloth, hides, sheepskin clothes, tea, crude ironware, foodstuffs, felt, rope and tawdry knicknacks, seemed to be the only wares, although trading was busy and the different types were interesting. The soldiers seemed the poorest, eking out their miserable pay by hawking cakes and bundles of firewood. They were mostly old, one-eyed, opium smokers, lame or otherwise unfit, and represented the one class of the population that was least capable of bearing arms. Their rifles were of very ancient patterns, and their uniforms so ragged and worn as to be almost unrecognisable as such, so that the soldiers' only conceivable function was to increase the prestige of their hirer, according to the number of men on the pay-roll, for each official had his own troops. I suppose two worn-out old coolies look more impressive than one lusty youngster, and probably cost less.

The Consul told us that in the summer of 1919, an undisciplined band of Bolsheviks, who apparently had had their homes looted by Chinese bandits, advanced to Chuguchak to demand reparation, and had so terrified the officials that not a shot was fired, the Russians were received with open arms, and sent away loaded with gifts of sheep and horses.

The feasting continued until the sixth, but none of the dinners were as bad as the first two, and we managed to come through without any further casualties. Morgan, however, had a touch of rheumatic fever, and was laid up for a few days, being attended by a Russian *feldsher*, or unlicensed doctor. He passed much of the time teaching me what he knew of the Kirghiz language, and I rapidly picked up enough to make myself understood. This or similar dialects of Turki are used all over Western China, so I thought it important to learn a little for future use.

Being anxious to get some information to the British Mission in Vladivostok as to the situation in Semiryechie, I decided to send a message in clear, as ciphers were not allowed by the authorities, but written in such a way that no one but an Englishman would understand it. After puzzling for a long time, I finally concocted the following:

To British Embassy,
Peking.

January Second. Repeat Britmis Vladivostok please mum. In southern league first round sorry hear Crimson Ramblers succeeded by an innings. Second round late boss stonewalling up wicket liable get stumped while semi rich Edward Carson slugs sixes from other wicket. Edward takes large size in toppers but probably hiring stable at Vyerni by last meet of Garth. His scrum wobbly heaps three-quarters capable taking ball on tackling not strong figure agincourt by ten to five. Our circus three by armada full rabbits and tarts.

HODGES.

This I hoped would be interpreted as follows:

Repeat Britmis Vladivostok please keep secret. On the southern front (*i.e.* where the Orenburg Army had been operating) the Reds have won easily at first. In the second phase my late commander Dutov is on the defensive in northern Semiryechie but is liable to be defeated, while Annenkov (Semiryechie's 'King,' Edward Carson was always known as the 'King of Ulster') attacks vigorously in the south. Annenkov is over-confident but will probably take Vyerni by the end of March. His infantry is weak but he has plenty of cavalry capable of action, though their powers of attack are poor, his strength being between 14,000 to 7,000 (1415 by 10 to 5). The Orenburg Army has about 4,700 (1588 by 3) and is full of slackers and women.

Whether that message ever reached its destination, or was understood when it got there, I have never been able to discover, but it gave me a lot of amusement, especially when I pictured some conscientious Chinese secret service agent trying to decipher it!

Meanwhile, my efforts to secure transport for the journey to Urumchi, fourteen days away, were meeting with no success. Although the Russian Consul had promised us money and carts, it soon became apparent that he had no resources of any kind, except what he received from Annenkov, and the influence he could bring to bear on the Chinese officials. The latter, however, were unable or unwilling to help us, and the Governor would refer me to the Chief of the District, and he in turn to the Diplomatic or Foreign Representative. Although each was hospitable and professed a desire to help us as far as their resources permitted, they were still suspicious of us, and were apparently waiting for instructions from Peking or Urumchi. As the telegraph line was constantly out of order, it was with growing uneasiness that I realised our awkward predicament. Our expenses since leaving Petropavlovsk in October had been nearly 24,000 Siberian roubles, exclusive of the cost of our own personal disbursements for food. Even reckoning this at 800 roubles to the pound, we had only spent £30 in travelling over a thousand miles, but all I had left was a sum of 46,000 roubles, which were of practically no value in Chuguchak, as the traders would not accept them. Luckily, Gordon Smith's carts and horses brought us in 5600 Tsarist roubles, which were considered much more valuable than the Siberian notes and passed as legal tender in the town. We were therefore able to live for a time on this amount, but had no other resources, and I began to doubt the wisdom of asking Peking to credit me with money at Urumchi, when it looked as if I could never reach there. There was also the possibility that when we got to Urumchi no account would have been opened if Peking had never received my wire. Then we should have been in a terrible hole.

Our five thousand odd Tsarist roubles, then worth about £10, were not sufficient to pay for one cart on the next stage of the journey, and our living expenses and stores for the road were rapidly eating into this small amount of money, for £10 doesn't go very far with twelve men to feed, even in the wilds of Mongolia where food is cheap.

It would be necessary to carry all our provisions for the

fourteen days to Urumchi, except for mutton, which we could obtain at several places *en route*. Morgan acted as our quartermaster, and laid in supplies of dried apricots and raisins, frozen potatoes, a few dried vegetables, coarse sugar (very expensive), two or three kinds of meal for porridge, salt, pepper, garlic, wild onions, and large quantities of bread made especially for long journeys by Mohammedans and baked with certain fats which prevented it from becoming stale. Moss and I had had sufficient crockery and cooking utensils when we left Omsk, and there were still small amounts of tea, coffee, and tobacco, but the engineers and the French Mission were without any utensils or stores whatever, and so we bought some rough bowls, an enormous iron pot, and two circular sheet-iron stoves which proved invaluable.

On the 5th of January, Ataman Annenkov arrived for a short conference with some of the Chinese officials. He told us that Dutov had handed over the chief command and was to become Governor of Semiryechie, while Bakich was to take over the remnants of the Orenburg Army and go into action south of Semipalatinsk. All the other generals were to be sent away to various places on unimportant missions. News from Siberia was to the effect that Kolchak had fallen, and the Bolsheviks were chasing the last of the White troops towards the Manchurian border. He did not know what his future plans were but was apparently considering a retirement across the border, and an eventual junction with Ataman Semenov by retreating through Mongolia in the spring and re-entering Siberia east of Lake Baikal.

As regards ourselves, he could only lend us 3000 Tsarist roubles, and hope that the Chinese would advance the rest. He returned to Urdjar that afternoon and I never saw him again.

After continuous and unavailing efforts to secure some assistance from the Chinese, the Russian Consul hit on a scheme, which promised well, and eventually succeeded in getting the necessary transport for us. He approached our Tatar host, Ramazon Chaneshev, pointed out that we had already been ten days in his house, that we were unable to provide ourselves with carts for the journey, and that we should probably stay with him for ever if transport was not forthcoming. Chaneshev was only too glad to get us out of his house, and finally agreed to find six large carts and advance the money for them provided we paid him back on reaching Urumchi. This I agreed to, and by the evening of the 8th, he reported that he had arranged matters for us satisfactorily at a cost of 51,000 Tsarist roubles. The next day the Governor promised us an interpreter and 200 Kwanpiao taels.

It may seem strange that we should have paid for transport in China with paper money of a defunct Tsarist Government, but the town of Chuguchak and the border country had once carried on a lucrative trade with Russia, and as the merchants and traders had large sums in paper roubles, which were at a premium on the other side of the border, this money circulated as freely as before the revolution, although at a depreciated value. At the same time silver was at such a premium and so hoarded by its possessors, that it had practically disappeared from circulation, and the Chinese authorities printed their own notes, but were unable to supply the demand. In Siberia, the only money was of paper, Tsarist, Kerensky or Siberian, the first being the most valuable. In Mongolia the old Tsarist money was used more than any other, in that particular part near the border, but the other two issues were so depreciated as to be almost valueless. In working out my accounts at the exchange of the period:

1000 Siberian roubles equal 4·80 Kwanpiao taels.
25 Tsarist roubles equal 1·00 Kwanpiao tael.

The Kwanpiao tael was the official currency of Sinkiang Province, of which the capital was Urumchi, and was then standing at 180 to 100 Shanghai dollars. In Urumchi, where I obtained a better rate of exchange than I could have done at Chuguchak, my 46,618·85 Siberian roubles brought me only 223·77 Kwanpiao taels. My accounts were therefore quite complicated, and became more so as we penetrated further into the country and encountered fresh currencies.

Finally, on the 10th, all was ready for our departure, which I set for the following day. Our stock of food and cooking utensils had all been bought, deficiencies in clothing made up as far as possible, and all our kit packed and corded for the journey. I was anxious to get away, as quite a number of Russian refugees arrived during the 9th and 10th, and it was only a question of time before the defeated and demoralised White troops would pour across the border, followed probably by the Bolsheviks, as the Chinese were incapable of putting up a defence, and were already in a state of panic as to what the future would bring. Further delay might have involved us in a repetition of the flight from Karkaralinsk across the steppe, and I was not keen to go through that again. It occurred to me at one time that if I chose to remain in Chuguchak, I might

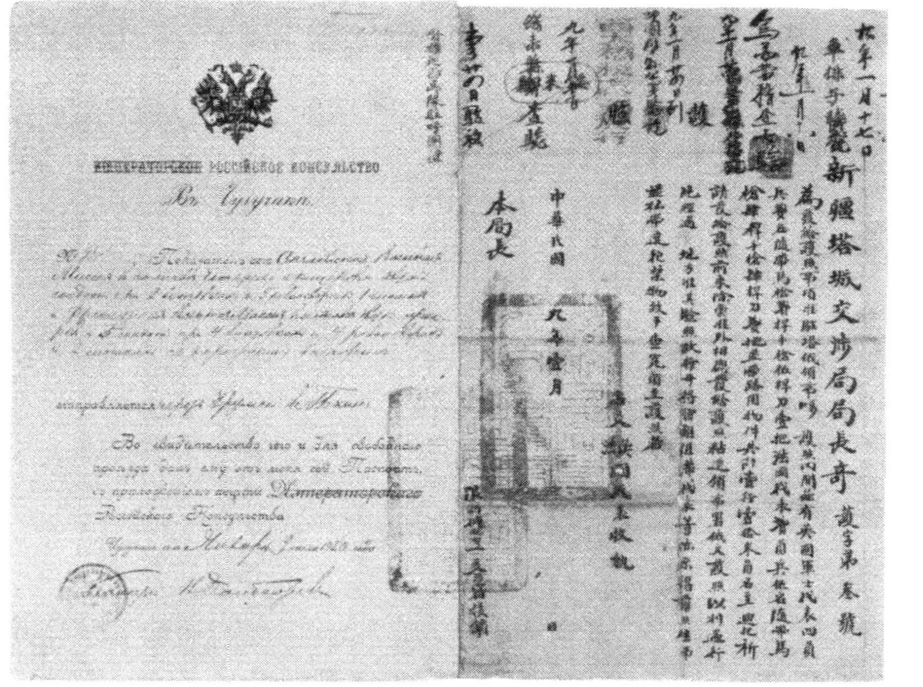

ИМПЕРАТОРСКОЕ РОССІЙСКОЕ КОНСУЛЬСТВО

Въ Чугучакѣ

新疆塔城交涉局局長奇

中華民國

本局長

MY PASSPORT FROM CHUGUCHAK TO PEKING, ISSUED IN RUSSIAN, CHINESE AND TURKI BY THE CONSUL OF A NON-EXISTENT GOVERNMENT

Facing p. 228

be of some help to the unfortunate refugees, most of whom were destitute, but I had no money or authority. and it was extremely doubtful whether I could get into communication with Peking, await their decision, secure funds, and still have time to be of assistance. If I reached Urumchi, and the British Government decided to keep me there for political or relief purposes, I should still be in a position to do something, and probably better situated near the Provincial Governor, and in closer touch with one or two other frontier towns. As it was, I decided to get away while I had a chance, especially as the French and the remainder of the party could not be asked to wait around indefinitely on the improbable chance of relief measures being decided upon by the Allies or the people at home.

I have already described briefly the town of Chuguchak with its snow-covered streets, massive walls crumbling in decay, the pitiful soldiery, and the mixed population. Although the officials were mostly Chinese, the people consisted of Mongols, Kalmucks, Kirghiz, Sarts, Tatars, Dungans, and other tribes of Mongolian or Turkic origin, and there was a fair sprinkling of Russian traders and refugees, and, of course, a large number of Chinese also. It was an extraordinarily interesting place, and under other circumstances I should have liked to stay longer, for there one was living under conditions such as existed in Europe in the Middle Ages. There were the walled city, the hired mercenary troops, the rival barons (represented by each local commander), the primitive life almost devoid of luxuries, bribery, corruption, intrigue, the lack of justice and weak central authority. There were to be seen the long camel caravans arriving from the East with chests of tea or other merchandise, the primitive metal-workers, and crude flour mills, the down-trodden and miserable labourers no better than slaves, and all the tyranny and wretchedness which one associates with the chaotic days of seven or eight hundred years ago. The single telegraph line, and the ancient rifles, were all that showed of modern civilisation, and they had made no impression whatever on the customs or standard of life of the people. It seemed impossible that such a place could exist in modern times, and stranger still that my oddly assorted companions and myself should unexpectedly find ourselves transported from the Europeanised plains of Siberia to this ancient and barbarous country, and faced with the prospect of a two-thousand-mile journey across its forbidding mountains and deserts.

De Kerangat, whose spirits never flagged although he must have been bored to death by all these English people, and I, managed to get a few maps, some Russian, some Japanese, and with the help of Mr. Ota, obtained a fair idea of the route to be travelled, although the exact character of the country was little known. Enough desert places, mountains, and rivers were visible, however, to show us that the road would be no easy one especially as the extreme cold made travelling an occupation to be avoided, even over good roads and with every preparation as to comfort and food. We were faced with a difficult road, little money, and hardly sufficient clothing, for we had not been able to secure much in Chuguchak, except rough sheepskin coats which were so badly made that they lasted no time at all.

The last night, we gave a dinner in the large and expensively furnished 'Salon' adjoining our room, to half a dozen Russians, men and women, whom we had met during the last few days, greatly to the horror of Chaneshev, who disliked having women in his house for fear that they would cause a scandal, which might reach the ears of his several wives, who were securely guarded in another wing of the house. His fears were not realised, however, as we broke up early to make ready for the beginning of the first stage of our journey in Chinese territory.

CHAPTER 19

THE ROAD TO URUMCHI

ON the morning of 11th January we said good-bye to the hospitable Chaneshev, who refused all payment for the quarters we had occupied, and drove out through his gate, escorted by half a dozen of Annenkov's Black Hussars and the Russian Consul.

Halting a couple of versts outside the town, the latter pointed out our road across the desolate plain, the escort shouted a last *Privyet*, and then left us to continue on our lone road through the Central Asian wilderness.

The caravan consisted of six light carts drawn by ponies, and with us rode a guard of half a dozen Chinese troopers. The driver of the cart in which Moss and I rode was the leader of the party, and in honour of his white beard was called Ak Sakal, a term of respect. He was an old Kirghiz, who spoke fair Russian, and acted as our interpreter.

Shortly after leaving Chuguchak, we had been joined by another party consisting of an old Russian General and a stout priest, who naïvely offered us their protection on the road. The priest was an ignorant, conceited ass, and a perfect nuisance, so we lost no time in requesting him and his companion to take themselves off. This did not occur, however, for several days.

A strong wind was blowing from the north-east, but it

was fortunately not too cold in the clear sunlight, and we journeyed southwards over the flat, barren plain, which was covered with a thick layer of snow. A number of small streams delayed our progress as they were often hidden beneath a treacherous coating of ice, and our wheels sometimes crashed through, to our great discomfort, and with considerable danger to the carts.

The first day we did twenty-five versts, and after crossing some frozen marsh land, halted for the night at a miserable hovel called Malo Ur or Tow Tai. With difficulty some brushwood was collected, a sheep killed, and we ate our mutton stew, thanking Heaven for the sheet-iron stoves, which had been bought in Chuguchak.

The next day was much the same, we crossed the River Emil on the ice and halted at the small village of Kurte, the population of which was Kirghiz or Tatar chiefly. On the 13th the mountains to the south were appreciably nearer, the amount of snow increased, and our ponies had hard work dragging us through the drifts. Passing the western end of the Urkashar range, we rested a couple of hours at the miserable picket of Sarai Kōl Sin, which stands on a small hill overlooking the plain, while to the west rose the rugged slopes of the Chaghan Oba.

After a further twenty-five versts of stony track covered with snow, a halt was made at Tolu for the night. We were now close to the foothills of the Djair mountains, which with the Maili range to the west are called the Djamantau or Bad Mountains by the Kirghiz. It was much colder, and we were hard put to it to keep warm, all crowding into one small room in a mud hut, where the entrance served both as a door and chimney, for our stoves were essential to keep us from freezing, and the pipe had to go out the only exit.

The so-called inns or rest-houses in Western China differ little from one another, except in size. The majority have a courtyard surrounded by mud walls and the row of hovels which shelter man and beast from cold and storm. They are nearly all in the last stages of decay, and where there is an innkeeper, he is usually an opium addict in the last stages of disease and poverty.

As soon as we halted at one of these caravanserai, I would select the least filthy of the huts, and stoves and necessary kit would be taken from the carts and a quantity of brushwood collected. As soon as a fire was started, an acrid smoke filled the hut, driving us all coughing and weeping into the freezing night. When the cold forced us to return, a large iron pot of brackish water was heating for tea and washing purposes. Meanwhile, a sheep had been found by the Kalmuck messenger, who preceded us each day, and this was killed and dressed by a Mohammedan, either the innkeeper or one of the drivers. The butcher had to be a Moslem, or the drivers would not touch the flesh.

Tea and ablutions being over, Morgan and the two servants prepared a mutton stew, which gave forth appetising odours, and partially made up for the filthy surroundings, the cold, the discomfort, and the acrid smoke from the stove.

After supper, we rolled ourselves up in every piece of clothing and covering we had, and lay down packed like sardines on the earthen *kang*, a mud platform which filled half the hut.

Each morning, stiff with cold, we rose about five,

breakfasted on tea, Mohammedan bread baked with fat, and some kind of porridge made of coarse meal. It was a hard, but healthy life.

Pushing on through hilly country, where the rough track wound in and out over stony ground we came to the Djair Pass, a narrow defile some six thousand feet above sea-level. On both sides rose sheer walls of sandstone and porphyry, and before us, in the floor of the gorge, ran the dry bed of a mountain torrent. Great boulders strewed the way, and at times the track was only just wide enough for our carts to pass. Struggling slowly upwards between the towering walls and over loose stones and hard rock, it was often necessary to man-handle the carts over rough places, and at one point we skidded fearfully on a sheet of ice, which covered the bottom of the defile and stretched ahead for several hundred yards. The ponies slipped and fell, the carts skidded, and we slithered back and forth, giving a hand here and there, and urging the tired beasts to further efforts.

This rough going lasted for twelve versts, and we then emerged on a small plateau, the summit of the pass, and began the descent on the southern side of the range. Here the defile was bordered by low hills. Darkness came on, our ponies stumbled along the stony track, and the carts swayed and jolted until I thought the axles would go at any moment. Halting at Köl Denin, we spent a miserable night as the hut was more dilapidated than usual, fuel scarce, and it was very cold.

The last twenty versts had been so hard on the horses that most of them went lame, and I found old Ak Sakal resorting to strange veterinary practices. One of his animals had gone lame in front, so he had tied a piece of rope very tight above each of the horse's knees, explaining that the lameness was caused by too much overheated blood reaching the hoof, and that he was therefore stopping the flow to let them cool off. I expostulated, but he shook his white beard stubbornly, and the horse was all right next morning.

On we went through rough hilly country, passing Otu, where there were a number of decrepit-looking soldiers, who arrived limping in twos and threes. They belonged to the new Governor of Chuguchak, who was on his way to take over from our old friend there. The road was bad and steep in places, but we managed to reach Sarjak, a very dilapidated picket.

Next day at noon we reached Olin Bulak, where there were a couple of huts in good repair, and I decided to halt and give the ponies a rest. This picket stands on the edge of a plateau some two thousand feet high, and commands a marvellous view of the great plain below. As far as the eye can see east and west is undulating country, sometimes barren, sometimes covered with dense forest, while to the south tower the great snow-capped mountains of the Tian Shan.

Standing with this great panorama spread out before me, I could look back through the centuries, and see the felt tents of the ancient Uigurs dotted here and there on a land more fertile than it is to-day; I imagined the sudden attack of their old enemies the Karaits, perhaps led by the great Wang Khan, Prester John himself; and then the *yurtas* disappeared, and the vast countryside was covered with the Mongol hordes of Genghis Khan marching westward on the long road that led to Moscow, and the plains of Poland and Hungary.

These scenes were not difficult to picture, for this far-off corner of the world had changed but little in a thousand years, or more. Gone were the days of Mongol glory, but around me were descendants of those ancient warriors clad in the kind of garments their forefathers had worn for generations, living the life of a nomad, eating boiled mutton, drinking koumis, and delighting in horse-racing and hawking. Except for the Russian *telegas* that carried us, we might have been travelling in the days of Marco Polo or Fra Rubruquis.

On the 17th, our caravan descended to the desert plain, which was covered here and there with low scrub, and halted at a picket of two huts called Köl. Here we met Djang Djar, the new Governor of Chuguchak, who seemed much interested in us. He sent a present of two pheasants, a box of cakes, and a bottle of rice brandy, requesting us to return the bottle when we had finished with it, and not to forget the cork!

Some of his soldiers wore the old leather belt of the British Army, and I noticed that the brass buckles bore the names of the Royal Sussex Regiment and Prince Albert's Light Infantry.

That afternoon we entered a tract of country covered with stunted trees and tall scrub, where the deeply rutted track wound in and out through dense thickets. There was quite a lot of small game, partridge, pheasant, and hare.

The next night we reached Lao Chen or Karasume, a small town on the main caravan route between the capitol of Sinkiang Province, Urumchi, and Kuldja over the frontier in Russian territory.

Here we decided to rest a day, and Morgan and I strolled through the streets, followed by a motley crowd of Tatars, Sarts, Kirghiz, and Chinese, who joined good-naturedly in our bargaining at the various small shops. We also watched two traders bargaining together, both seated cross-legged at the entrance to a shop. Having reached a stage in the negotiations when a settlement was near, and the public not supposed to know the final price, they each placed fingers on the other's right wrist, under the long loose sleeve of the coat, and the bids and offers were continued in silence by means of finger pressure. Our Tsarist paper roubles were not accepted here, as they had been previously, and we had to spend a number of our small stock of paper taels.

The caravanserai had proved too dirty for us, and so we had secured a lodging in a Sart's house. Our host had been ill for some time, so his womenfolk seemed to have more freedom than is usual. There were four or five of them, unveiled and quite good-looking, and they seemed to be having the time of their lives examining all our possessions, crowding round Albert and Peter when cooking was going on, and asking innumerable questions in Turki. Morgan did his best to satisfy their curiosity and I chimed in occasionally with a few words.

They had with them a beautiful little girl of ten or twelve, who watched us shyly from behind her mother's skirts, and seeing me smile at the child, the latter asked me if I wanted her for my wife. I inquired the price, and was told she was worth two hundred camels!

When we set out next morning, Moss and I waited behind to get a couple of new stove-pipes which a local Sart tinsmith had been ordered to make for us. The usual crowd collected as we waited outside the shop, and at last the smith, a swarthy, hairy-chested man, came out and handed us one pipe. I was surprised at seeing only one, as we had ordered two, but I paid him for the one at half the price agreed on. He immediately raised his voice in protest, and before I could find out what the trouble was, he and our old driver Ak Sakal were engaged in a furious dispute, clutching at each other's beards, and making such a din that I could get no sense out of them. I shouted to Ak Sakal to drive on, but the Sart seized the horse's reins and the row became more deafening than ever.

The crowd, which had been delighted at first, quickly changed its temper and was getting ugly, when Moss got out of the cart and tried to push the man away, so I called to him to get out his revolver. It was probably a foolish thing to do, but at the sight of the gun the crowd scattered in all directions, the Sart fell back sullenly, and we drove off, followed by screams and curses. I found out when we rejoined the others, that the Russian priest, who had attached himself to our party, had taken the other pipe from the smith, but had not informed me, so that the smith was entirely right in kicking up a row. I was already annoyed with this Russian as he had appropriated a sheep the night before, although it had been sent to us as a present by a local official, so I requested him to travel his own way in future, and leave us to ourselves.

For three days, our little caravan pressed eastwards, now over desert country, now through forests of cottonwoods, for we were skirting the southern edge of the Forest of Susat Kan. To the south rose the steep slopes of the Tian Shan, at which we never tired of gazing, as we emerged from some low-lying belt of woods on to a higher and more barren spur.

On the second night it snowed heavily, and our crazy

hut was not proof against the swirling eddies, which drifted in through countless cracks and covered us with a light blanket before dawn. With four inches of snow on the ground, the going was pretty bad next day, as we ploughed through drifts and over stony paths, and wound through woodland hollows and stretches of tall rank weeds seven or eight feet high. Then came a waste of stones, an occasional stunted tree, and at last the banks of the River Manass. Its broad shallow bed was two or three hundred yards across, and covered with a sheet of ice except for three boiling torrents which swept northward in narrow channels. The main torrent passed under and around a decrepit wooden-looking bridge, which stood desolate and forlorn, spanning its fifty yards in the centre of the field of ice. As we looked at this obstacle to be crossed two bare-footed Chinese came toward us fording the freezing streams, and kicking at the floating ice as if the water were as warm as the sea in summer.

With my cart leading we slithered down the steep bank on the frozen surface of the river, plunged into the first torrent, where the water foamed above our axles and the wheels sank deep into the soft ice, crossed twenty yards of ice again, and then crept fearfully over an ice bridge under which the water boiled and seethed as it raced past. I heaved a sigh of relief when the last cart had come over that safely. An hour later it must have been worn away.

Before us lay the main stream which overlapped both ends of the high-arched desolate bridge. Dropping a full three feet into the water, our cart was dragged slowly to the bridge, crossed it and set out over the ice to the far bank. Just as we left the bridge I happened to glance up-stream and saw a wave of foam approaching, cutting through the ice and racing towards us at a considerable speed. I shouted to the others to hurry, and just as the last cart neared the bank, the wave rushed past, cutting a new and wider channel.

A stretch of desert and we entered Manass, after passing many ruined and empty houses on the outskirts. The fierce struggles during the great Mohammedan Rebellion in the '60's had destroyed many a prosperous town, and this was evidence of some long-forgotten massacre. We entered through the West Gate, and as the inns were bad, we put up at the house of a Sart, Aiew Pa Djee, whose name had been given us at Laochen.

Manass was dirty, half-deserted and uninteresting, and we left it gladly to travel for three more days until we reached Urumchi.

Travelling of this kind is monotonous in the extreme. The carts are uncomfortable, the cold intense, walking is difficult in thick clothes, and the scenery hardly varies from day to day. Only the brilliant sunshine and the wonderful air make life worth living. Hardly a living soul is met from morning start to evening halt, and the inns are mere mud hovels by some brackish well. The towns or villages are poverty-stricken and filthy, and the inhabitants miserable to the last degree.

No sign of beauty, but for the cold serenity of the mountains to the south, no lovely trees, no grass, no colour but the drab rocks and stones, stunted trees and patchy scrub, nothing but mile after mile of stony track, the creak of harness, the scrunch of wheels. A deathlike stillness broods over desert and mountain, as the weary travellers plod heavily onwards, or lie listless and cold in the swaying carts.

During those three days from Manass to Urumchi, the destruction brought by the great rebellion was evident in ruined pickets, half-empty villages, and a crumbling temple.

The day before we reached our destination, I had another glimpse of Kirghiz veterinary work. One of our ponies got colic badly, and began bleeding from both nostrils. After walking the animal up and down for several minutes, the driver brought out a rusty old razor. The pony's head was held by two other men, and then his owner cut a shallow horizontal slit under each nostril. This exposed the ends of two bits of white gristle, which were promptly sliced off, and the operation was complete. Unfortunately, it was not successful, and the horse died that night.

On the 25th, we crossed the eastern branch of the frozen Hobali River, passed more desert country and reached the River Arhotu, where there were some trees and more vegetation. As we approached Urumchi, the Boghdo Mountains grew nearer, and soon a gap was visible, where the descending slopes, crowned with many-storeyed pagodas, gave access to the town through an easy pass. Soon the outskirts of the place were reached, a couple of stone bridges crossed, and we drove up a winding street lined with mud huts of Sarts and Tatars. Men, women, and children stared at us curiously as we went by, and then we swung under the massive gate, through narrow walled streets, through a noisy bazaar and out once more through another gate to the Russian Consulate.

CHAPTER 20

URUMCHI

THE Russian Consul was a short red-headed man, who had lived so long in this out-of-the-way place that he spoke a mixture of French, Russian, and Chinese in a very funny but almost unintelligible manner. We soon found ourselves in the empty house of the late Vice-Consul, a cheerless place in the Russian compound, where three bare rooms and a kitchen were allotted to us. A few Russian refugees occupied an upper floor.

We were too hungry and tired to cook anything, so attacked some frozen sausage and Tatar bread, and had just finished, when a tall Englishman accompanied by a short Japanese entered our room. I don't know whether he or we were the most delighted, but at any rate, we fell on each other's necks, and all sat down to ask innumerable questions. He was Postal Commissioner of Sinkiang Province, and his name was Boyers. The Japanese was Mr. Otaki.

Boyers was furious with the Russian Consul as the latter had asked him to put us up, and had then forgotten all about it! It was now too late to move, as the gates closed at five, and Boyers' house was at the other side of the city.

We gave him an account of our adventures, and then asked him for news as we had been out of touch with the world for over three months. He told us that the Bolsheviks had come in contact with Japanese troops near Lake Baikal, that the Czech General Gaida had attempted a *coup d'état* at Vladivostok, but had been defeated, that Annenkov had already crossed into Chinese territory with the remains of his own and Dutov's forces, and that Denikin in South Russia was on the verge of collapse. We were well out of Siberia at any rate.

During the next two days we moved our belongings to Boyers' house, where he and his wife welcomed us hospitably. Bielenky, the two French soldiers, and the two Letts remained at the Russian Consulate, Peter, Albert, and Samstag (de Kerangat's one-time chauffeur) were lodged at a nearby inn, and the rest of us were given two rooms by our host.

He had an attractive little house, surrounding the usual courtyard, in what had been the Manchu quarter before the massacres that took place during the revolution in 1911-12. We were very comfortable, and had good reason to be thankful that Boyers was there for he helped us very much in making ready for our further journey.

Urumchi, or Tihwa-fu, as it is called by the Chinese, is the capital of Sinkiang Province, and a most interesting city. The population of about 100,000 is chiefly Moslem. In its narrow crowded streets one sees types from all Asia: bearded Sarts, squat Kirghiz, yellow Mongols, turbaned Dungans, fierce Kalmucks, Chinese officials, traders from Turkestan, Afghanistan, India, and Persia. There are veiled Moslem women, Kirghiz women with their white headdresses, and silk-clad Chinese peeping through the curtains of a Peking cart. The edict against foot-binding and pigtails finds little sympathy and obe-

IN THE MOUNTAINS SOUTH OF CHUGUCHAK

Morgan, Gordon Smith, Buffet, Lieut. Moss and Capt. de Kerangat

URUMCHI, FEBRUARY 1920

To the right is the wall of the Boyers' house

Facing p. 244

dience here. Nearly all the women and young girls hobble painfully on deformed feet, while most of the Chinese cling tenaciously to the shaven head and queue which were once a badge of servitude.

Great crumbling walls, pierced with four gates, surround the city proper, and within are the chief bazaars, the yamens of the officials, and countless houses hidden from the narrow streets by high mud walls. Only their tiled roofs and richly-carved eaves show sometimes as one passes. Behind the walls are little courtyards, gardens, and many passages.

In the bazaars are cheap goods from the coast; coal brought from nearby mines in great creaking wagons that block the narrow streets; sheepskins; felt of goat or camel hair; cheap bowls of earthenware; dried fruit; vegetables; mutton; iron-ware of local make; blue clothing padded with cotton wool; skins of wild animals; jade ornaments and beads. Occasionally one spies a box of Huntley and Palmer's biscuits, or a packet of English candles.

Some of the streets are wider than in most Chinese cities, and along them pass little Peking carts, drawn by a mule with the driver running alongside, coal carts creaking and lurching over the frozen ground, horsemen from the surrounding country, ragged soldiery eking out a miserable existence hawking firewood, Mongol women with great daubs of scarlet on their cheeks, moon-faced Chinese children, fat officials in black silk and honourable spectacles.

The Governor of the province, Yang Tsen Shing, was a man of humble origin, who seized power by a *coup* during the revolution and has kept it ever since. His yamen held about two thousand of his relatives and dependents when I was there, and he ruled with an iron hand. He was reactionary, despotic and cruel, paid scant regard to Peking and appropriated the revenues for his own use. There were many stories about him.

One of them, which I have good reason to believe true, was as follows. In 1916, a plot to kidnap his eldest son was unearthed, and the Governor discovered the names of the conspirators. Without giving any inkling that he knew of their designs, he gave a large banquet, inviting the guilty ones and a number of other important officials and merchants. When the feast was well under way, he rose as was the custom, sat down next to one of his enemies and began playing the famous finger-guessing game with him. This was a signal. The doors were thrown open, a number of officers and soldiers with drawn swords entered, and the doors were then locked and guarded. The armed men made at once for the unfortunate conspirator with whom Yang was sitting, dragged him from his seat and murdered him on the spot. The horrified guests rose in terror, but were commanded to keep their seats. There was no escape.

The Governor, a large, powerful man, rose slowly and approached another trembling victim. He in turn was seized, dragged to the floor and hacked to death. All the plotters were dispatched in this way and then the terrified remainder were let go with a few words of warning.

Yang Tsen Shing was awarded the K.C.I.E. by the Indian Government for services rendered during the war, and news of this honour was received when I was there. I was therefore able to congratulate him personally, much to his delight.

De Kerangat and I called on him once in the yamen,

and a few days later dined in the very room where the murders had taken place. I was a little apprehensive lest he try his finger-guessing game with me! He also paid us a call at the Boyers' house, preceded by two bugle bands and a guard with fixed bayonets. The visit lasted for about an hour and he asked us many questions about the situation in Siberia. The state of affairs on the border was disturbing him greatly, as Annenkov's troops had been driven across the frontier into Chuguchak and Kuldja. They were still armed, as the local Chinese were powerless to do anything, and the Bolsheviks were writing threatening letters to Yang, demanding the immediate expulsion of all 'Whites' from Chinese territory.

He was, therefore, between two fires, and didn't know what to do, as his own troops were useless, and he knew it.

Some time after I left Urumchi, Annenkov actually appeared before the town with the remnants of his Army. The Governor closed the gates, and both sides sat down for a long period of negotiation. Yang appeared friendly, and Annenkov, lulled to a false feeling of security, soon accepted an invitation to dine at the yamen. Accompanied by only a few officers, he rode into the city, and by nightfall was lying bound hand and foot a prisoner. There he languished for many a long month, a victim of overconfidence, but a brave and capable man for all that.

Ataman Dutov, who had been relegated to an unimportant post by Annenkov when we were still in Chuguchak, was treacherously murdered in Kuldja about this time, and so the last two leaders of the anti-Bolshevik forces in Central Asia met their fate.

Shortly after my arrival in Urumchi I received a telegram from Colonel Etherton, our Consul-General in

Kashgar, asking who I was, what I was doing, and requesting a detailed report on the situation in Siberia and Urumchi. Most of my time was occupied in typing this on de Kerangat's portable Corona. I also began a long report for the War Office, which was eventually sent to the proper authority, who did not even acknowledge its receipt!

There were several Europeans in the city besides the Boyers, Fathers Joseph and François Hoogers, two brothers of the Belgian Missionary Society of Brussels. The former was Superior of the Ili District and had a small church at Manass. De Kerangat paid them a visit one evening and had a wonderful time. The two old men, both grey-beards, were dressed in Chinese fashion, smoked long, small-bowled pipes and drank a delicious local wine. The Frenchman made them laugh till the tears came with his witty account of our adventures, and they only let us go reluctantly at a late hour.

Two English missionaries, Messrs. Hunter and Mathers, were extremely kind and helped us a great deal. Mr. Hunter had been there for many years and was translating the Bible into Turki.

Three Japanese officers in mufti lived in the city, and we dined with them one night. They were delightful, and one played to us excruciating tunes on a violin – *Annie Laurie* and *Marching through Georgia*!

All the while we were there preparations went forward for the further journey. The British Minister in Peking had wired 2500 Shanghai dollars to the local Russo-Asiatic Bank, and with money at last I could hire carts, buy supplies, and repay the loan from Ramazon Chaneshev. The money was given me in rough shoes of silver weighing anywhere from five to ten taels apiece. Each of these lumps had to be weighed and marked, as each was different, and when one wanted change a shoe had to be cut up and each small piece weighed again. Every shopkeeper and merchant carries his own scales and needless to say they all disagreed.

For the two months' trek across the Gobi, I hired six large two-wheeled carts, and made arrangements for them to be covered with hoods of matting and felt, with wooden doors in front, to protect us from cold, winds, and sandstorms. These carts are heavy wooden vehicles, the wheels being over five feet in diameter, with wooden axles and two shafts. One mule in the shafts bears the weight of the load and steadies the cart, while three lead mules, harnessed abreast, do all the pulling. The driver carries a long whip, but there are no reins, and he controls the team by voice alone. Owing to the load and to the rough going the teams never go above a walk and average two and a half to three miles an hour.

While staying with the Boyers we got our only look at a thermometer and found the temperature at thirty-five degrees below zero. Sixty-seven degrees of frost is something to be prepared against, so I laid in a stock of rough sheepskin coats and trousers for every one, and more lengths of grey felt to heap over us in the carts and at night in the caravanserais. It was impossible to buy any crockery or utensils, except for earthenware bowls, and iron pots and spoons, so our own battered tin mugs and plates had to suffice. As most of the journey was to be across a desert, with only occasional oases, large stocks of provisions had to be carried. The intense cold enabled us to take with us numerous sheep carcases, besides the necessary sacks of coarse meal, dried vegetables, Turfan raisins, Mohammedan bread, and strings of garlic.

My efforts to obtain an interpreter had met with little success, as no English or Russian-speaking Chinese could be found. Finally, after much search, a half-baked young Sart who spoke Turki and Chinese was induced to come with us as far as Lanchowfu. As Morgan spoke a Kirghiz dialect of Turki, and I had got hold of a Turki grammar and was studying hard, we took him on. An agreement was signed with his father, and he was immediately nick-named Tilmach, which means interpreter in his language.

We were all, of course, great objects of curiosity to the officials and local inhabitants, especially those of us who wore uniform, for no British or French officers in uniform had ever been there, or been allowed to pass through the land fully armed with a party of soldiers. One of the officials who was something of a scholar invented Chinese names for us, mine being Ho Dji Si, meaning a good, eminent scholar, or a noble, heroic gentleman. On Mr. Boyers' advice I had cards printed in Chinese, my full title being Da Yin Kaw Gow Djee Chun Kwan, which being interpreted means The Great British Country's High Military Officer. If I had used the Chinese equivalent for Captain I should have been very small fry, so the more important, though somewhat vague title, was used to impress officials along the road.

At last on 9th February, fourteen days after our arrival, we were ready to start on the long and arduous journey across the mighty Gobi. Our party had suddenly been reduced by the decision of the two Letts and Samstag, de Kerangat's servant, to stay behind. The Gobi looked too threatening to them. This gave us more room, and as these men were the least desirable members, we were more pleased than otherwise.

We were now eleven men, including Tilmach, and being armed with rifles, revolvers, and shotguns, besides the French machine gun with its two thousand rounds of ammunition, felt ready to face the unknown dangers of another three and a half months' journey. Besides, if the worst came to the worst, de Kerangat and I had our swords!

Our fortnight in Urumchi had been enlivened by intercourse with other foreigners, calls on the Governor, rumours from the border, and quiet evenings of bridge with the Boyers. We thought with regret of the warm, comfortable evenings in the old Manchu house, and looked forward with distaste to the filthy inns, the long monotonous days of slow trekking across the desert waste, and the everlasting mutton stew. But it was time to go and we loaded our clumsy carts, made our last purchases, received passports from the yamen, and prepared to set out.

Our small party had already spent over two months at close quarters, and the prospect of many more weeks of enforced companionship might have been far from pleasant, if we had not shaken down so well together. We were all so totally different that we got along extremely well, and there was far less friction than there might have been in a group composed entirely of Englishmen, or of soldiers. The monotony, the cold, the discomfort, and all the thousand and one little things that can irritate so easily, could have made life unbearable, if we had not been so mixed.

I find I have given very little space to my companions,

except to mention a name occasionally, but I have had so many events to describe that personal incidents have not had much scope. In fact, when one travels hard all day in such weather that keeping warm is one's chief aim in life, one halts for the night hungry and tired, eats as soon as possible and then falls asleep. Interesting incidents are few and far between, and conversation is only about the next day's journey, food and so on. Sometimes days passed without half a dozen words spoken by any of us, all being in a sort of coma of boredom and discomfort.

On the whole, however, we were quite cheerful, and if there was anyone who set us an example it was Captain de Kerangat. He was some eight years my senior, and from a military point of view, in command of our party. Actually, the French being in the minority, and his Government having supplied him with insufficient funds for the journey, I made most of the arrangements, such as hiring of carts, buying of food, and so on, while my party, especially Morgan and the two ex-prisoners, did all the work. De Kerangat was therefore left with nothing to do, and no man of his own class and nationality to talk to. My French was no more than fair, and his English on a par with my French, so that he was dependent for most of his conversation on the young interpreter Bielenky.

De Kerangat was always cheerful and polite, always singing away in the mud huts at night, usually lying face down on a strip of felt and beating time with his toes, while the stew simmered in the pot. Or on innumerable little scraps of paper he jotted down notes for a future book. Occasionally, I would get him started on Napoleon, or some period of the war, or of French history which interested him and he would become animated, but on the whole he was quietly cheerful, and a delightful companion.

Our two mining engineers were very different types. Gordon Smith, a man in his middle forties, humorous occasionally, but very quiet most of the time. He liked to talk of his South American experiences, and I remember him most cleaning out his pipe, which had a very small opening in the mouthpiece and clogged every few minutes.

Morgan was in his thirties, a small wiry man, with a weather-beaten, pugnacious face. He was an indefatigable worker, and a wonderful man to have on such a trip as ours. Work was what he wanted, and he got plenty of it, running our food department extremely well, and training my two batmen to work as he did. I don't know what I should have done without him.

Moss had a placid temperament which stood him in good stead, for my own outbursts of ill temper were usually visited on his head, and he took them philosophically enough. He was quiet, too, but had been invaluable to me on the Russian side of the border, for he spoke the language perfectly, and never seemed to feel fatigue. He sometimes irritated me by his slowness, for he was a big man and thought slowly, but we got along well together, and I could always rely on his getting things done.

My two batmen were invaluable. Albert, with his thin face and long lanky figure, and Peter, a short, dark inarticulate Magyar. Both worked like slaves, and could not have done more for me than for one of their own officers. Always up first in the mornings long before dawn, and to bed only after all the washing and cleaning had been done, always ready and willing to fetch and carry, to clean and mend, and to load or unload, they were a marked contrast to the two French soldiers, who never did a hand's turn, and groused eternally.

I became very attached to both my ex-enemy batmen, and I believe that they worked for me as splendidly as they did because I treated them as I would have treated two of my own men.

CHAPTER 21

ACROSS THE GOBI DESERT

FROM Urumchi to Lanchowfu on the Hwang Ho is a distance of nearly eleven hundred miles as the crow flies, and over twelve hundred by road, and the intervening country consists largely of desert, a part of that great waste known as the Gobi, which stretches from the borders of Tibet across Mongolia to Manchuria. Our road ran first along the northern slopes of the Boghdo Ola range, then south-eastwards through the mountains to the oasis of Hami or Qomul, across more deserts and mountains into Kansu Province and to the sandswept city of Ansichow, through the western gateway of the crumbling ruins of the Great Wall to Suchow, along the northern slopes of the great Nan Shan, which forms the border of Tibet, to Liangchow and finally to our goal, the city of Lanchowfu.

Two months of arduous travel lay before us, months of monotonous, uncomfortable riding and walking, intense cold, dust storms, brackish water, coarse food and filthy inns. I cannot say I looked forward to it with any particular enthusiasm, but the novelty of the experience, and the possible excitements of the journey in the way of game or bandits counterbalanced to a certain degree the prospect of long hours of desert scenery viewed from the felt-covered floor of my heavy cart. Most of the road we were to follow was the main caravan route across the Gobi, where our weather-beaten carters spent their lives doing the two months' trip backward and forward with passengers or merchandise. I was lucky enough to get copies of a road map by the late General (then Lieutenant-Colonel) Pereira for the whole distance, except that he followed the southern route from Urumchi *via* Turfan, and we the northern one *via* Kuchengtze until our roads converged at Chi Ko Chingsa, some two hundred and fifteen miles further on.

The morning of 10th February dawned clear and cold, the thermometer showing sixty-seven degrees of frost, and we rose to our last day at Urumchi. The majority of the stores had already been packed the day before, and it only remained to say good-bye to the Boyers and the English missionaries, and to collect the servants and French soldiers before we set out. We assembled in front of the old Manchu house that had sheltered us for nearly a fortnight, made our farewells, and climbed into the heavy carts. The drivers cracked their whips, and with a creaking of wooden wheels and a strain of ropes and harness we swung out on to the street and headed north. As we left the city a desert plain stretched before us, while on our right hand were the foothills of the Boghdo Ola. The plain continued for twenty *li* to Chitauan, and we then entered a narrow lane bordered by trees, which lasted for almost another ten *li* to Kamuti, a village of about twenty-five houses where we halted for the night. The inn was fair. Our carts filed into the courtyard, came to a halt, and all was bustle and confusion for a time. The carters unharnessed the leading mules, propped up the heavy shafts, and then led out the shaft mule that carried all the weight while travelling. Released from the chafing harness the animals all proceeded to roll vigorously on the hard ground, raising a cloud of dust and refuse until their backs were eased, and they stood patiently waiting for the evening meal. Rows of earthen troughs usually filled one corner of the courtyard, and into these was poured a mixture of dried peas, beans, and coarse chopped straw, which was all the fodder they seemed to get. Meanwhile our stoves had been taken into two of the least dilapidated rooms, and the pipes adjusted to lead out through door or window as the case might be. The only firewood was as usual green scrub, which gave forth such clouds of acrid smoke that we were driven coughing and weeping into the open until the fire had got under way properly, and some of the smoke had drifted out. The old routine was resumed. First water would be boiled for tea, and we would eat some Sart bread and drink one or two tin mugs full of the steaming liquid, sweetened with coarse sugar. Then a shave and wash in the water left over, and while the stew was cooking for supper, we would read what little literature we had, write up our diaries or discuss the road for the next day. The inevitable mutton stew, being our only square meal, was eaten with avidity, and then after an hour or so of bridge, which we played on a wooden box, all sitting on the *kang*, we would lie down in a row, cover ourselves with everything we possessed and go to sleep until dawn. The indefatigable Morgan was always up first, and with Albert and Peter soon had tea and a porridge of coarse meal and raisins ready, and as there was no washing or dressing to be done, we were soon ready for the road.

Still bearing north-east, we travelled slowly, walking most of the time, as sitting in the carts was too cold and monotonous, and after sixty *li*, halting at Fukan for the night. The country had been a dreary waste until we approached the picket when a few stunted trees and some scrub relieved the monotony. On the 12th, we passed the picket of Santara about midday, and met a large caravan of two hundred shaggy, heavily-laden camels pacing slowly towards Urumchi, and reached Tze Ni Chwan about dark, having come ninety *li*. A *li* is about a third of a mile, but is more a measure of time and distance combined than any definite linear measure. At least so it seemed to us, as a short day's trek over difficult country seemed the same number of *li* as a long day over easy roads, the time taken being about the same in each case. Sixty *li* or twenty miles was an average day's journey, as it took us seventeen days to cover the 335 miles to Hami.

Some excitement was caused by volumes of smoke pouring from Gordon Smith's cart in the inn yard, but it was only a feather pillow which had been set on fire by a guttering candle. The two engineers were much put out, however, as their pillows were their proudest possessions!

We were now marching due east over rolling country dotted with scrub, and cut by the beds of several dry watercourses. The morning of the 13th was misty, and it was not until early afternoon, when the deserted village of Ulungai (Narit) had been passed, that it cleared up and the snow-capped peaks of the Boghdo Ola were again clearly visible to the south. After ninety *li*, we reached the small village of San Tai, in the one street of which a deer and many lean, fierce-looking dogs were prowling. The next day the country was the same, we passed Yu Dau Za (Yun Chan) a miserable place where, according to Tilmach our young Sart interpreter, the Little Gobi starts, and

Shikho. From here a more fertile tract began, with trees and scattered farms, most of which were in ruins. Several streams were crossed, and one fair-sized river before we got to a dirty, half-deserted village of some size, called Fu Yuan (Tsimsa).

The trees and farms continued for about half the way to Kuchengtze, which was our halting-place on the following night, and then ceased, giving way to coarse grass and low scrub. Kuchengtze, to our surprise, was quite a large place, with a good bazaar or market, and we laid in a fresh stock of provisions to guard against accidents, and would have liked to rest a day, but the only available inn was so bad that I decided to push on as soon as the mules had been shod on the following morning. At the local 'post office,' a batch of old Reuter's telegrams sent on by Mr. Boyers were waiting for us and proved a valuable addition to our reading matter although they were over two months old.

It was now nearly four months since Moss and I had set out from Omsk for a few weeks with the Orenburg Cossacks, and in all that time we had been practically cut off from the civilised world. Life in these wild regions was becoming almost our normal existence, just as during the war one became so used to the danger and monotony that the resumption of a peaceful occupation seemed an impossibility. It seemed perfectly natural that we strangely assorted people should be travelling slowly across the mountains and deserts of Central Asia, halting at miserable pickets or dirty towns, and sleeping in a row on a *kang*. The long days were so devoid of interest that I went through them almost in a coma, sometimes sleeping for hours in the cart, or trudging slowly in heavy kit along the rough track. By day the desert stretched away far to the north, the barren mountains to the south, and never a living soul passed us on the road, except for a very occasional post rider, mounted on a shaggy pony, or a caravan of camels. The whole world seemed a desert. At Kuchengtze the caravanserai was a replica of all the others, with its crumbling mud walls, unsavoury guest-rooms where a ragged piece of matting on the *kang* was the only pretence to furniture, and yard crowded with carts, mules, and idlers. The deeply-rutted streets were frozen hard now, and the cheap booths in the bazaar housed blue-nosed merchants, who shivered in their padded coats and stamped their feet for warmth.

Later we were to pass many towns and villages, some deserted, others with but a handful of inhabitants. The terrible massacres that took place during the great Mohammedan rebellion of the '60's and '70's was the direct cause of this. Only by long and costly efforts did the Chinese put down the rising, and in doing so millions of Moslems were put to the sword. The Chinese General Tso Ch'ing T'ang accomplished his mission by marching his troops from the Yellow River to Kashgar, a feat which earned them the name of the Agricultural Army as they advanced a certain distance and then sat down, sowed their crops and waited for the harvest before pushing on again. It was the only way the men could be fed.

The desolation caused by this long and bloody war is felt to this day, and from Urumchi to Lanchow and beyond, half-empty villages, whose imposing walls had once enclosed a prosperous community, still lay in ruins, with but a few inhabited hovels outside one of the gates.

Everywhere in this vast inland region the heavy hand of poverty and disease showed all too plainly. The cringing

MY CART ON THE GOBI BETWEEN URUMCHI AND HAMI

Facing p. 260

beggars in their unbelievable coverings of rags were more deformed and frightful than in any other land, and the petty traders, carters, smiths, and farmers who eked out a bare living, spent their lives on the desert or its outskirts in various stages of poverty. In describing a journey such as this it is difficult to give even an idea of the awful dreariness of the arid plains and mountains where not a living thing existed which was not stunted and wizened by the aridity of the soil, the great extremes of heat and cold and the lack of progress, intelligent development, capital, good government, and all those other factors which enrich a country and make it livable. Life in those far-away places is so primitive and monotonous that it astonishes and appals one, and conjures up imaginary pictures of Europe a thousand years ago, except that Europe never had such deserts.

Everywhere the flat Mongol face predominated in Kirghiz, Sart, Tatar, Kalmuk, Mongol, and Chinese. Occasionally a hawk-nosed Tatar or Kirghiz was met, showing another strain, and sometimes a Chinese would pass by with a more aquiline cast of features. Western China was scarcely Chinese at all, so many were the Moslems of Turkic and Mongol blood, and of the Chinese population, the majority seemed to be soldiers, the most despised (except the barber) of all their castes, or escaped criminals, and adventurous petty farmers, who probably had trudged the whole distance from cities near the coast, and were now rueing their arduous journey to this inhospitable country.

Our inability to understand the language often caused humorous incidents, and on leaving Kuchengtze, about midday on the 16th of February, one of these occurred.

We had just cleared the walls of the town, when an uproar at the rear of the caravan caught my attention, and I went back to investigate. The rear cart had halted and in front of one of the wheels lay a Chinaman, apparently anxious for it to pass over him and end his career. A gesticulating group of carters, traders, and others had collected and added their chatter to the lamentations of the man on the ground, so that I had some difficulty in getting at the bottom of the trouble. Bielenky, who was de Kerangat's interpreter, had apparently been approached by the Chinaman, who handed him an old briar pipe, and the former, thinking it was one of Gordon Smith's which had been dropped on the road, gave the man a few cash and turned to follow the carts. The Chinese had then become very excited and eventually threw himself under the wheel, and refused to budge. Tilmach was called in and I eventually found out that the pipe had been offered for sale for a silver tael, and the seller thought himself cheated when the few cash were given him. It wasn't Gordon Smith's pipe at all, so I returned it to its recumbent owner, who suddenly ceased his complaints and made off, while we resumed our march.

An hour from Kuchengtze, there was a fair-sized stream crossed by a good bridge, and a little further on we passed several camel caravans camped on the roadside. Men and beasts were resting in sheltered ground behind some rocks, while the heavy packs were lying in regular rows on the ground. It was very cold even in the bright sunlight, which showed up every fold and hillock of the coarse grass-covered country with wonderful clearness. A couple of hours after midday a halt for a few minutes was made at a hovel by the road, and we then pushed on in the same south-easterly direction we had taken on leaving Kuchengtze that morning, until our ninety *li* trek for the day ended at Las Kitai (Chi Tei Sian), where the caravanserai was so bad that most of us slept in the carts.

On the 17th, I walked nearly all day. The country was a little less barren, with quite a number of stunted trees until we had passed Shi Tze Yer, a small village with a few poverty-stricken shops. The road became stony, trees ceased, and as the mountains to the south were nearer, it was also more hilly than usual. Again ninety *li* ended at Mu Li Khe, a tumble-down place with several inns, of which ours proved better than usual.

Next day the mountains were perceptibly nearer, and the country undulating and barren. After forty *li*, the carts halted at a hovel called Yuan Chuan Tsui, which had a running stream close by. The road grew worse, being alternately sand and loose stones, while the hills which we had to climb were steeper than before. We halted for the night at San Chiao Chwan, where there was a post office in a mud hut. Here de Kerangat received a letter from Boyers in which he gave the news that General Knox had passed through Shanghai on his way to England. How far away the coast seemed to us! Fuel was very scarce, but Morgan managed to get a little low-grade coal, which had been brought from the mines near Urumchi.

On the 19th, having a long day before us, we left before six and set out through a hilly but not difficult country, and over a very stony road, covering 120 *li* to Ta Shi Tao, a place consisting of four caravanserai and a ruined temple. The green scrub used for fuel produced such an acrid smoke that we were driven repeatedly from our room into the bitter cold outside.

This was the eve of the Chinese New Year and the carters celebrated it with joss-sticks, drink, and opium, so that we were late getting away on the following morning. Leaving the main road to Barköl, our caravan turned further south, making for a pass which would take us between the Boghdo Ola and the Barköl ranges and bring us to Hami. The road was difficult as it was stony and fairly deep in snow, so only sixty *li* were covered before reaching Tow Chi, a picket of four rest-houses situated in a narrow cleft in the hills.

In the bitter cold of the early morning, we went on, entering a narrow gorge, a short distance from Tow Chi. The towering walls of rock rose steeply on either hand, and for the first five hundred yards the pass was covered with a sheet of treacherous ice. By skilful driving and good luck, the heavy carts made their way slowly towards firmer ground, as the cracking of the ice which partially gave way sounded like revolver shots echoing from wall to wall. Once across the ice, the road was fairly good, although there were plenty of loose stones, and it wound through the mountain pass, which was very narrow in places.

About thirty-five *li* from the start, the pass ended, and we emerged on the northern side of a large plain, surrounded by a ring of snow-peaked mountains. This valley was covered with sand and stones, without a trace of vegetation, except that from where we stood there appeared to be a wood in the very centre of the plain. We had walked through the pass, and as the carts were still some distance behind, and it was too cold to sit and wait for them, we went ahead thinking that the next inn would not be far off. The distance, however, was very deceptive, as in the clear atmosphere objects look very much nearer than they are. In our heavy sheepskins, we walked on and on, never seeming to get any nearer to the cursed wood, and at last, with sweat streaming down my face, I stopped and said I thought it was a mirage. I couldn't stand still and be frozen, so we stumbled on again, and after covering close on thirty miles since the morning, reached the gnarled and twisted stumps of prehistoric trees, which in the distance had seemed to us a forest. Half covered by sand, these petrified stumps must have been a forest, or perhaps vegetation in swampy land, or at the bottom of a lake, and the whole place made as desolate a scene as can be imagined. While examining the edge of the 'wood,' I came across a wild-looking Mongol of twenty-five or thirty, dressed in a ragged skin coat and trousers, who eyed me with great interest, and eventually came up and spoke in some unintelligible language. I tried the little Turki I knew without success, and he then led me to a collection of miserable hovels among the stumps, where some wizened members of his family were squatting. The surrounding desolation, and these primitive people, living as near to nature as it is possible to do, might have formed a picture representing Adam and his family some time after the eviction from the Garden of Eden!

The picket of Chi Ko Chingsa consists of four inns and a few Tatar or Kirghiz huts. The only water obtainable is from a series of *kars*, or underground tunnels, which are used to convey the melting snow from the mountains in spring-time. A number of deep wells are sunk at regular intervals, stretching from the picket towards the hills, and beneath the surface each line of wells is connected by a tunnel, so that as the melting snow collects in the furthest well, it overflows along the tunnel to the next well, and so on. Water is stored in this way during the other months of the year.

It took us about four and a half more days to reach Hami, over terrible roads and desert country, but interesting in that there was plenty of game, especially antelope, which gave us some sport although we did not bag any. Chi Ko Chingsa is 2360 feet above sea-level, and in the valley between the mountain ranges it seemed quite warm. As we pushed on, next day, we passed a large sandy basin marked on Pereira's map, and continued across the stony valley which had a certain amount of scrub as vegetation, and climbed steadily all day, sighting several antelope, but not getting a chance at a shot. After covering seventy-five *li* of sandy road, during which we had climbed over 2700 feet, we halted at the entrance to a pass, where the hills rose up a hundred feet on either hand, and where we found three inns almost in ruins, called Che Kulu. Wood was scarce and the rooms almost uninhabitable, but our evening meal was a thing to remember, as Morgan made us some delicious pancakes of precious eggs bought in Kuchengtze, mixed with meal and horrible-looking Mongol butter.

On the 23rd we entered the pass, and shortly afterwards emerged on a rocky plateau, where the small narrow ridges stretched away like the waves of the sea. After forty *li*, we halted at I Wan Ch'uan, where there were an inn and a house almost in ruins. No fuel was to be had, and we pushed on over a very rocky and bad road for another sixty *li* to Liao T'un, a place of eight inns and houses and one *kars*. A covey of partridges was put up soon after leaving next morning, and a number of antelope were sighted. As the road was bad and the carts moved slowly, I took my rifle, crept up one of the narrow gullies through which the melting snow from the mountains descends in spring, and stalked a small herd of antelope for some distance. My rifle was a short Lee-Enfield which I had never used, and we had so few cartridges, that I was anxious not to waste any. After some time I got a chance, took careful aim at a fine-looking buck, and fired. He sprang in the air, wheeled, and made off with the rest, going in great bounds, and travelling like the wind until out of sight over a ridge. I felt sure I had hit him but was unable to follow. When I rejoined the carts, mine was stuck in a rut, and it took ten mules to pull it out. After seventy-five *li*, which were covered in nine and a half hours, we halted for the night at Taranchi (Ti Tzu Ch'uan). During the last two days we had descended two thousand feet. The stony undulating plain continued next day, and a few antelope were sighted, but not near enough to get a shot. I got very annoyed with Moss, as his method of stalking was to walk straight towards them as if marching on parade, and he seemed surprised when the animals made off when he topped a ridge! There was a certain amount of snow on the ground, and the road was often soft sand, into which the wheels sank, making it hard work for the mules. We reached San P'u (Togouchi), a place of twenty or thirty Sart houses, and halted for tea, then went on, coming to a plain covered with grass and a few stunted trees, in places crossed by several streams flowing south. At five we reached Erh P'u (Astin or Astance), where there were several inns and Sart houses, but the accommodations were so bad that it was decided to push on to Sum Kara Ga (Tou P'u). The country was now a little more fertile, with a few trees and scattered farms, and we halted for the night about seven. T'ou P'u has only about ten poor Sart houses, while Erh P'u must have shrunk considerably since Pereira's visit as he gives ninety-eight houses, which is too large an estimate now.

On the 26th we left at dawn, and sent Tilmach ahead to secure us good lodgings in Hami. When the sun had risen, it became so warm, that we shed our skins for the first time in many days, and sat out on the front of our carts breathing in the fresh spring air, and taking comfort in the more hospitable-looking country. As we approached the city outskirts the farms increased, and a few real trees appeared, and then as we got nearer we passed through acres of crumbling Mohammedan graves. Ahead of us appeared a crenellated gateway, massive walls, graceful towers, minarets, buildings, and mosques with a distinctly Moorish style of architecture mixed with the Chinese. De Kerangat, who had served in Morocco, said that the whole scene reminded him of Northern Africa, especially when we came opposite to the great gate of the Wang's (Prince's) Palace, where a group of Sart women and children with cheeks daubed scarlet and dressed in brilliant colours, watched our approach with amazement and then fled screaming. We skirted the wall of the palace, entered the Sart city of Qomul (Hami) and halted at a very dirty inn.[1] The stupid Tilmach hadn't succeeded

[1] Marco Polo, the famous traveller, gives his impressions of Hami as follows: 'Kamul is a district situated within the great province of Tanguth, subject to the grand khan, and contains many towns and castles, of which the principal city is also named Kamul. This district lies in the intermediate space between two deserts; that is to say, the great desert already described, and another of smaller extent, being only about three days' journey across. The inhabitants are worshippers of idols, and have their

'AHEAD OF US APPEARED A CRENELLATED GATEWAY, MASSIVE WALLS . . .'

Hami, February 192[illegible]

Facing p. [illegible]

very well in getting us good quarters, but luckily a Russian-speaking Sart came up, and we asked him if there were any better caravanserai. He led us a little further on to a new place, which was very much cleaner, and we filed into the yard and prepared to spend a day or so of rest. A crowd of curious Chinese and Sarts followed us, and even came into our rooms, some poking their fingers through the paper windows to get a view from the outside. Tilmach was sent off with our cards to the Mohammedan Prince of Hami and to the Chinese Governor, and we were soon supplied with a guard of soldiers, who cleared the yard and put a sentry at the gate so that we finally had some peace.

The Chinese Governor called early next morning while

peculiar language. They subsist on the fruits of the earth which they possess in abundance, and are enabled to supply the wants of travellers. The men are addicted to pleasure, and attend to little else than playing upon instruments, singing, dancing, reading, writing, according to the practice of the country, and the pursuit, in short, of every kind of amusement. When strangers arrive, and desire to have lodging and accommodation at their houses, it affords them the highest gratification. They give positive orders to their wives, daughters, sisters, and other female relations, to indulge their guests in every wish, whilst they themselves leave their homes, and retire into the city, and the stranger lives in the house with the females as if they were his own wives, and they send whatever necessaries may be wanted; but for which, it is to be understood, they expect payment: nor do they return to their houses so long as the strangers remain in them. This abandonment of the females of their family to accidental guests, who assume the same privileges and meet with the same indulgences as if they were their own wives, is regarded by these people as doing them honour and adding to their reputation; considering the hospitable reception of strangers, who (after the perils and fatigues of a long journey) stand in need of relaxation, as an action agreeable to their deities, calculated to draw down the blessing of increase upon their families, to augment their substance, and to procure them safety from all dangers, as well as a successful issue to all their undertakings. The women are in truth very handsome, we were still asleep, so we had to dress hurriedly and have Albert get some tea for him while we sat around and exchanged compliments. The call was returned by us at midday, and we rode on hired ponies through the streets to the Chinese city, watched by curious crowds. I do not believe the Governor carried as much weight as the Prince, as the population was mainly Moslem, and I cannot recall much of the visit, as nothing beyond the entry of the actual event in my diary remains to jog my memory. The chief event of the day was the discovery of a Chinese bath-house, a long narrow building lined with cubicles on both sides, in which a narrow wooden trough served as a tub, and one poured the water over oneself from wooden buckets. I had my first bath in nearly three

very sensual, and fully disposed to conform in this respect to the injunction of their husbands. It happened at the time when Mangu Khan held his court in this province, that the above scandalous custom coming to his knowledge, he issued an edict strictly commanding the people of Kamul to relinquish a practice so disgraceful to them, and forbidding individuals to furnish lodging to strangers, who should be obliged to accommodate themselves at a house of public resort or caravanserai. In grief and sadness the inhabitants obeyed for three years the command of their master; but finding at length that the earth ceased to yield the accustomed fruits, and that many unfortunate events occurred in their families, they resolved to dispatch a deputation to the grand khan, in their names, to beseech him that he should be pleased to suffer them to resume the observance of a custom that had been solemnly handed down to them by their fathers, from their ancestors in the remotest times; and especially as since they had failed in the exercise of these offices of hospitality and gratification to strangers, the interest of their families had gone progressively to ruin. The grand khan, having listened to this application, replied, "Since you appear so anxious to persist in your own shame and ignominy, let it be granted as you desire. Go, live according to your base customs and manners, and let your wives continue to receive the beggarly wages of their prostitution." With this answer the deputies returned home, to the great delight of all the people, who, to the present day, observe their ancient practice.'

weeks, and was informed that for most of the inhabitants it was only indulged in once each year. The other two entries in the diary remark on our relief at getting some beef, after weeks of mutton stew, and the severe sandstorm which rose early in the evening and blew with violence during the night.

Soon after breakfast on the 28th, the Prince of Hami arrived in state, riding in a smart closed carriage of English make, drawn by a fine pair of horses, and escorted by forty or fifty wild-looking Sart horsemen armed to the teeth, who galloped through the streets, driving all and sundry into door and alley-ways. The Prince was a short, handsome man, almost entirely bald, with a brown wrinkled face, hook nose, and white beard. He was dressed in rich Chinese silks, with a round fur cap, and looked an exceptionally intelligent and educated man. Tilmach proved a sorry interpreter and after a halting conversation which lasted for half an hour, our visitor left us.

As soon as we could procure ponies, and the services of the Russian-speaking Sart, whom we had met the day before, we rode through the narrow streets to the palace, passed through the massive gateway, and several stone-flagged courtyards in the shadow of the crenellated walls until the guide signalled us to dismount. Our volunteer interpreter grew visibly more nervous as the time for the interview grew nearer, and finally disappeared by the time we had entered the Palace, and been received by the Prince. The rooms through which we passed were richly furnished with beautifully-carved chairs and tables, rich hangings, cushions, and soft rugs from Persia and Bokhara, much finer than anything I had seen so far. In a small, but imposing council chamber, de Kerangat and I were given the seats of honour on a raised dais, and there were a few moments of silence while Moss went out to find the interpreter. He was soon brought in, and stood terrified in the farthest corner of the room with bowed head, probably fearing the possible displeasure of the Prince, who was, I believe, the religious head of not only all Moslems in China but also of those in Russian Turkestan.

A curious conversation followed. The Prince was very interested in our travels, and asked a great many questions as to our doings in Russia. Knowing of the German attempt to picture the Allies as enemies of Mohammedanism, I asked whether any propaganda to that effect had been distributed among the people. He said no. I then asked whether he had heard of Germany's defeat, and he replied that there had been rumours to that effect, but no confirmation! From his attitude he didn't believe it. Our interpreter, when translating my remarks from Russian into Turki always coupled 'Germans' with 'Mussulmans,' for example, when I said, 'Germany has been defeated,' he repeated it as, 'The Germans and Mussulmans have been defeated.' The Prince's face naturally showed polite incredulity, but he must have had some inkling of the truth, for he asked anxiously as to the fate of Stamboul and of Mecca.

Hearing that there were to be some 'games' in an open space outside the city that afternoon, we kept the Mongolian ponies, and after lunch rode out across a sandy plain to a small wooded valley, where a company of strolling players were performing in a rude open-air theatre, while a crowd of the poorer Sarts and Chinese watched in a dense mass. Around the outskirts were booths, where sweetmeats, cakes, fruit, and tempting bowls of food were being sold, and hawkers pushed in and out crying their wares. We dismounted nearby and started walking among the people, until our presence became known, and the entire crowd forgot about the play and came surging round us. The excitement was so great, that although every one was perfectly good-humoured, we soon became separated and crushed in the seething mass until luckily we bumped against the ponies, managed to mount and force our way out without any other damage than sore ribs.

After dark, the inn yard was invaded by a troop of actors, who gave us a realistic performance of a furious battle between an enormous, writhing dragon and an armed warrior to the accompaniment of drums and clashing cymbals. Ten minutes of pandemonium were enough, however, and a few taels soon rid us of the whole crowd.

The Chinese Governor called again next day, and presented de Kerangat, Moss, and myself with three small flags, which bore our rank and names in black characters and were stamped with his chop. They were to be hung outside of the carts and would inform passers-by who we were. He also ordered one of his officers, a Chinese Mohammedan, to accompany us as far as Lanchowfu, and to help us on the way in case of trouble with any of the local authorities. When I asked about conditions further on, he told me that the weather would be milder except in the mountains, that the road was bad on the whole but not impassable, and that there would be water available everywhere though very brackish at certain points.

A fresh supply of provisions had been bought, including two hundred and fifty eggs to relieve the monotony of breakfast on meal and raisins, and as the carters wished to travel at night for some distance, while the moon was up, we decided to leave at nine that evening. The carts had been overhauled, the mules re-shod and rested, and as soon as the kit and stores were loaded, we paid our reckoning at the inn, said good-bye to our Sart friend, filed out through the almost deserted streets and made for the desert once more, leaving behind the old Mohammedan stronghold and marching into a country which became less and less Moslem as we proceeded further east.

CHAPTER 22

ACROSS THE GOBI DESERT (*continued*)

THIS next stage of the journey to Ansichow took us 225 miles over some of the most desolate country we had yet seen, and lasted for ten days. Most of the travelling was done at night as the moon gave plenty of light, and the mules stood the work better when they could rest during the day in the sunny yards of the inns.

After leaving Hami the desert wastes began again and for three nights our carts swayed and bumped for more than two hundred *li* over the rough road, giving us little chance to sleep. Resting by day in the carts, or basking in the brilliant sunshine was something of a change, however, and we were also able to go stalking antelope, though the scarcity of ammunition and the danger of straying too far from the tumble-down caravanserai prevented us from shooting any.

On the fourth night, the road climbed steadily. In many places the soil was soft sand, and our wheels sank so deep that the teams had to pull for ten seconds, rest, pull again and so on, dragging the heavy carts from one deep rut to another. After an exhausting march of 140 *li*, during which we climbed 1500 feet, a halt was made at K'u Shui, where the water was so brackish as to be almost undrinkable. It was bitterly cold again, and we had to go back to our sheepskins.

The night of the 4th of March, we did eighty *li* to Sha Ch'uan Tzu, a picket of three Chinese inns, surrounded by low hills of sand and gravel, where there was plenty of antelope. We had climbed another 1300 feet, and were now five thousand feet above sea-level. Our next stage took us over one of the worst roads yet encountered. Leaving at nine, the track crossed a series of rocky ridges, and at times the wheels ran on the solid rock which had been worn down into ruts by generations of passing caravans. As we climbed higher, the road resembled a gigantic staircase, each tread being formed by a flat ledge of stone, so that we bumped and swayed up the interminable steps until it seemed impossible for the carts to hold together any longer. After over eighty *li*, we halted at the top of a ridge called Ta P'an Shan, where a lonely temple, reached by a flight of stone steps, stood guard over the receding waves of rocky hills. The porch and interior of the temple were hung with tablets and banners of all descriptions, left there by devout travellers wishing for good fortune on their further journey. Our carters also left their small offering to the gods, and we then pushed on a few *li* to Sing Sing Hsia, where a dilapidated fort with a small garrison, three or four inns, and a holy shrine are situated in a narrow defile. On the surrounding hills were hundreds of little cairns of rock built by travellers, who look on this place with some veneration, and consider it an act of some importance to leave their own little pile of stones on a high point of the hills for good luck. We each built one, too.

We were now on a plateau six thousand feet high, which stretched almost to Ansichow, four days' journey away to the south-east. The road was bad most of the way, run-

SING SING HSIA

In the foreground, the Inn Yard. Above, the Shrine, and the Cairns built for good luck

Facing p. 276

ning over undulating country of sand, gravel and rock, where low hills about fifty feet in height and separated by gullies where a little scrub grew, ran at right angles across our path. This plateau was the Pei Shan range, while to the south rose the lofty snow-covered peaks of the Nan Shan. By day the brilliant sunshine poured down in the clear cold atmosphere, accentuating the terrible desolation of the scene, where only an occasional herd of antelope gave a touch of life to a region devoid of human habitation. By night the soft radiance of the moon and the myriad stars that covered the entire expanse of the heavens, gave an almost unearthly appearance to the stony waste and to the distant mountain peaks.

On the night of the 6th, we did 130 *li*, passing Ma Lien Ching, and halting at Ta Ch'uan next morning, where there were two dilapidated inns. Early in the afternoon a sandstorm sprang up and gradually increased in intensity, so that the drivers refused to go on, and we spent a bitterly cold night, as the sand filtered in through holes and cracks in walls and roof. By eight next morning the wind had died down sufficiently to let us proceed, and we reached Hung Lien Yuan soon after dark. The Chinese innkeeper told us that the River Su Lu, just this side of Ansichow, was in flood and that we might have to wait for a week or more before it would be possible to cross.

Fortunately this was not the case and our two days' trek to Ansichow was without incident, except that it snowed on the second night, and we again suffered severely from the cold.

At one time the city must have been an important one, as the walls enclose a large area, but it is almost deserted now, and many of the houses are in ruins. A large proportion of the population is still Moslem, in spite of the massacres which followed the great Mohammedan rebellion sixty years ago. In some places the city walls had been pulled down, and on the eastern side close to the gate huge sand drifts practically reach the crenellated battlements, and the eroding action of the sand has worn away the soft brick, leaving the harder mortar to stick out a couple of inches from the wall, which looks like a honeycomb. A gale was blowing all day, and the dust soon discouraged our exploration of the miserable bazaar. We had hoped to rest here, but the place was so dirty and uncomfortable, that we decided to push on the next morning.[1]

Accordingly, on the 11th, our caravan set out to cross the 160 miles which separated us from Suchow, the weather being very cold, with a high wind.

During the next five nights we crossed four small rivers, which ran northwards into the Su Lu. As before, most of the country was desert, except for occasional patches of cultivation. Three or four walled villages were met, too, but the majority of the houses were in ruins and only a few miserable hovels sheltered half a dozen poor families. At one place, we had to cross the River Pa

[1] Marco Polo describes Ansichow as follows: 'When the journey of thirty days across the desert has been completed, you arrive at a city called Sachion, which belongs to the grand khan. The province is named Tanguth. The people are worshippers of idols. There are Turkomans among them, with a few Nestorian Christians and Mahometans. Those who are idolaters have a language distinct from the others. This city lies towards the east-north-east. They are not a commercial, but an agricultural people, having much wheat. There are in this country a number of monasteries and abbeys, which are filled with idols of various description.'

Chia Chuan, which was really a frozen marsh that presented a serious obstacle, as the thawing ice was so soft that the carts sank almost axle deep and were only pulled out with the utmost difficulty.

Those five nights brought us to the village of Hui Hui Pu, a poor village of thirty or forty houses, which was only remarkable for a shrine to the first Mohammedan missionary in China.[1]

Already we had been nearly five weeks on the road from Urumchi, and the deadly monotony was hard to bear. Jolting over terrible roads at night, often half frozen, and crowded together in cramped quarters at each halt, our frayed nerves were beginning to grow unruly. Luckily the very cosmopolitan character of our party was a blessing, as each was loth to show signs of temper or impatience. Peter and Albert worked valiantly and well under the able direction of Morgan. Together they unloaded all necessary kit at each halt, collected firewood, boiled water and prepared the meal. While waiting for supper, which was always mutton stew plentifully seasoned with garlic, de Kerangat would lie face downward on the *kang* singing *Madelon* to himself or recalling some amusing incident of the Orenburg Army's campaign to Bielenky. Moss and I would be shaving silently, and Gordon Smith cleaning his pipe. Fortunately we had enough tobacco, although some of it was mouldy.

In the next hovel, the two French soldiers groused eternally, but as they never did a hand's turn of work they had little to complain of. Around and about hovered the foolish round face of our Sart interpreter, who always managed to get in the way, or do something wrong, until

[1] 'Hui Hui' in Chinese means Mohammedan.

Morgan had cursed him fluently and he would then fade away.

So we got through the endless days and nights somehow without any of that wrangling and rowing which might well have marred our journey, but it was monotonous. No one can realise how terrible the boredom of the waste places of the earth can be, until he has trekked for months over their barren sands and rocks. The monotony of food, of sun, of scenery, and of companionship is almost too much to bear, and the most trivial idiosyncrasies and irritating habits of others assume tremendous proportions.

Moss good-humourdly bore with many an outburst on my part, but on the whole we kept our personal grievances under control, and tried to make the long days pass as pleasantly as possible. If we had only had something to read, besides the very few tattered papers and books we had collected *en route*, things might have been easier, but my library consisted of a coverless volume of Thackeray's *Yellowplush Papers*, and some handbooks on gunnery and gun drill, and the others were no better off. I longed for a volume of Marco Polo's travels, and books on China, for here we were making this unique journey through little-known country, without the slightest conception of its history, and even without an interpreter through whom one could ask intelligent questions of the inhabitants.

It would have been far more interesting to read of Genghis Khan, Marco Polo, Yakob Beg, and many others, emperors, soldiers, and travellers, who had trod this desert road, while we were actually travelling as they had done. One would have felt so much more sympathy with that stout-hearted Father John de Plano Carpini, who at the age of sixty-five, and in spite of a very ample paunch, made one of the most wonderful journeys in history. In 1245, after the disastrous battle of Liegnitz, which left Europe almost defenceless against the Tatars, Father John was selected by the Pope to go as ambassador to the Khan. Leaving France at Easter, he made such progress that he crossed three thousand miles in four months and presented his credentials to the great Khan at Karakorum in Mongolia.

Or I would have delighted in the tale of Su Wu, a Chinese General, who in 100 B.C. was captured by the Huns. For many years he was kept a captive, tending flocks on the steppes near Lake Balkhash, his only possession being his old staff of office. His fate was finally discovered when a wild goose, with a message tied to its wing by the exile, was shot by the Emperor in the Imperial hunting grounds and Su Wu was rescued.

Traversing a road which had witnessed the age-long struggle between ancient Chinese civilisation and the uncouth barbarians of the West, and the growth of trade between the Celestial Empire and far-off Europe, it was tantalising to ride day by day through country rich in history, and yet to miss everything that was worth seeing and hearing.

To have known that close on two thousand years ago, along this very track, similar heavy carts, laden with furs, silks and pig-iron destined for Rome itself, crawled slowly towards the setting sun, would have increased our interest in the crumbling inns and ruined cities which we passed. Little did I realise then that the interruption of this trade with China and the Indies by the Turks many centuries later, sent European sailors on those great voyages of discovery which gave us the Americas. Unfortunately the adventures of a cockney yellowplush and the uninspiring diagrams of 18-pr. guns could not give us what we really needed, and the phantoms of marching Hun and Eleuth, Mongol and Scythian with their spears, their bowmen, their tossing yak-tail standards, and their sturdy horses, passed us by unseen.

The country became absolute desert again after leaving Hui Hui Pu, and early next morning we spied in the distance the watch towers of the Western Gateway of the Great Wall of China. At first only the fort, some two hundred yards square, was visible, but as we drew nearer, the wall itself came into view, stretching southward over the gravel ridges as far as the eye could reach to the foothills of Nan Shan. It was a miserable affair ten to twelve feet high and three or four feet thick at the top, made of sun-dried brick fast crumbling away, and in places already demolished to allow travellers or herdsmen to pass in and out. Even in its early days it could not have offered much of an obstacle to Mongol horsemen.

The fort itself has massive walls faced with good brick, but it is also in a bad state of repair and there is only a small garrison. The village on the eastern side is called Chia Yu Kwan, and consists of about thirty houses and a few temples. From the watch-towers of the fort we could look southwards to the glittering slopes of the Nan Shan, and eastwards to Suchow over a vast flat plain, while to the west stretched the gravel and sandy wastes through which we had just come.

No matter how unimpressive the Great Wall appeared at this point, it had obviously served its purpose at times, for many a warlike race from the north, the Huns among

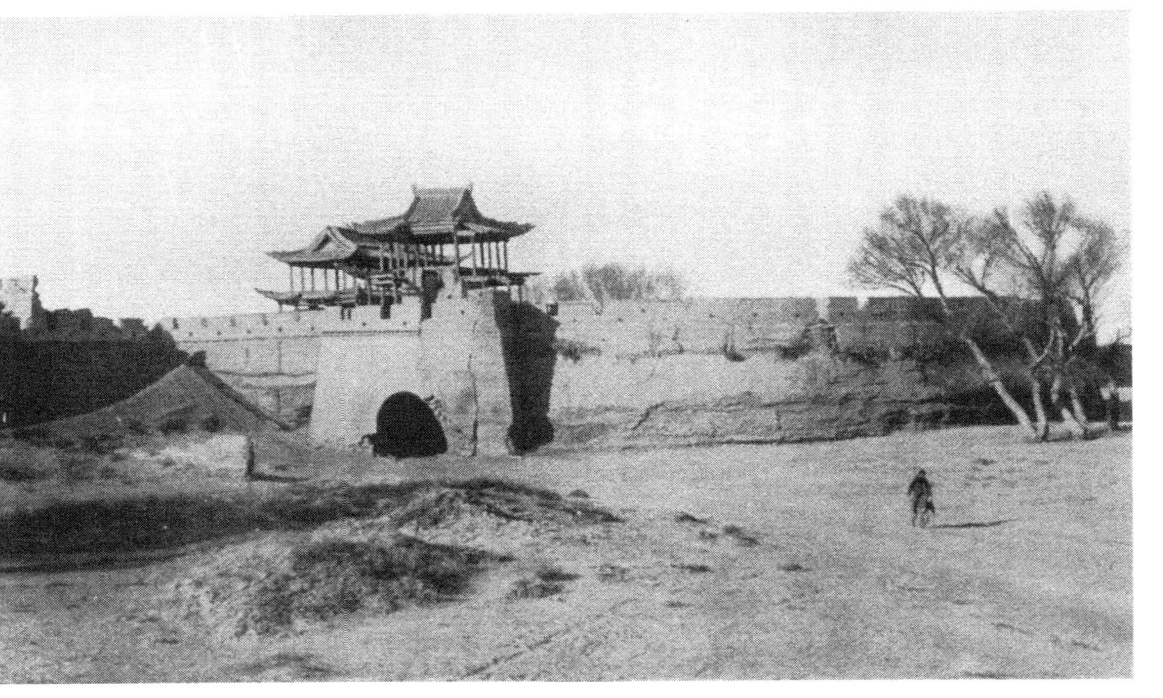

THE NORTH GATE OF ANSICHOW

Facing p. 282

them, had turned back from the great barrier to seek their fortune further west, to the misery of European peoples.

There being no reason to halt here we left again that night, the 17th, and reached Suchow next morning, entering the city by the north gate. The road was better than any we had traversed for some time, but close to the city the country was very marshy and crossed by several small streams, which made the going difficult at times. Our inn was poor and the Chinese very curious, crowding into the courtyard and examining ourselves and our possessions with great interest, but we had to rest a day so that the carters could alter the carts. Inside the Great Wall, the roads are narrower and the gateways lower, so the wheel base was reduced by fitting new axle-trees and lowering the cart covers. Another batch of Reuter's telegrams was received here from Boyers in Urumchi, and I also got two telegrams from Peking with reference to money, which was waiting for me at Lanchowfu. Suchow was one of the Mohammedan strongholds during the great rebellion in the '60's, and put up a long and bloody defence.

On the 20th we left, heading for Kanchow, 160 miles away, along a sandy road bordered by tall elms and scattered farms. About forty *li* from the start, we approached marshy land near the River Lin Shui, where there was a horrible smell of decaying vegetation, crossed the fifteen-foot wide river, and a few *li* further on entered Linshui, an old walled city now deserted, with a small village outside the west gate.

We moved on again before dawn over desert country, where the ground was covered with deposits of salt and nitrates, and the only vegetation was tufts of coarse grass. A halt was made at Shuang Ching Tzu, a small village without a wall, where we breakfasted. As we pushed on, the road was flat and sandy, with old watch-towers visible on the north every mile and a half, and we passed Ku Shui, where there were only two houses, before reaching Yen Ch'ih. We had done ninety-five *li* that day, and were very tired. This place was dirty and primitive in the extreme, with about thirty houses and a few shops, while to the north lay great salt marshes covered with wild fowl. I took our Belgian twelve-bore, and walked out to where a low bank gave me some protection from the cold, and waited patiently for the chance of a shot. As the sun went down, thousands and thousands of duck, geese, and crane came flying from the south and settled with shrill cries on the waters of the lake and on the tufts of coarse grass that bordered the shore, but I was too close to the village and none came within range.

We again left before dawn, and crossed similar desert country covered with salt deposits, reaching Shen Kou about half-past eight. Here there were fifteen houses and the remnants of a wall, while to the north were a few salty ponds. As we resumed our march, the River Pei Ta Ho was visible at times, covered with wild fowl, and we passed quite a number of carts and men going westwards. Hua Chiang Tzu, a place of fifty houses and walls two hundred yards long, was reached about two, and we halted for the night. Buffet and Moss each shot a duck, sitting, I am afraid!

Hearing that there was a foreign priest at our next stop, Kao Tai Hsien, de Kerangat and I borrowed some ponies from our Chinese escort, and taking with us the Chinese

Lieutenant, who had joined us at Urumchi, set out before dawn ahead of the caravan. In the darkness we lost our way, and reached the banks of the Pei Ta Ho before turning back southwards to regain the road. After traversing marshes and a sandy waste about a mile long, we caught up with the carts, having wasted over an hour, and pushed on in the growing light. It was bitterly cold, the wind cut like a knife, and at the first village we three dismounted at an eating-house and consumed steaming rice mixed with plums, all neatly wrapped up in some kind of leaf. The country now became more fertile, there were tilled fields and scattered farms, each like a miniature fortress. It was an ideal country for wild-fowl, of which we saw plenty. We also met a cart covered with blue cloth, with a Chinese dressed like a foreigner sitting on the front. He was a postal clerk going to Urumchi and talked with us for a few minutes in English. He looked as out of place as we did in those strange surroundings. A mile or so from Kao Tai we crossed a marsh on a narrow causeway, and finally entered the town, where we met a jovial Belgian priest, Father De Smet, dressed in Chinese clothes. He lived in a Chinese house, and we were soon sitting down to an excellent lunch, and being warmed by bowls of local wine. De Kerangat was in good form and we talked hard as if there was little time to lose, smoking Manila cheroots the while. There were newspapers too, and we read of the world's doings as recently as 31st January. Two hours later the carts arrived, and the whole lot of us were asked to dine, which we did, with the exception of Peter and Bielenky.

Father De Smet told us of his two hundred Chinese converts and of the resources of the surrounding country.

In the immediate vicinity of Kao Tai cotton is grown as it is more profitable than grain; salt is secured from the marshes; coal comes from primitive mines in the mountains; and jade from near Suchow. All the industries are in the hands of, and almost paralysed by, the officials.

We left next morning, passing through a narrow belt of fertile land, bounded on the north by the marshy banks of the Pei Ta Ho and on the south by desert, made a detour to avoid soft ground, passed through the walled village of Hui Ti Pu and halted at Sha Ho Pu on the main road again.

On the 25th a start was made before 4 a.m., as another detour was necessary. Being anxious to reach Kanchowfu early, de Kerangat, the Chinese officer, and I again rode ahead along a very stony road, finally reached the cultivated belt again, and after fording several swiftly-flowing streams where the water reached our ponies' bellies, arrived at the west gate where a sentry halted us. We gave him our cards and he finally let us enter the city, which has tremendous walls and about fifty thousand inhabitants.[1]

[1] Here is Marco Polo's impression of Kanchow: 'Kampion, the chief city of the province of Tanguth, is large and magnificent, and has jurisdiction over all the province. The bulk of the people worship idols, but there are some who follow the religion of Mohamet, and some Christians. The latter have three large and handsome churches in the city. The idolaters have many religious houses, or monasteries and abbeys, built after the manner of the country, and in these a multitude of idols, some of which are of wood, some of stone and some of clay, are covered with gilding. They are carved in a masterly style. Among these are some of very large size, and others are small. The former are full ten paces in length, and lie in a recumbent posture; the small figures stand behind them, and have the appearance of disciples in the act of reverential salutation. Both great and small are held in extreme veneration. Those persons amongst the idolaters

We were looking for missionaries, but by mistake were taken to a house where a young Chinese medical student called James Hillington Gow greeted us warmly. After a short talk, in which he told us that there was fighting going on the other side of Lanchow, he took us to the Roman Catholic Mission, where Father Stoppers, a Dutchman, welcomed us, and gave us cigars and wine of his own making. It was excellent. He had no later news than Father De Smet, but we sat and talked to him and to another priest, a Belgian, who had left Brussels after the German occupation in 1914, and was most interested in the war. The carts arrived at dusk. The inn was crowded and poor, but we had Dr. Gow to dine, and he seemed to enjoy our stew very much! I had seen and admired some

who are devoted to the services of religion lead more correct lives, according to their ideas of morality, than the other classes, abstaining from the indulgence of carnal and sensual appetites. The unlicensed intercourse of the sexes is not in general considered by these people as a serious offence; and their maxim is, that if the advances are made by the female, the connexion does not constitute an offence, but it is held to be such when the proposal comes from the man. They employ an almanac, in many respects like our own, according to the rules of which, during five, four, or three days in the month, they do not shed blood nor eat flesh or fowl; as is our usage in regard to Friday, the Sabbath, and the vigils of the saints. The laity take to themselves as many as thirty wives, some more, some fewer, according to their ability to maintain them; for they do not receive any dowry with them, but, on the contrary, settle dowers upon their wives, in cattle, slaves, and money. The wife who is first married always maintains the superior rank in the family; but if the husband observes that any one amongst them does not conduct herself well to the rest, or if she becomes otherwise disagreeable to him, he can send her away. They take to their beds those who are nearly related to them by blood, and even espouse their mothers-in-law. Many other mortal sins are regarded by them with indifference, and they live in this respect like the beasts of the field. In this city Marco Polo remained, along with his father and uncle, about the space of one year, which the state of their concerns rendered necessary.'

of the Chinese wooden saddles and elaborate leather saddle cloths, and told him I was going to buy one at the first opportunity, but he immediately went to his house and returned with a very fine set, which he insisted on my accepting as a present in spite of all I could do to refuse. He also made us a present of some vegetables and tinned meat.

Early next morning we set out for Liangchowfu 170 miles away following a flat, fairly good road, which ran along close to the south bank of the Pei Ta Ho. The weather was fairly warm, but misty, and to the north we caught glimpses of the lofty Pei Shan range. We were at that time over five thousand feet up ourselves. A halt was made for breakfast at Ku Ch'eng, a walled village of about fifty houses, and when we left there I walked on ahead, feeling the need for exercise after a morning in my cart. The road was sandy, sometimes full of stones, and bordered by desert with occasional small oases, and weird coffin-shaped mounds of earth, which appeared at regular intervals.

The last half-mile to Tung Lo Hsien, the road ran between banks twenty feet high, and as I emerged from this cleft in the hills, I came upon an open space in front of the gateway of the village. To one side, against the crumbling wall, a rough stage had been erected, and on it was a troop of strolling players engaged in one of those interminable Chinese tragedies. A crowd of villagers and petty farmers in tattered clothes stood spellbound before the stage, and in rough country carts, equally intent on the play, sat their womenfolk in cheap but gaudy silks, their faces painted white and scarlet, and their hair carefully greased and secured behind by long steel pins.

Little painted girls, their hair decorated with paper flowers, also sat here and there, while a local official had a private box set up for himself and his friends at the back of the audience and watched at a dignified distance. In and out of the crowd moved hawkers with cakes and small pieces of appetising pork stuck on little sticks. It was a picturesque scene, and not wishing to distract the attention of the people, I passed through the gate and climbed on to the wall. From here I had a good view, undisturbed, and soon saw de Kerangat and Moss arrive. They were at once surrounded by a curious crowd, and I called to them to come and join me, which they did, and we stood watching until the carts arrived. This place has over one hundred houses.

On the 27th we left before dawn, crossing the Pei Ta Ho twice, before halting five hours later, close to a large temple called Ta Fo Shu, perched on a nearby hillside. As there was said to be a famous Buddha there, we all walked over to the building, and on entering beheld the enormous figure of the deity reaching far up under the eaves of the temple. I could not estimate the height, but the great toes were fully four feet high, and the figure sat enthroned with the supports of the building rising from its body, so that it was impossible to view the whole at once. It had originally sat unprotected on the hillside until the weather had threatened its destruction, and the local priests had built this temple as protection in four tiers, or setbacks, the supports for the first tier resting on the ground, the next on the knees, and so on, so that the sightless eyes look out of the paper windows of the topmost gallery.

The road continued between banks from six to fifteen feet high, the Pei Ta Ho was crossed again, and we entered

Shan Tau Hsien, a town with walls about a mile long on the north and south, but only a couple of hundred yards apart. The single main street was both prosperous and dirty, and we halted at an inn for breakfast. The desert country continued, and with difficulty we forded the river once more, at a point where the Great Wall, here in ruins, crosses it. In the soft earth of the plain were many great clefts, twenty feet or more deep, and for the fifth time we forded the river, passing two small walled villages, and continuing along a bad road. There were many hawks and cranes overhead. I walked as far as the walled village of Erh Shi Ho Pu, and then slept in the cart as far as Hsin Ho Yi. This place is 6660 feet above sea-level.

Early next day we pushed on. The sun rose on a clear sky, but it soon clouded over and snow began to fall heavily. A village of six houses and many ruins was passed and we reached Hsiao Kou Chen seven hours from the start, and halted for breakfast. This place had only a few miserable houses and dilapidated walls. As we moved on, the Great Wall was seen at intervals, but it had disappeared completely in places, and was not more than eight feet high at its best. We had been climbing steadily all day, and now entered a pass nine thousand feet up, where the road was all stones and boulders, difficult at all times, but doubly so then, as a snowstorm drove in our faces and half blinded men and beasts. A miserable village of ten houses, called Ting Chiang Miao, 9428 feet up, was reached and we then began a gradual descent, over a road deep in mud from the rapidly-melting snow. As we struggled onwards through the storm, and over the deeply-rutted track, a shepherd with his flock passed by on a neighbouring hillside. His dog, with tail tucked tight

THE GOBI AND THE GREAT WALL EAST OF SUCHOW

Facing p. 290

between its legs, kept the huddled sheep in motion, while the shepherd stumbled over the rough ground, his head covered with a piece of ancient felt, his naked body showing through the tattered clothing, and his feet swathed in other rags. As a picture of primitive life and the depths of human poverty that scene has stuck in my mind for many a long day.

Soon after the snow ceased, and we walked on. A mile and a half from our destination we came to a post some ten feet high standing by the roadside. Near the top was a short cross-piece, and from it, suspended by its pigtail, hung a human head. The nose and both cheeks had been slit, and this gruesome object, so said our Chinese Lieutenant, was a warning to horse and cattle thieves, it being the head of one of them caught by the local soldiery. We reached the walled village of Shui Chuan Tzu, a place of about fifty houses, soon after this and halted for the night.

Early next morning we were on the road again. It was still cloudy and cold, and we had some snow during the afternoon. The village of San Tiao Kou was passed, and on the low hills to the north we saw what looked like a dozen or more small temples. For breakfast a halt was made at the small and dirty village of Hung Miao Tun, and we then pushed on about eleven, crossing the River Pai Li Ho, and passing some ruins. The road became terrible, with many small streams crossing it, some of them almost torrents with treacherous and rocky beds, and the road itself was covered with stones and boulders. We halted for the night at Yung Chiang Hsien, a walled village of about fifty houses. The inn was small and very dirty. Tilmach came into our room while we were waiting for supper and told us that one of the carters was very ill, so I went out to look at him. I found him in agony on the ground, surrounded by the other men, and eventually discovered that Bielenky had given him a box of laxative pills, without telling him to take only two at a time. The poor devil of a carter had apparently swallowed the whole lot and now thought he was going to die. One of his companions decided to try a little Chinese doctoring and after tying a piece of string tight round one of the patient's fingers, proceeded to dig a rusty needle into the flesh right under the finger-nail, and also to jab it into his back near the spine! The man was all right next day! Here I received a letter from an English missionary in Liangchowfu, saying he was expecting us, and would like us to stay with him.

On the 30th, our caravan started a couple of hours after midnight. The road was very rough and stony all day, and the country desert, although there were a few farms wherever there was water to be found. We passed through the villages of Pei Pa and Sha Ho Pu and halted at Feng Lo Pu early in the afternoon. Here there were fifty odd houses and a small fort, while the inn was better than usual.

On the 31st a start was made soon after midnight, and we passed over some of the worst pieces of road yet experienced. It was made up chiefly of large, loose stones, which shook the carts at every step, and successfully prevented our getting any sleep. At dawn we halted at a small village, washed and breakfasted, and then de Kerangat and I rode forward on borrowed ponies toward Liangchowfu. The same terrible stony waste continued for some time, and was succeeded by a great area of crumbling graves and tombs, which extended for acres on either hand, while a range of hills some 1200 feet high stretched parallel to our line of march and slightly to the south. Not far from the city, we were met by Mr. Belcher, an English missionary, who was dressed in Chinese costume except for a soft felt hat, and was riding a large and handsome mule. A servant who was with him was left to guide the carts, while we ourselves rode on with the missionary, a man of about forty, very shy and difficult to talk to. He told us, however, that Admiral Kolchak had been taken by the Reds, and shot at Irkutsk. I was very sorry to hear the news, as Kolchak had always seemed to me a pathetic figure struggling to play an honourable part among a crowd of incompetent or cowardly advisors.

After passing through one of the main gateways, our guide turned to the right and we moved through some mean and narrow streets to the mission. In the outer courtyard, a Miss Mellors, who had been conducting a class of Chinese women, came out to greet us, and we then passed into an inner court, on three sides of which were the living and sleeping-rooms of the missionaries. The living and dining-rooms were comfortably furnished and beautifully kept, in fact much more like civilisation than anything we had seen for six months or more, and it was wonderful to sit on a cane chair in a warm room and look at the most recent copies of English newspapers. Mrs. Belcher then came in, and we sat talking until the rest of the party arrived. After a most excellent lunch, during which we had the greatest difficulty in keeping the conversation going, as our hosts were remarkably shy, Morgan, Mr. Belcher, and I walked through the city to the east suburb, where the carts and servants were billeted. The streets were narrow and dirty, and we attracted a good deal of attention. De Kerangat was anxious to see some Roman Catholic missionaries who lived nearby, so I went with him to their mission house, but found no one there, although there was a note (as they were evidently expecting us) asking us to call next day on the Bishop, who lived outside the town. That evening was memorable for three things, to wit, a bath, a good dinner, and a bed with a mattress and clean sheets.

Being with missionaries we rose early next morning – it was 1st April – breakfasted and had prayers afterwards, singing 'Rock of Ages,' and listening to a lesson from the Bible. It seemed so curious, sitting there in the low-ceilinged Chinese room, far away from the Nonconformist chapels of England, and surrounded by hundreds of square miles of desert and mountain country, populated by thousands and thousands of yellow 'heathen.' Inside the compound the narrow, but conscientious spirit of middle-class England prevailed, undisturbed by the age-long, decaying civilisation beyond its walls. I wanted to smile at the thought of our freethinking and often blasphemous party, solemnly singing hymns in a room of the China Inland Mission, but the sincere and kindly faces of my hosts restrained me.

A word here on missionaries will not be out of place. I had always been rather prejudiced against them by the opinions I had heard expressed so often by Anglo-Indians, both soldier and civilian. According to these critics, the zealous workers in the cause of Christ did more harm than good, making dishonest and hypocritical Christians out of honest and respectful heathen. I suspect that the natives thus educated are not so willing to kowtow to their white masters, and hence the opposition in certain quarters to missionary work, but whatever the cause, soldier and merchant do not like the ministers of the Gospel, and take no pains to hide their feelings. My experience in China, both at that time and later, was that the missionaries were a distinct asset to the community in which they lived, healing the sick, caring for orphans, educating and helping those who cared to profit by their teaching. As in the western parts of China, the number of converts was very small, and the Christian religion can hardly make any important impression on the mass of the population, but the example set by the devoted workers of all sects does have an effect, and where the missionaries have enough sense not to interfere in politics, or side with one faction against another, they are respected by all intelligent Chinese. While the majority of the men and women, who spend their lives in the interior, are comfortably housed and fed, and their hardships few, a great deal of self-denial and hard work is necessary to achieve even a slight success, and they give up all that most people hold dear to help the unfortunate inhabitants of another race. The great majority of Roman Catholics, for instance, never see their native lands again, and the Protestants only at long intervals. I have a great respect for most of them, and except in a few cases, found them hospitable, kind and helpful in the extreme. Their greatest fault is their intolerance of other sects, and this is sometimes carried to ridiculous extremes, especially in cases when there is so little difference in belief that a layman like myself can see no difference at all.

In order to call on the Roman Catholics, de Kerangat and I, together with a guide, rode on mules through the west gate and struck south-west along a stony track for thirty *li*. After about an hour and a half's riding, we came to a small group of buildings, topped by a wooden crucifix, and dismounted on a terrace, overlooking what must have been a pretty garden in spring-time. In the dining-hall, we came on a young priest, who seemed so delighted or astonished at the sudden appearance of two white men in uniform, that he was almost unintelligible. A few minutes later the Bishop and two other priests came in, and we were soon sitting around the table smoking cigars and discussing world events. De Kerangat, as usual, let off steam, and entertained us till the arrival of lunch, a coarse but excellent meal at which a delicious red wine was served. The Bishop, who was, I believe, an Italian, could almost hold his own with the Frenchman, and we stayed there till after four, having inspected the church, school, garden, and vineyards. They could hardly let us go, but we finally succeeded in getting away and returned, riding through a miniature dust storm. On our arrival, the Belchers had lost their shyness and we spent a very enjoyable evening, keeping them up till the late hour of ten-thirty.

Next morning our kit was sent off to the inn, and we walked over with Mr. Belcher, to find nothing ready for our departure, although the Tilmach had had orders to move on as soon as we should arrive from the mission. He was a lazy and stupid youth, and seems to have spent his time in Liangchowfu buying hats! He appeared that day in a purple sun-helmet with a green pugaree, an importation from the coast evidently, which made him look so ridiculous that we had to laugh and forget our anger at his incompetence. Before leaving I sent through

Mr. Belcher twenty taels to Dr. Gow, who had presented me with the saddle in Kanchow, for use among the poor, and also gave my host some money for the same purpose. He walked with us for the first five *li*, and then, after we had thanked him again for his hospitality, turned back, and we continued on our way.

CHAPTER 23

LANCHOWFU AND THE LAST OF THE GOBI

THE end of our two months' journey across the great Gobi was in sight, for we had already covered 1050 miles in fifty-three days, and only 185 miles lay between us and Lanchowfu, the city on the Yellow River where we would have to halt, pay off our carts, and make fresh arrangements for our further journey. On my arrival at Liangchow I had received a letter from an English missionary in Lanchow, a Mr. Mann, who said that he was looking forward to our arrival and was making tentative plans for transport for us. I replied by letter, and also wired him and Mr. Chan Butto, the Postal Commissioner, the probable date of our arrival. I had been given a letter to the latter by Mr. Boyers before leaving Urumchi.

After saying good-bye to Mr. Belcher, we walked on, although the road was bad, snow was falling heavily, and a cold west wind made matters worse. At Ta Ho Yi, thirty *li* from the city, we waited for the carts, in a Chinese eating-house. Only a few hovels inside the walls of the village were occupied, the majority of the inhabitants living in houses which straggled for some distance along the road outside. We pushed on through Hotung Pu, the track being appallingly stony most of the way, bordered by many ruins, and reached Ching Pien Yi after six. The everlasting mutton stew for dinner was made more palatable by cakes, sauces, and cocoa given us by the Belchers.

On the 3rd we had a very hard day passing over a terrible stretch of road. We left before 4 a.m., and had no difficulty until we reached Ku Lang Hsien, a straggling village on the banks of the River Ku Lang. This stream flows north-eastwards into the sandy wastes beyond the Great Wall, and either loses itself in the desert or flows into a brackish lake some eighty miles away. The village itself stands 7030 feet above sea-level, or two thousand feet higher than Liangchow, and is surrounded by steep hills six hundred to eight hundred feet high, between which the river flows, confining the road to a precarious shelf along the steep slope on the western bank. We set out from here about midday, climbing, twisting and turning along the slippery and stony track, now edging carefully past narrow places where parts of the road had fallen into the swiftly running waters below, now plunging into a raging mountain torrent where the mules sank to their bellies in icy waters and the wheels bumped over boulders and sank into deep holes. Just before reaching Hei Sung Pu, we had to cross the main river, which was a raging torrent, rushing down the hillside with great noise and violence. My cart was the first one to cross, and only succeeded after four attempts had failed. The ford was difficult to locate, and we kept sinking into treacherous holes, which threatened to upset the cart, and made us return to the banks three times. The fourth try was nearly disastrous, as the shaft mule suddenly dropped into a hole, and remained there for five minutes with nothing but part of its head above water, while the anxious carters stripped themselves and plunged into the icy waters to help out the unfortunate animal, which bore the whole weight of the shaft on its back and could make no effort to climb out of the hole without the combined efforts of all the men and the three lead mules.

The other carts crossed without mishap, and we climbed up the winding road past Hei Sung Pu, where the ancient village walls had been worn down by time and sheltered only a few miserable hovels, and An Yuan another poor place of half a dozen huts. Half a dozen crude water-wheels were seen on the river bank, now west of us, which apparently drove mills for grinding corn, or were used for irrigation. The thawing snows made walking difficult, and as the sun went down the cold became intense, so that we were glad to reach the dilapidated inn at Lung Kou Pu, which is about ten thousand feet up and no place for a traveller if he can find better quarters. To the east were the high rugged peaks of the Ma Ya Shan which forms the water-shed between the Ku Lang, which flows north, and the Ping Fan, which flows south.

On the 4th we crossed the highest point of the mountains, over ten thousand feet up, near Wu Shao Ling, where a large white boulder carried up there in some glacial era lies in a bed of reddish soil. It is regarded by the Chinese as excellent medicine, and they chip off small pieces, grind them to powder, and swallow this with great success. After passing through a crumbling section of the Great Wall, we crossed the headwaters of the Ping Fan and halted at Chen Chian Yi for breakfast. As we descended the mountain slopes and followed the river valley, the weather became warmer and shoots of green could be

OUR CARTS IN A CARAVANSERAI ON THE GOBI, MARCH 1920

Facing p. 300

seen here and there, while the road too improved and the desert began to give way to more fertile country. After passing the night in a wretched inn at Shi Ya Kou, we pushed on at 2 a.m. next day, forded the river again, passed outside the Great Wall for a time, and reached Pin Fan soon after one in the afternoon. Here the walls were two hundred and fifty to three hundred yards square and in good preservation, but most of the people lived outside the gates on the south side, where saddle and harness shops seemed to predominate in the bazaar. I received a letter from Mr. Chan Butto, and a wire from Peking asking for information about some Englishmen of the 'Irtish Corporation,' which I had never heard of. Presumably people like ourselves, lost in the steppes of Siberia or Turkestan. We also heard that the new Postal Commissioner for Sinkiang Province, a Mr. Guaita, was on his way to relieve Mr. Boyers at Urumchi, and that we should probably meet him the next day.

The road on the following morning was rocky and extremely rough until Ching Sau Erh was reached, and we then entered a cultivated area as far as Hung Ching Tzu, quite a big place, where we halted for the night. Mr. Guaita did not turn up, but a note came from him, which began 'Dear Party,' and said that he was at a village thirty *li* away, expecting us to arrive at any moment. He also sent us some fairly recent copies of *Punch* and *The Bystander*, which we fell on like wolves, and looked on the smartly dressed inhabitants of London, or the pink-coated horsemen out for a day with the hounds, as dwellers in a different world.

On the 7th, we made our usual early start, about 2 a.m., and some four hours later I was roused by a Chinese officer, and told that the new Commissioner's caravan was approaching. Cursing at our meeting at such a time, I crawled out of the cart, and walked over to where Mr. Guaita, in obvious ill humour, was struggling into some clothes. Conversation soon brought us both to a better frame of mind, and as he had only just left Hsien Shui Ho, he decided to return with us, letting his caravan go on. Earlier in the morning we had turned eastwards through the Great Wall, leaving the valley of the Ping Fan, entering a narrow valley or pass, and, after meeting Mr. Guaita, reaching the small village where he had spent the night. We gave him some breakfast, and our guest then insisted on opening a bottle of Italian champagne, which we drank to each other's good fortune. Morgan had been the first to clamour for the wine, which had been presented to us, but I opened the bottle, and after we had finished I said, referring to our necessarily 'dry' journey, 'Morgan was the first to fall!' He seemed so amused at this feeble joke, that we finally discovered his cup had been forgotten in the excitement, and he hadn't had a drop at all. However, Mr. Guaita gave us in addition two bottles of Johnnie Walker and one of gin, so he felt better.

After giving our Italian friend much information and advice about the road, we said good-bye, and each set out on his way, ours taking us along a road many inches deep in dust, which wound in and out between low hills of reddish-brown and greyish-green, very steep in places. After climbing to 6200 feet, the road dipped down into a valley beyond, where a small stream flowed in a river bed with banks twenty or more feet high. We followed this stream for several *li* and then crossed by a bridge, passing Ha Chia Tsui, a place of about a dozen houses, and continuing along the winding and dusty road, meeting a fair number of travellers, mostly in small carts. Near Hsiao Lao Chih, the red hills assumed extraordinary shapes, where constant erosion of the soft soil formed tall columns with large round heads, like the domes on the towers of mosques. A halt was made for the night at Yu Chia Wan, a scattered village of about fifty houses and without a wall. A miserable place some six thousand feet up, where the *kars* system of wells was necessary to maintain the water supply. In fact the water all day was brackish and distasteful.

There was great overhauling of battered valises, clothing, uniforms, and equipment that night, as we were to enter Lanchow next day, and wished to look our best for the occasion. Our two months of monotonous and arduous travel over the mighty Gobi were about to end, and every one felt lighthearted and happy at the thought of a few days' rest, and the gradual approach of civilisation.

A start was made at midnight and we reached Shi Li Tsin about eight. The surrounding country, which was very hilly, was cultivated on every possible square foot of level ground, even up the hillsides in little terraces, while the road wound through the valleys, often between steep banks, and always deep in dust. In the caravanserai, de Kerangat and I changed into our best uniforms and prepared to ride forward to the city. We were having breakfast, when a Chinese N.C.O. and two soldiers made their appearance, with a note of welcome from Mr. Geerts, the Commissioner of the Salt Gabelle, and waited to guide us on the right road. We were soon ready, and set out, I on the *Tura's* (Chinese officer's) horse, and rode through the hills, sometimes crossing small ravines, and sometimes passing cultivated land. To the south could be seen the broad ribbon of the Yellow River, flowing calmly toward the distant sea. Soon scattered dwellings appeared, and we ascended a steep slope to an old gateway built on the side of a hill, passed through it and entered that part of the city which lies north of the river. As we rode down the sloping street, two British missionaries, Messrs. Mann and Botham, met us, both wearing sober Chinese clothes, except for their Homburg hats. Both appeared surprised at our smart appearance as they thought we would be in rags after our long journey. We dismounted and walked on with them, meeting Mr. Chan Butto, the Postal Commissioner, on the modern suspension bridge, then in great need of repair, which spans the Yellow River here. Beneath us ran the broad yellow waters of the great Hwang Ho; behind us on the hills which came right down to the river banks, were the houses of the northern suburb, while to the south, standing out in bold relief against the not far distant mountains, were the massive crenellated walls of the city, surmounted at intervals by towering watch-towers and gateways.

With the Chinese Commissioner talking volubly, we crossed the bridge, turned to the left along the south bank, skirted the walls for a couple of hundred yards, and entered the city by the north gate. The old Manchu Club had been prepared for us as a billet, and I found that we were to have a large reception hall, a room for Moss and myself, another for Smith and Morgan, and one for the servants and soldiers, while there was also a kitchen. De Kerangat was to stay with Mr. Geerts, the Belgian Salt Commissioner. The rooms were bare and cheerless, but far better than any inn we had yet seen, so I was well content. Mr. Botham, a young English missionary much interested in the Moslems, and who was learning Turki and Arabic, guided de Kerangat and myself through the narrow streets of the city with its typical crowd of black or blue-coated Chinese, beggars, hawkers, soldiers, merchants, officials, carters, coolies, and priests, out of the west gate to the suburb on that side where we were to lunch with Mr. Geerts. Mr. Mann was to bring on the remainder of the party as soon as they arrived. Soon we were being greeted by the grey-haired Belgian and his sister, were conducted into a comfortable Chinese house furnished in European style, and found ourselves reclining luxuriously on cane chairs, sipping an excellent glass of cognac. De Kerangat, being with people who talked his own language, was soon chatting in his charming and amusing way, and kept us entertained until Moss and Smith turned up an hour later.

On our return to the billet, we found that a great many Chinese officials had called in our absence, and Morgan had had an awful time finding out who they were and what they wanted. Our carters had returned to an inn across the river as soon as our kit was unloaded, but came in to see us that afternoon, saying that their agent had arranged for a return trip to Urumchi with a load of merchandise in a few days' time. That was their life. We gave a tip of five taels to each driver, instead of a lump sum to the head-man, and this unusual procedure, while delighting the others, caused him great surprise and annoyance so that he pestered us for days with a claim for money due him owing to our two days' stay in Hami. The cost for the entire journey of two months for the six carts was a thousand Kwan Piao taels, or about £60, which had all been paid in advance.

Our ten days in Lanchow were busy ones, as there were all the preparations to be made for the journey to Sianfu, some 470 miles away. Fresh carts had to be hired, our old covers reduced in size to fit the smaller carts, provisions bought, kit overhauled, and many other details attended to. There were official visits to be paid too, and that and our preparations kept us busy all the time.

Our first duty, of course, was to send cards to the Governor and other important officials, and this was supposed to be done by the Sart interpreter, Tilmash, but apparently he made a mess of things, and the Governor never got our cards at all. I had to humbly apologise for this breach of etiquette when I called on him a couple of days later. On this occasion de Kerangat and I, accompanied by Messrs. Geerts and Chan Butto, were carried to the yamen in chairs, marvellous creations covered on the outside with emerald-green silk. From each corner of the roof, which was surmounted by a silver ball, hung long black silken tassels, and the inside was lined of the same material in red and green, and furnished with cushions and arm-rests. A door curtain hid one from the inquisitive glances of the passers-by. Each chair had four bearers and two soldiers as escort. In this magnificent manner we were carried at a swift shambling walk, with frequent cries from the soldiers to clear the streets, to the gates of the yamen, where a number of troops in blue-grey uniforms armed with what looked like Japanese rifles were on guard, and past them into an inner court. With our cards held aloft by a black-coated servant, we passed through several small courtyards to a waiting-room, where, after a few moments' delay, word was brought that the Governor was ready to receive us. The palace seemed to cover an enormous area, for we crossed still further courts, before coming to a modern one-storey building of stone, where the Governor, a fat, medium-sized man, received us in his private office, or study. This was a large 'L'-shaped room, but so filled with scrolls, photographs, and other things that it was difficult to move. On the walls were many scrolls, some written by the Governor himself, who rather fancied his penmanship, and some by well-known officials. Scattered among these were hundreds of photographs of our host in different poses. In some he was dressed in native fashion, and in others in full uniform, one being a life-size enlargement in the uniform of a general. After the usual formal conversation, he took us into the next room and showed us beautiful paintings on silk, copper and brass vessels thousands of years old, ancient pottery, urns, inkwells, porcelain, all jumbled up in inextricable confusion on tables, chairs, and floor with such incongruous articles as packets of American breakfast food, a dirty towel, cheap photographs and modern wicker furniture.

He returned our call next morning, and seemed interested in our arms and equipment, especially in the engraving on the blade of my sword. That afternoon we all went to dine with him, de Kerangat and I riding in chairs as before. The same maze of courts and passages was traversed to the very back of the yamen where in a reception-room we were met by Mr. Chan and half a dozen officials, all dressed in the usual black silk. Mr. Geerts was with us, and in a few moments we were joined by the Governor. The meal was served in the garden in a sort of summer-house, which was supposed to represent a ship, and consisted of eight or nine courses, served in semi-European style. The knives and forks of local manufacture were of pure silver, and so soft that any undue pressure bent them in half. There was very little drinking. Afterwards we went for a stroll in the garden, were shown the private zoo, where a four-horned goat, and a number of large, mangy-looking deer formed the chief attractions, and then climbed to the top of the city wall. This section of it was reserved for the Governor and inmates of the yamen, and from it we could see the extent of the palace grounds, the numerous watch-towers, myriad roofs, snow-capped mountains to the south and west, the Yellow River at our feet, and the Mission Hospital on the north bank. For half an hour, we listened politely to the excruciating efforts of a military band, and then just before leaving were shown a spot at the base of one of the towers, where a beautiful princess in bygone times had knocked out her brains, after the defeat of her husband in battle. The supposed bloodstains were pointed out to us, and we were told that they came out fresh every year.

Mr. Geerts, and all the missionaries, were extremely hospitable, and helped us in every way to hasten our departure, for in spite of our long months on the road, we were anxious to reach the coast and get the journey over. I had grown tired of walking day after day over stony or dusty roads, and as the weather was now quite warm, I decided to buy a horse, or rather pony. After looking at quite a number, I selected a fine-looking black, for which I paid fifty-five taels, and also invested in some smart-looking saddlery of blue silk webbing, ornamented with brass, with two red horse-tails to hang at head-stall and breastplate. He made a fine show. According to the

Chinese, a black is the best, and then in order of excellence came bay, chestnut, grey, and white.

Here in Lanchow, as in other places we had visited, was the same story of corruption and poor government. 'Squeeze,' or bribery, was the only means of getting anything done, from the smallest official to the Governor himself. Peking was practically ignored. Laws and proclamations were posted on the city walls and gates, but never enforced unless it suited the pockets of the officials to do so. The wretched peasants and shopkeepers were taxed almost out of existence, and yet little money ever found its way into the treasury. A little stuck in the palm of each through whom it passed. The soldiers were seldom paid, and consequently extorted money from all and sundry, torturing those whom they suspected of having buried treasure, by pouring boiling oil into their victim's ear. The troops were always on the verge of mutiny, and seemed able to secure their back pay only by threatening a serious disturbance, thereby frightening their officers and forcing the official by whom they were employed to disgorge. Even then the pay was in a debased paper currency, which the soldiers forced on the population at par value, and part of that would be 'squeezed' from them by their officers.

The province is rich in coal, copper, salt, musk, and other things, but it was impossible to develop any industry owing to the 'squeeze' demanded in advance by the officials concerned. The irrigation of the land was done in such a primitive way, that even near the Yellow River no water could be brought up to the ditches at low water, as the heavy, clumsy water-wheels only worked when there was a strong current. The great possibilities of water-power were not understood at all, and the electric light in the yamen was produced by an ancient plant, which consumed much coal and gave so dim a light, that candles or oil lamps had to be used invariably in order to see at all.

As an instance of the incompetence and procrastination of the governing class, I give the following. The Central Government had ordered a new map to be made of the Koko Nor district west of Lanchow, and had sent surveyors for this purpose. They were to be supplied with funds by the Governor of Kansu. On their arrival, they were kept waiting for months without pay, while the Governor had reported to Peking that the work was progressing satisfactorily. Just before my arrival, he wrote that the new map had been finished and would be published shortly, and the Director-General of the Chinese Postal Service thereupon wrote to Mr. Chan Butto for two copies. Mr. Chan had to reply that far from having completed the work, the surveyors had not even left Lanchow for the district they were supposed to map, but were expected to start in ten days!

On one of the highest points in the mountain range to the south of the city stood a new pagoda built by the Governor, and but recently finished. The inside story of its inception is amusing and shows how little the Chinaman has progressed beyond the superstitious beliefs of our own Middle Ages. The story goes that the principal wife of the Governor went to her photographer for a special portrait (she seems to have been as fond of these modern wonders as her lord and master), and told him to work quickly on it, so as to let her have it with all speed. Probably in the excitement of receiving so important a personage the photographer unfortunately placed an exposed plate in the camera, and discovered when the negative was developed that the lady appeared with several arms, another shadowy form nearby, and a radiance above her head. Being a clever man, instead of acknowledging his mistake, he called at the yamen, approached the great lady with every appearance of awe and respect, showed her the plate, and proclaimed her a deity. She fell at once, became deeply religious and caused a pagoda to be built at the top of the highest mountain near the city, to the opening of which all important officials of the city were bidden. Up the steep mountain trails went the Governor, weighing a good two hundred and fifty pounds, carried in a chair by relays of sweating coolies, and after him came the unhappy mandarins, each borne in his chair also, and being roughly shaken on the steep hillsides. Some came nasty croppers and rolled down steep places, with chair and coolies following after, and great was the unpopularity of the photographer, who had discovered the holiness of the Governor's wife.

The East has always been famed for the number of eccentric foreigners who live in Treaty Ports or further inland, but not one of them can have chosen a stranger career than a certain Mme. David Neill, a Frenchwoman, who was then living in the great Buddhist Monastery of Kumbun, at Sining, near the Tibetan border. I was told that she had been in different parts of Tibet for seven or eight years, wearing native costume, professing Buddhism, and had been made a Llama. She travelled fearlessly from place to place, accompanied perhaps by only one servant or companion, and according to local gossip had first become interested in her new religion when travelling in India. Her object in life was now to find certain ancient documents relating to Buddhism, which had been taken from India into Tibet centuries ago, and which would prove of tremendous importance to students and historians of that great movement. I tried to imagine this cultivated and apparently comely Frenchwoman living among the wild and superstitious inhabitants of that little-known country, and devoutly taking part in the religious ceremonies at some great monastery perched high on the rugged slopes of an unnamed mountain range. Curiously enough, de Kerangat had met her husband some years before in Algeria.

The missionaries had a great deal of suspicion and superstition to overcome in their work. Even the higher officials gave ready credence to tales of babies being eaten at night in mission compounds, and similar absurdities. On the whole, however, they were all treated well, and I never heard of a foreign woman being attacked, although they often travelled practically alone through country swarming with bandits. There have been cases of kidnapping and holding for ransom, but men were usually in the parties seized. I believe the Roman Catholics made a practice of buying small children from starving peasants, a policy bitterly opposed by the Protestants, but this was usually done only in extreme cases when the child would probably have starved to death, if the priests had not taken her in, and the purchase money merely concluded a business transaction so that the parents could not reclaim the child at a later date. She would naturally be brought up as a Roman Catholic. As far as I know only girls were bought, but that was probably because the Chinese have little use for girls and would not be likely to sell a son.

The Chinese women of the interior are practically uneducated, and much more ignorant and unintelligent than the men, as among the better classes they are virtually prisoners in the women's quarters, and lead a life similar to that of a Turkish woman in a harem. We never saw the wives of any of the officials, and when out of doors they always rode in carts with the curtains drawn. Foot-binding was the rule wherever we went, and it was exceptional to see even a peasant woman among the Chinese with unbound feet. Although this practice had long been forbidden by law, the poor, ignorant girls insisted on going through the tortures it entailed, rather than suffer the disgrace of having normal feet. They even did it against the wishes of their parents.

Although Kansu is not as Moslem as Sinkiang, there is still a large proportion of the population who follow the prophet, and there were signs of unrest among them at that time, although the ferocious repression by the Chinese of the great Mohammedan rebellion in the latter half of the nineteenth century was still fresh in the minds of all. Recalling the far distant days when the Mongol hordes held most of China, the present day Moslem of the West still chafes at the alien rule of Peking as the recent troubles have proved. During the Great War, German and Turkish emissaries were very active in certain parts of the country, trying to start a holy war to the embarrassment of the Allies, but their efforts had had little or no effect. There were said to be Persians and Afghans in Sinkiang and Kansu at that very moment carrying on pro-Bolshevik propaganda. However, the constant failure of all the Moslem risings, makes one think that the Mohammedans are weak in popular support, or torn by dissensions amongst themselves. Perhaps now that the western provinces of China have practically declared themselves independent of Peking, the predominating race will have a better chance of regaining some of its lost power. The Central Government is so weak, and China will be so torn by civil war for some time to come, that the Moslem West will have an opportunity during the next few years to develop along lines of its own choosing.

Lanchow has left an impression on my mind of a great city surrounded by imposing walls, dominated by the four great gateways and many watch-towers, its yamens, bazaars, barracks and suburbs spread anyhow along the banks of the Hwang Ho, and behind it the barren mountains rising range after range and stretching south and west in an unending panorama of snow-capped peaks to the far-distant horizon. Through its narrow streets life went on as it had for countless centuries; here were the shops displaying leopard, tiger and other skins brought from the mountains of Tibet and Szechwan; there the workers in brass, silver and gold, producing bowls and ornaments with almost prehistoric tools, clever in the intricacy of the work, but copying the ancient designs, unoriginal, always the same; here would be the mender of broken pottery painstakingly twirling his drill with the aid of a loosely strung bow, and piecing together the little fragments with clamps of metal; there would be a group of ragged little children, their noses running, and with small brass locks hung round their necks to guard them from evil spirits; at the gates, and in countless other places, crouched those terrible beggars, clad in the most impossible rags, filthy, covered with sores, and existing on infrequent donations of copper cash or the refuse thrown into the street. Overhead in the cloudless sky would circle a flock of pigeons, making the air sing with the music of their flight, for attached to the leg of each was a hollow tube of bamboo, which produced a flute-like note when the birds were in the air.

Everywhere was discomfort, poverty, ignorance, and disease. Only too evident were the effects of a corrupt and oppressive Government, grinding down with its 'squeeze,' its taxes, its extortions, and its lack of enterprise, a people too long occupied in the worship of its ancestors. To me China is but a replica of Europe in the Dark or early Middle Ages, in spite of her boast of centuries of culture, before the white man had emerged from the savage. Her walled cities, powerful war lords, private armies, bandit rulers, lack of justice, archaic methods and lack of communication are a perfect reproduction of Christendom a thousand years ago. The new awakening, brought about by contact with Western civilisation, inclined at first towards Moscow because no other Power would attempt to help the Nationalists in their long struggle against the incompetence of the Central Government. China's new nationalism, however, is not likely to tolerate Russian interference, now that she has achieved some form of stable government, but how long it will take for her to complete the pacification and unification of the country is hard to say. Lack of communications, the ignorance and superstition of the mass of the population, and the inexperience of new rulers will make it a hard task.

Slowly our preparations for departure went forward. Six carts were found at last, the old cart covers altered, and provisions were laid in. We dined each night with the hospitable Manns, who insisted on our coming to their compound. I can never thank them enough for their hospitality and the help they gave us in getting ready for the journey to Sianfu.

Having seen some of the Governor's scrolls, I greatly delighted him by asking him to write one for me. This he did and I received two beautiful ones written by his own hand and sealed with his chop. The first one translated read, 'To the Great English Kingdom's High Military Officer Ho Dji Si passing through Kansu given,' and the second one, 'Great Chinese Republic Ninth Year Fourth Month Kansu Governor Chang Kuang Kien gives.' On the scrolls was an inscription referring to the great Army of many corps which I should command. I was delighted!

At length on 18th April all was ready and I decided to start next day, as all of us were impatient to reach the coast with all possible speed.

CHAPTER 24

THE ROAD TO SIANFU

BEHIND us were the sandy and stony wastes of the Gobi, and the months of travelling at a temperature far below zero. From now on, with occasional exceptions at high altitudes, the weather was warm and spring-like, it even rained occasionally, and our road led us through the soft soil of the loess country, where the traffic of centuries had worn the road bed down so that frequently one travelled fifty or a hundred feet below the level of the surrounding country, ploughing through dust inches thick, and sheltered from the sun's rays by sheer walls on either hand.

This country of rich red soil was long ago the cradle of the Chinese race, and its peculiar properties have influenced and moulded the national character. Like the fertile and fantastic loess, the people are both yielding and obstinate. To this day, the cultivation of the land is as easy and as difficult as it was three thousand years ago, for while the fields yield large crops, they can never be counted on to remain in the same place. The soil erodes so easily that a heavy rainstorm may wash away several acres, if there are not enough men to prevent their land from flowing into their neighbour's.

A Chinese proverb says that farming in the loess country is good if one can keep track of the farm.

This farming problem encouraged the solidity of the

family group, which has been such a feature of Chinese life, and the immunity from constant warfare gave no chance to the development of martial characteristics. The loess area seems to have been empty, there was no clearing to be done, no permanent works to covet, and it was easier to take new fields than to seize someone else's. Thus the men who became leaders were not the soldiers, but the cultural innovators.

These centuries of agricultural life passed in peaceful preoccupation with the land, and involving ceaseless co-operative effort to control the shifting soil, have made the Chinese both weak and strong. They are defenceless against more warlike races, but once conquered they impose their culture and their philosophy on their new rulers.

About a year after I crossed this section of the country, a terrific earthquake caused such an upheaval that whole villages and farms disappeared, roads were obliterated, trees moved hundreds of yards, and the courses of rivers altered. It is not so necessary therefore to give a detailed description of our journey to Sianfu, for the road has changed considerably, and only the general character of the country remains. I shall therefore give a less precise account of the three weeks which we took to reach the capital of Shensi.

On the morning of 19th April we said good-bye to our hospitable missionary friends and to the Geerts, assembled the carts and set out across the city, jolting over the uneven streets, which were so bad in places that a number of boxes and sacks were shaken off the carts, and had to be picked up every few steps. A large crowd watched our departure and accompanied us to the gate. For twenty *li*, I rode on my new black pony, followed at a jog trot by a *mafu* on foot, through cultivated land, and then up a long steep hill, which gave a magnificent view of the city to the west, and the gorges of the Hwang Ho to the north. The road became very hilly, and we plunged into those deep cuts which we were to experience in many parts of Kansu and Shensi. My pony ambled along, so that I felt as if I were riding in an arm-chair, and the *mafu* ran ahead or alongside pointing out the road, and thus keeping me from losing my way amongst the maze of tracks that forked off at frequent intervals.

The inns, during the first few days, were poor, the water brackish very often, and as the weather was now too warm to carry meat as we had done across the Gobi, we found that the lack of anything but fat and unpalatable pork was rather trying. Once see a Chinese pig and you never want to look pork in the face again. It was a curious hilly country, with the roads often a hundred feet below the surface, sometimes coming out near the crest of a hill, and following a precarious route along its edge, with an almost perpendicular drop to the valley far below.

On the 22nd we left the river valley we had been following in a south-easterly direction, and turned east over the Ching Hang Shan range. Upon reaching the top, after a steep ascent, the road ran along a razorback ridge for some distance, so that we could see the valleys away below on either hand, and the terraced fields of cultivated land rising one above another almost to the hilltops. The descent was extremely steep, fully one in three in some places, so that the wheel mules almost slid the whole way down.

The next day we reached Hui Ning Hsien, quite a large

town with ancient crumbling walls, but poor and uninteresting. From here the road had originally run along the river-bank, but in course of time the water had so cut into the soft soil, that the banks fell in, taking the road with them. It was now necessary to follow the river bed, which was deep and wide, with only a small stream, perhaps thirty feet across, meandering from one side to the other. Trekking through the gorge, we had to ford the winding river every two or three hundred yards, so that we must have done this literally scores of times during the day. De Kerangat, who had set out to walk had himself carried over the first two fords by a dirty-looking ruffian who offered his services, but gave it up when he realised he would have to spend most of the day on the coolie's evil-smelling back.

On the 24th after leaving the walled village of Shui Kia Tsui, and passing a poor place called Chai Ping Lien, I rode ahead, and about five *li* from our destination followed a footpath, which offered a short cut to the other side of the valley. The path led down to a muddy ravine, and I had almost crossed when my pony suddenly sank into a bog. Luckily we were near firm ground, and he got out without much difficulty, after knocking me down in the process. A Chinaman, who had followed me on his pony, had worse luck, for he sank in the middle of the ravine, and his poor beast floundered hopelessly, for half an hour, getting further and further from a secure foothold. When my carters arrived on the road above they finally pulled the exhausted pony out, but it died that night.

On the 25th we reached Ching Ning Hsien, a large walled town, comparatively clean. The best inns are in the west suburb. The Chinese there were very curious, and we had difficulty in securing any privacy at all. Several officials called, and one of them brought in a substance that looked like graphite, as he had heard that there were engineers in the party. Smith and Morgan scanned it but could not make out whether it was graphite or molybdenite. The official showed his gratitude at our interest by sending us a duck, a chicken, and a sack of potatoes!

The next day I had another view of Chinese veterinary work, when one of their horses and one of their mules got colic. The horse doctor jabbed each animal below the eye and below the nostrils with a rusty needle, then threw the animals, pinched their sheaths and jumped on their tails! Thinking, I suppose, that it would be preferable to conceal their aches and pains than endure this treatment, the two beasts recovered.

Between Ching Ning Hsien and Lung Teh Hsien, the road was flat and ran between an avenue of trees. We reached the latter place, inside the decaying walls of which are only a few hovels, on the afternoon of the 26th, and the next day crossed the high ridge of the Lo Pan Shan. The approach was so precipitous, although it zigzagged up the mountainside, that only two carts could be taken up at a time, three teams of mules being necessary to drag each one to the summit. The descent was even steeper, and it took us nine hours to cover the thirty *li* which separated one side of the mountain from the other. Riding on I passed through Ho Shang Pu, merely a collection of hovels, then Wating, where the large area covered by the crumbling walls contained only a few houses, and a little later I came to a marshy valley where in a number of huts lived a clan of primitive woodcutters and basket-weavers.

About ten *li* from How Tien, I rode through a narrow and rocky defile, where there were several temples and a great number of pink blossoms, cherry or apricot, which made the gloomy place quite beautiful in the fading light.

On the 28th, starting out as usual about 4 a.m., we travelled along a flat and fair road, bordered by trees in some places, and late in the morning met Dr. Parry and young Mr. Tornewalle, who had ridden out from Ping Liang to meet us. They were missionaries, the latter belonging to some American Scandinavian Mission, and the former to the Mission Hospital in Lanchow, now on a visit to this place to care for the sick. They told us that a good deal of fighting was going on in Shensi, and that our road was not safe further on, as bands of rebels or robbers were pillaging, burning bridges and cutting telegraph lines. It might be necessary for us to return to Lanchow and seek another route to Peking. As we approached the city walls, past which flows the King Ho River, we saw groups of soldiers and civilians digging away the heaped-up sand, which had banked up against the ramparts so high in places as to make them easily scaleable by a determined enemy. The city inside the walls was very poor and dirty, but the mission had a semi-European house, which was quite new, and after leaving the carts and servants at an inn not far away, de Kerangat, Smith, Morgan, Moss and myself went there to stay during our sojourn in the town. Supper was at five, and we had sat down at the table, when the missionaries suddenly broke into a hymn, which startled us so that we all nearly fell off our chairs. Besides the two men we had met, there were Mrs. Parry, Mr. and Mrs. Tornewalle and their daughter, all most kind and hospitable, and much interested in our travels.

Being anxious to get more definite information as to the state of affairs in Shensi, de Kerangat and I dispatched our cards to the Governor, but he could not see us that day, and sent word that the road ahead was not safe. On the following morning, the news appeared worse, as the local troops defending the Kansu border had withdrawn to Chang Wu (a small place just over the boundary in Shensi), many refugees were reported coming west, and the robbers appeared to have destroyed a bridge, which might mean a delay of over a fortnight for us. Mr. Tornewalle advised us to turn back and make for Ning Hsia, from whence we could obtain rafts and float down the Yellow River till we struck some town within reach of Peking.

All day the gangs continued their work on the fortifications, and in the afternoon de Kerangat and I paid a visit to the Governor. He was very depressed and said that he could not possibly hold out should the robbers attempt to enter Kansu. He also advised us to make for a place called Ning Hsien near Ning Hsia, and float down the river until we got close to Kalgan, from whence there is a railway to Peking. We decided, however, that we could not leave the missionaries as the robbers might be hostile to foreigners, and we ought to protect our hosts as best we could.

From what I could make out of the fighting in Shensi, the situation was as follows. The Governor of the province, Cheng Shu Fan, was practically besieged in Sianfu, the capital, by General Hsu Jan Cheo, who had been sent down from Peking in 1918 with Manchurian and Mongol troops to take over the governorship of the province. Cheng, having good pickings where he was, decided to stay and a deadlock ensued, both parties refusing to move. This had been going on for over a year. To complicate matters, two independent bandit leaders, Ko Chien and Fan Lao Ri, coquetted with the northerners, defied Cheng, and ravaged the western half of the province. These were the men feared by the Governor of Ping Liang.

One of the curious things about travelling through this part of China, was that we were constantly passing through districts held by bandits or semi-bandits. A local commander might hold a town and a certain number of villages, and yet be at enmity with the provincial governor and the government troops. Outwardly it was impossible to tell the difference between soldiers and bandits as both wore the tattered blue-grey, with the five-pointed star of the Republic on the caps, and carried the five-coloured national flag. The 'five families' represented in the flag being:

Chinese . . .	Red
Manchus . . .	Yellow
Mongols . . .	Blue
Tibetans . . .	White
Mohammedans . .	Black

Our passports, however, and the letters carried one day ahead of us by a trusty messenger, procured our safe passage through the land, just as the postal service, even in the wildest parts, is always respected and allowed to pass unchallenged.[1]

[1] The Chinese postal service has the longest land route in the world, *i.e.* Peking to Tihwa-fu (Urumchi).

Fortunately a truce was arranged by which the two bandits, and the northern troops, were to leave the province, and we received news of this on the 30th. It was decided to move on next day, and meanwhile we paid a visit to the barracks and arsenal. The latter was little more than a primitive workshop, which had been started by a poor and ignorant man, who had salvaged some old hand lathes and machinery from a sunken dredger, and was turning out about fifty primitive brass fuzes a day. He also made shells and rifle stocks. The shells were about one and a half inch calibre. In the barracks were two 1885 Krupp field guns and half a dozen smaller models of 1893 pattern. They were well kept, and the N.C.O. in charge had obviously been trained by European officers. We had tea with the senior officer in the barracks, and heard from him that the bandit troops had moved nearer to Sianfu, thus giving up any intention for the present of invading Kansu. The northern troops then occupied the towns vacated by the bandits, thus extending their lines about the capital, which was said to be in a state of siege with the gates barred and sealed.

After an early supper, young Tornewalle produced a football from somewhere and suggested a game of 'soccer.' This was hailed with delight, and it was decided that the Army should play the Civilians, the sides being represented by de Kerangat, Moss, and myself against Dr. Parry, Tornewalle, and Gordon Smith. In an incredibly stony field near the mission, we tossed up for ends, made goal posts out of our coats, placed de Kerangat in one and Smith in the other, and kicked off. The spectators consisted of a score or more of little Chinese girls aged from about six to twelve, from the mission school, and I have never seen any audience so amused as these little yellow babies at the antics of us foreign devils. They were so convulsed that we became convulsed too, and after five minutes of very strenuous play, had to lie down and recover our breath. In spite of months in the open air, and many miles of walking a day, the violent exercise winded us in an incredibly short time, and after half an hour, when I was approaching exhaustion, the Army had to own its defeat by five goals to four!

Owing to the fear of pillage should the bandit troops arrive, everything of value, including food, had miraculously disappeared from the bazaars and all we could buy to add to our supplies were a few potatoes. One would have thought that the town had already sustained a siege, so short were the provisions and so empty the shops.

Next morning, 1st May, escorted by four troopers we set out along a road bordered by fine old trees, and through cultivated country with here and there young shoots of green in the fields and clusters of fruit blossoms in the orchards. Dr. Parry and young Tornewalle accompanied us for about ten *li*. After forty *li*, a thunderstorm came on, so we stopped at a poor place for the night, and were presently disturbed by the blare of bugles, announcing the arrival of about a hundred infantry, carrying many brightly-coloured banners and having three buglers to hearten them on the march. They were headed for 'the front.' As the whole country was infested with bandits, and I did not know what to expect I gave orders to all of the British members of the party to keep together at all times, never to walk more than two hundred yards ahead of the caravan, and to have arms ready at hand in case of emergency. We each had a revolver, except the two servants, and to these I issued a rifle apiece. The French had a light machine gun, but it was so carefully wrapped up that it would have taken half an hour to get into action. I also divided the night into two-hour periods, and arranged that one of us should be on guard at all times in case of trouble. I had heard sufficiently unpleasant tales about the famous bandit leader, White Wolf, who had ravaged the country some years before, to know what one might expect, and was determined to take no chances.

On the 2nd, the road was flat, running along the south bank of the King Ho. Eighty *li* out we halted for breakfast, having started at 2 a.m., and then pushed on along the pleasant valley in the warm and sunny afternoon. There was quite a lot of traffic both ways, on foot, on donkeys and in carts, and there were scattered farms too, from which ran little Chinese boys begging for cash. There were beggars not a few beside the road, also, whining and holding up their maimed limbs or exposing disgusting sores, though many of them looked young and able-bodied. About ten *li* from King Chow, we forded a swiftly running river, and caught sight of the city walls, in a hollow between two hills. The sunshine lit up the towers and crenellated walls against the more sombre background of the hills, and made the place seem like some lovely mediæval castle towards which we were riding to rest a night under the protection of its lord. As we approached, however, the glamour faded, and we rode along a dirty and noisome street full of soldiers in tattered uniforms and with difficulty found two tiny rooms in a poor inn.

Hearing that there was a missionary in the town, Smith and I went off to find him, and came upon a little church. Entering a court to one side we came upon a tall blond man in a black frock-coat, string tie, and broad-brimmed hat, who appeared as surprised to see us, as we were to behold his costume in this out-of-the-way place as he looked more like a Kentucky Colonel than a missionary. His name was Jelsethe, and he soon introduced us to his wife and a younger woman, Miss Sieverson. They had not heard of our coming, as all the other foreigners had before, and were all the more curious, asking innumerable questions. They were Americans of Scandinavian blood, but Mrs. Jelsethe talked with what appeared to be a strong Irish brogue. They were very stiff and shy at first, but soon thawed a little and gave us an excellent supper. According to them the accounts of the fighting were much exaggerated, and only forty or fifty wounded, nearly all slight cases, had been brought in. The bandits had been driven off to Fung Hsian some forty miles from the main road, and they did not think there was any danger. Missionaries were not molested in any case, and they intended to go to the coast themselves in a few weeks. There seemed to be some sort of estrangment between this mission and that at Ping Liang, an example of the friction and lack of co-operation between missions of similar belief, that goes far to nullify any good they may otherwise do in China. Quarrelling among each other can hardly help to convert the Chinese, who cannot comprehend the absurd differences that arise over questions of dogma.

For the first ten *li* next day the road climbed steeply, and then became flat until we reached the Shensi border, and halted for breakfast at the village of Yao Tien. That night we stopped at Chang Wa, and had the same difficulty in securing quarters owing to the number of troops. There were some more missionaries here, Mr. Jacobson, a Dane, his wife, a Swede, and another woman who was a Scandinavian American. They were curious, but hospitable, and gave us supper. The town is famous for a special kind of baked chicken, which looks as if it had been pressed flat and then varnished!

The local commander at first refused to supply our usual escort for the morrow, but on seeing our passports promised eighteen troopers.

The road was pretty bad next day, partly owing to the rain which had fallen during the night, and flat most of the way except that we descended a steep hill to enter the village of Hei Chwan, where we breakfasted, and climbed another bad one some fifteen *li* from Pin Chow. During the day we passed many fruit trees, temples on the hills, and hundreds of caves cut high up on the steep hillsides or in perpendicular cliffs. These caves are only reached by precarious paths, or footholds cut in the rock.

While some of the caves are only used by the peasants as a place of refuge in times of civil war, or bandit raids, there is still a race of cave-dwellers. They live, just as the contemporaries of the mythical Yu Ch'ao (the Nest Dweller), who persuaded men to leave their nests in the tree for holes in the ground more than five thousand years ago.

Pin Chow has great walls a mile square, but most of the place is in ruins, and almost every house was full of soldiers. There was a nice young Swedish missionary there, called Mr. Neilsen. We gave him some tea and made him talk, but he had lived so long with the Chinese that, as he said himself, he was practically a native. His English was biblical, and he was very earnest. He told us there was no danger from the bandits as they had been driven off, and would not come back for some time. I therefore cancelled the orders about guard duty at night, but continued the other precautions. We found the people in Shensi far more unpleasant than anywhere else in the interior, as they were not only curious but impertinent, possibly because the missionaries were used to 'turning the other cheek,' while we were not!

The 5th of May was a bad day for the mules. We set out at 3 a.m. and climbed a terrible hill to a plateau, where the road was fair, and then descended another steep slope to the village of Tai Yu Chen. It had taken us seven hours to do about thirty *li* (ten miles). We had hoped to reach Hao Tien, sixty to seventy *li* away, but soon after leaving Tai Yu Chen, the road became appalling, the ascent steep, and we finally reached Yung Shu Hsien at 8 p.m., the mules being absolutely exhausted, after a day's pull which had covered about twenty miles in seventeen hours. The view from the crest of this range was magnificent to the west and south. We had left the valley of the King Ho, and were now marching almost due south on the eastern side of another broad valley, whose waters emptied themselves into the River Wei, fifty miles to the south. Yung Shu is a small village, outside a large walled fort now in ruins.

All through this rich land from Lanchowfu on the west to Sianfu on the east, one came across the same thing – extensive ruins, where great crumbling walls and roofless yamens gave evidence of former culture and wealth. Outside the walls would be a miserable cluster of mud hovels, or in the once imposing city, only a fraction of the houses would be inhabited. Although civil war had had much to do with the destruction of the cities in years gone by, the poverty of the people in a land which is extremely fertile, is largely due to opium, which has sapped their vitality and left them to live miserably.

As a means of revenue, much opium was grown in various parts of these provinces, although its cultivation was forbidden by the central Government. The local governors, however, could not resist the temptation of easy money and therefore winked at a practice which was so profitable, as opium commanded a high price and could be heavily taxed without difficulty.

The main road from here runs through the town of Kien Chow, but for some reason we made a detour to the east, keeping up in the hills and making for Li Chuan. It was a hot, sunny day, and we halted at Yan Tze Pu for breakfast, later pushing on past many farms and walled villages. At Li Chuan was said to be another missionary, so taking two troopers with me, I rode ahead on my black pony, going at a smart pace, and leaving the high ground for the plain twenty-five *li* from my destination. The soldiers at the gates refused to let me pass, but after much flourishing of my passport and gesticulation I was admitted, only to find the missionary away. I returned to an inn outside the walls, and waited for the remainder of the party to arrive, which they did about seven.

The country we were now passing through seemed to be growing chiefly maize, barley, peas, and clover. The maize only in small patches.

On the 7th, the road was better and we made good time. I rode all day followed by six troopers, taking pleasure in the balmy spring weather and the brilliant patches of fresh green in the fields. There were the usual scattered farms, and walled villages, some of which were in ruins, and quite a lot of traffic going and coming, heavy country carts, light Peking carts, donkeys, soldiers, and pedestrians. About ten *li* from Hsien Yan, we came in sight of the broad ribbon of the River Wei flowing majestically through the wide and fertile valley. As we approached the massive walls of the town, a half-naked coolie ran past us in the fields, followed hard by a soldier mounted bareback on a restive pony. Much to the delight of the peasants, the soldier was thrown on to the dusty ground, but remounting quickly he soon caught up with the coolie and continued belabouring him with a strap until both were out of sight. The coolie made no attempt to defend himself but ran forward blindly and doggedly.

Our inn was very fair, and as Sianfu lay just across the river, we spent the rest of the day bathing, cleaning equipment, and polishing buttons, preparatory to our entry into the capital of Shensi. The local postmaster called on us and I gave him a note to send to Mr. Newman, the English Postal Commissioner, who already knew of our arrival.

The next morning we left the inn soon after four, passed through the streets of Hsien Yan, and half an hour later reached the banks of the Wei Ho, where there was already a crowd of carts and pedestrians waiting to be ferried across. Mr. Newman had sent a man to guide us to his house, and the latter was waiting for us with a great flat-bottomed barge, which was then unloading its cargo. Our mules were unharnessed and the carts run on to the barge by hand, the Chinese watermen singing a sort of chanty the while. As soon as the carts were on the barge, they were turned over on their backs with the shafts in the air. De Kerangat's cart was the first to go aboard, and when it had been tipped over, we heard much profane language issuing from within. His head then appeared out of the front opening, with a comic look of amazement as he peered over the side into the water. He had been asleep and oblivious of his surroundings till he awoke standing on his head! Four carts, with their complement of mules and drivers and a few barrows and foot-passengers, made up the first load, and we then pushed off. Six boatmen with long poles, and one man at the sweep, ferried us across, working in unison to a kind of chanty, and smelling all the while of concentrated and most pungent garlic. It took us a quarter of a hour to get across and by seven we were on the move and halted for breakfast at San Kiao. I then rode ahead with the Chinese officer, and soon met a mounted Chinese, who joined us and told us he also was from Mr. Newman, and would guide us to the city. The great walls and numerous towers of the city came in view, and we rode through the West Gate, and along streets paved with broad flat stones. I caused a great deal of curiosity, but we ambled along quickly, passed through the massive drum tower on to a wide street that runs from there to the East Gate, turned into a passage at the side of the Post Office, and dismounted at the door of Mr. Newman's house.

He was a grey-haired, handsome man of forty or forty-five, and was delighted to see a fellow human being who spoke his own language, and could appreciate the excellent tiffin he had prepared. I was overwhelmed with questions, and spent a very enjoyable time until the carts arrived. Quarters had been prepared for us in a nearby inn, a ramshackle two-storey building of wood, the rooms of which opened on an inner court, where the excruciating music of Chinese fiddles kept us awake far into the night. The servants and soldiers took their meals in this place, while the five of us had ours at Mr. Newman's house, and enjoyed his hospitality during our stay in the city.

In the afternoon, having duly sent our cards to the chief officials, and hearing that it would be impossible to pay our calls for a day or so, de Kerangat and I went to see the Roman Catholic Mission at the west end of the city, and there met the Italian bishop and a Spanish priest. They had quite a nice place, with a big church, schools, gardens and a nunnery, where there was a French Mother Superior and several foreign and Chinese nuns. The two priests spoke in halting French, but we managed to get along all right, and saw quite a lot of the Spaniard during our stay. There were also Swedish and Anglo-American Baptist Missions, with quite a number of missionaries, whom we called on in due course.

On the 10th, de Kerangat, Newman, and I, with Mr. Chang of the local Foreign Office, made our official call on the Military Governor, Cheng Shu Fan, a man of about thirty, reputed to be a good and brave soldier. His yamen was where the old Dowager Empress lodged when she fled from Peking after the Boxer Rising, and was the usual rambling affair with countless courtyards, passages, and ramshackle buildings. As he was in mourning for the death of one of his wives, we only stayed long enough to exchange the usual compliments, and then went on to call on the Civil Governor, a bored-looking individual, who asked us to dine with him the next day.

The Military Governor's mourning prevented his entertaining us for a few days, but did not postpone his marriage to another woman, a day or so after the death of his wife. Having thirteen or fourteen, I suppose, made him a bit callous.

That afternoon we all went off with a Swedish missionary to see the famous Forest of Stones, a collection of carved stone tablets, housed in dilapidated temples, which is too well known to describe fully. These tablets are nearly all of black stone five or six feet high, and covered with delicate carving and long rows of beautifully chiselled characters. The legend is that when the first great Ch'in emperor, some 200 B.C., ordered the destruction of all the books in the country, the contents of the volumes were cut in stone by lovers of the classics so as to preserve the learning of the sages and the history of bygone heroes. Of especial interest to the Westerner is the famous Nestorian Tablet erected at Sianfu in A.D. 781, which records the gratitude of a large number of Chinese and Syrian priests to the Emperor T'ai Tsung for his enlightened reception of the Christian movement, and records the hope that Christianity will make a speedy conquest of the land.

There are hundreds and hundreds of these great slabs, and quite an industry has sprung up, making copies of the inscriptions and selling them throughout the East. A number of men and boys are constantly at work covering the tablets with thin white paper, and then tapping it all over with little mallets soaked in ink, so that the finished product shows the characters and drawings in white against a black background.

Sianfu at the time of my visit had a population of about 300,000 people, but two thousand years ago when it was the Imperial Capital, there were several million inhabitants, and the city walls were nine miles square. Now trade was practically at a standstill, as the city was in a stage of siege, being almost surrounded by troops of the northern general, Hsu Jan Cheo, who had been sent to relieve Cheng Shu Fan. This was one of the internal wars, with which China is still cursed, where rival war lords were contending for the control of a province, and the consequent enrichment of the visitor and his entire family at the expense of the merchants and peasants. As in the other provinces we had visited, the cupidity of the official class strangled all attempts to develop the country, and at that time coal was still brought over a hundred miles from the railway at Kwan Yen Tang on wheelbarrows, the unfortunate coolie struggling over rough trails pushing his cumbersome load of a hundredweight or more. Yet the Belgian company which was constructing the railway to connect Sianfu with the main line to Peking, had countless difficulties to overcome at every step.

The local warring factions naturally weakened central authority in Sianfu, and throughout Shensi, robber bands roamed the country terrorising and living on the unfortunate people. Some day, when the Chinese masses face the truth, that all their ills do not come from the few thousand foreigners scattered along the coast, or from the concessions obtained long ago by these same foreigners, they will turn on these officials, military governors, and bandit chiefs and pay them back a little of what is owed them. Then there shall be much blood, and the French and Russian revolutions will pale beside this new and still more violent readjustment. I hope it comes soon, for there is no people to-day so exploited by their own as the Chinese, and the reckoning will be one well deserved.

On the 11th, there was to be a conference between the besiegers and the besieged, and the northern general or his representative was to meet Cheng Shu Fan and again try to come to terms. Being anxious to witness this interview, de Kerangat, Newman, and I rode to the East Gate and dismounted outside a building which was gaily decorated with republican flags. After crossing several courtyards, which were heavily guarded by troops, we entered a large audience hall where a number of military and civil officials were awaiting the arrival of the military and civil governors. These two turned up half an hour later and we stood talking about the Great War, and answering many questions asked by the Chinese officers. To pass the time, we had our photographs taken with the two governors, and then as the northern general had not arrived, we returned to the Post Office and lunched with Newman, later going to the Civil Governor's yamen for dinner. In addition to our host, there were also Cheng Shu Fan, the Italian bishop, the Spanish priest, Newman, and the five of us. We had an excellent feast, and there were polite speeches by the two officials, de Kerangat, and myself. A visit to the Baptist Mission ended the day, and we were glad to get to bed, as we were to start next day on the final stage of our long journey to the railway.

CHAPTER 25

THE LAST STAGE

We were astir soon after five on 12th May, and found nine small carts of the Peking variety waiting for us in the broad street outside the inn. All was bustle and confusion for a time, as the servants and soldiers loaded on our kit, provisions and cooking utensils, while Bielenky created a sensation by appearing in a dark green sola topee with a lilac pugaree. Hearing that it would be difficult to dispose of my pony further along the road, I sent him off to Mr. Harquist, a Swedish missionary, and asked him to have him sold and to give the proceeds to the church at Ping Liang. A pious act which I hope shall be counted for me some day!

The carts were very small, and except for the soldiers and servants we had one apiece. Unless one was accustomed to sitting cross-legged within or perched on the running-board next to the driver, with one's feet dangling on one side, they were uncomfortable in the extreme. I finally managed to lie down with my feet on the mule's quarters and thus obtain a certain amount of comfort, but as my driver encouraged his beast by pricking it with a pin, my feet had none too secure a resting-place.

We set out soon after eight, passed out by the East Gate, and rode through flat and cultivated country, which had plenty of fruit trees and green fields. Our escort consisted of two mounted troopers. Soon after leaving the city a squadron of Fengtien cavalry, belonging to the besieging force, passed us going east, preliminary, I suppose, to their withdrawal from Honan. About one, we reached Lin Tung, famous for its sulphur baths, and were kept waiting an hour and a half outside the gates, as the country was under martial law, and all travellers were closely scrutinised.

Late in the afternoon, after traversing a stony road, we got to Hsin Fan. There were luckily no troops here, but the place was crowded with carts, probably belonging to the Northern Army, and we had great difficulty in finding an inn. De Kerangat had picked up a Chinese in Sianfu who spoke pidgin French, and we had lots of fun talking to him. He had been a house-boy in Indo-China, and was allowed to travel with us, acting as interpreter and servant to the French captain.

Next morning we set out along the most terrible road I have ever experienced. It was paved for twenty to thirty *li* with great, uneven slabs of stone in need of repair, and jolted us so that every piece of crockery we possessed was broken, and our teeth chattered in our heads as if a giant were shaking us violently in his huge hands. I thought I should go mad after a time, but luckily it came to an end at last, and we journeyed along a muddy track to Hua Yin Miao. After breakfasting, we started again, caught sight of the junction of the Wei and Yellow Rivers to the north, and finally reached Tung Kwan, a walled city with fine gateways and stone-paved streets. In spite of the fact that we had two interpreters, two soldiers and a guide, we had the usual difficulty in finding an inn, our caravan wandered about aimlessly and at last ended up in a *cul de sac*, from which we had great difficulty in extracting ourselves. I finally discovered an inn myself and after a good deal of trouble got some of the soldiers turned out of their quarters, although they continued to crowd into the courtyard, and pressed around us in the most impertinent way, until a N.C.O. from the local commander came and ordered them out. The inns were as poor in this fertile country as many we have seen in the desert, for the Chinese traveller seems content to have a roof over his head, and asks for little else.

On the 15th, we pushed on again, feeling happier that our troubles would soon be over. After travelling twenty *li* along a road sunk in deep gullies, we passed through a small walled town full of troops with the numerals 105 and 310 on their collars, and then entered a more hilly country, halting at Pan Tao Chen for breakfast. There were no soldiers here, and we found a good inn, so our meal was the pleasantest since leaving Sianfu. From there a sandy road led up a long slope and then down again, heavy work for the mules for about fifteen *li*. To the north we could see the broad expanse of the Yellow River, covered with junks and other vessels. As I sat on one shaft watching the passing traffic, my driver, who smelled strongly of garlic, and had apparently smoked too many opium pipes the night before, kept falling off to sleep, and putting his weary head on my shoulder. As my polite protests were unavailing, I soon took to blows, but he was too sleepy to feel them and I spent an unpleasant afternoon. At one point we passed four men, each carrying a large monkey westwards, and at another two coolies trotting along, shouldering their bamboo poles with a basket at each end. In each case, one basket was full of vegetables and the other contained a little naked baby, sitting up complacently like a miniature yellow Buddha.

Next morning, after travelling four hours through deep gullies and across quite hilly country, we halted at the walled town of Lin Pao, and there met a French railway engineer, M. Jiroit, and his Armenian assistant. He had been prospecting for six years for the Belgian company that was building the Lunghai Railway towards which we were heading, and was delighted to see us. We went round to his place after breakfast for coffee and liqueurs, and were served by a pretty little Annamite girl. That evening, near Shan Chow, we met another engineer, this time a Belgian, M. Slosse, whose wife and three little boys were also there. We spent a cheery evening, as we were all beginning to realise that our long trek was nearly over. It seemed hardly possible that the next day we should reach the railhead, and say good-bye to our carts for ever. The monotonous grind had become so much a second nature that I could hardly picture any other sort of life. The approach of civilisation had been so slow, that when it was almost within reach I could scarcely believe that real beds, porcelain baths, beautiful women, and decent restaurants really existed and would soon delight my senses.

On the 17th, as if to punish us for our belief that all was over, the road was very bad, and we struggled through deep, dusty gullies, and over stony hills, bumping and swaying as the cart wheels struck the loose boulders in the track, and choking as the fine dust clogged our throats and noses. Two of the carts turned over at one particularly bad spot, but no damage was done, and at last we struggled into Kwan Yen Tang, a long, straggling, busy town full of cheap shops. An inn, about three-quarters of a mile from the railway station, was found, and we had tea. Our first sight of civilisation was at this inn, a dirty, dilapidated hotel, little better than a desert caravanserai, when a ragged Chinaman began pasting the green and white labels of the 'hotel' all over our luggage!

Very soon a note arrived from M. Faury, a Frenchman, in charge of the railhead, asking us all to dine with him and sleep at his house. As this would facilitate our entraining the next morning, I decided to accept his invitation. The drivers had all dispersed and we had great difficulty in finding them, and getting our luggage over to the station, a task which was not completed until after 10 p.m. We then had a late dinner with M. Faury, and turned in worn out, too tired even to get excited at the sight of the steel rails, the empty coaches, and the whistle of an occasional engine.

Next morning we woke to the unaccustomed sounds of a railway siding, and rose to find that our carts had already gone, while our eyes were gladdened by the sight of the station, and the lines of the rails which were to carry us swiftly towards our journey's end. Our kit was soon loaded on the waiting train, and our cosmopolitan party, looking more incongruous than ever on the platform, piled in, breathless with excitement to be on board a vehicle that could travel faster than three miles an hour. At nine, we started for Chengchow, and after an uneventful journey of eight hours, we reached that place, which is on the main line from Hankow to Peking, and where we descended to be welcomed by a number of foreigners. Our party was separated, the soldiers and servants sleeping in a special railway coach which had been reserved for our journey to Peking, and the rest of us staying at various houses in the town.

I had the good fortune to stay with Mr. Ainsworth, of the Asiatic Petroleum Company, until our special car was attached to the Peking express next day, and we started northwards.

Beyond a little trouble with some Chinese soldiers, who appeared to think the dining-car was a barrack-room, the trip held nothing of especial interest, and on the 20th May, exactly seven months after my departure from Omsk, we steamed into the station at the capital.

A British N.C.O. met me there, arranged the transport of our kit, and our travel-stained company assembled on the platform to say good-bye, as we were never to meet again as companions in adversity, and it was the last time I saw Peter Rigo, our silent but hardworking Magyar cook. Bielenky, in his worn British uniform and patched Russian boots; Peter and Albert, also in British khaki with B.M.M. in silver on their caps; Morgan in long boots and an old pair of corduroy riding-breeches once belonging to me; Gordon Smith also in riding-breeches and boots; the two French soldiers in faded horizon blue; and de Kerangat, Moss, and myself in our best uniforms, stood round awkwardly, making plans to meet again before we dispersed for the four corners of the earth, but as a unit we were no more, and it was sad to feel the days of hardship which had bound us together were over.

The French departed to the French Legation, our two servants to the Dutch Minister, then in the charge of the repatriarion of ex-prisoners of war, and ourselves to the British Legation. The Chinese officer, who had stuck to us all the way from Lanchow, disappeared too, joining friends of his own in the native city, while Smith and Morgan went off to an hotel.

I was met at the Legation by Major Brook, acting Military Attaché, and Moss and I were the guests of the Legation Guard during our stay. The officer commanding the Guard, which was composed of a company of the 18th Infantry of the Indian Army, was a Major Hammond, who had gone to my old school, Sherborne, although some years before I had been there.

Peking is an interesting city, with many beautiful palaces and temples, but I could raise little enthusiasm for sight-seeing and paid only a brief visit to the Forbidden City. The last two hundred miles from Sianfu to the railhead, which had seemed to pass so slowly, was still too recent for me to relish tourist jaunts in Peking carts or even rickshaws, and I had had enough of things Chinese to last me many a day. It seemed incredible, when I walked through the beautiful grounds of the Legation on Empire Day, and watched the little white children running races, and the stately Englishwomen moving about gracefully in their thin summer dresses, that only a week before I had been travelling over the rough roads of Honan, a refugee from Siberia in travel-stained uniform, while now I was among my own kind once more with those seven months of hardship far behind me.

To my relief the last of the British Mission to Siberia had passed through Shanghai some days before, and had already sailed for England on the *Professor*. I was therefore able to apply for leave to return home *via* Canada and the United States in order to visit my father in New York, as I had not seen him since September 1914. My application was granted, and a passage was obtained for

PEKING, MAY 1920

Left to right (Standing)—*Bielenky, Albert, Doumeng, Buffet.* (Sitting) *Morgan, Capt. Hodges, Capt. de Kerangat, Gordon Smith, Lieut. Moss*

Facing p. 344

me on the *Kashima Maru*, sailing from Shanghai on the 30th.

Of my late companions, the two servants, Albert and and Peter Rigo, were left in the hands of the Dutch Minister, and eventually returned to their own countries. I said good-bye to Albert with regret as he was a loyal and hard-working batman, and I hope he has found happiness and success in his native Saxony. Moss and Gordon Smith returned to England *via* Suez a little later than I did, and I saw them several times in London, until I returned to China again in the spring of 1921. De Kerangat, on his return to France, applied for service in Morocco, and has been there ever since, while Bielenky found some kind of occupation in Tientsin. Morgan remained in Peking for some time, and when last I heard of him, he was travelling back through Mongolia towards Siberia, with the intention of returning to the Spassky Mine near Karkaralinsk, where he had left his Russian wife. Whether he ever achieved his object and brought her out with him, I do not know.

My journey from Petropavlovsk to Kwan Yen Tang (the railhead) covered more than three thousand miles of some of the wildest, most barren and least known regions in the world, and was undertaken only by force of circumstances, without adequate preparations and accompanied by a considerable element of risk. Little as I liked the cold, the rough fare, the danger, and the other hardships at the time, it was an experience I would not have missed for many silver taels. Besides the fact that I was fortunate enough to travel through countries seldom visited by even the hardened globe-trotter, it has given me a picture of primitive civilisation in all its poverty, ignorance and filth, which no book can ever convey. I have seen the vast desert wastes, the cold grim mountains with their eternal snows, the dying rivers sinking slowly into the barren, rocky soil, and the endless Russian steppes. I have been cold and hungry, weary and afraid, too, in those far-off places, but with it all I have learnt many things.

Russia and China. Two colossal figures, but now awakening to the disturbing culture of the West. Russia for the moment has found stability under her able leaders, and is making a desperate effort to work out an ordered civilisation alien to the patchwork structure of Europe and America. China is in dreadful chaos. The seaboard provinces are likely to be torn with strife for years to come, but I like to think of my desert lands holding aloof, until a better day has dawned, and the march of progress up the old Imperial caravan route will be one of peace and prosperity instead of bloodshed.

Some day, perhaps, a new 'Agricultural Army' headed by the ghost of Tso Ch'ing T'ang will advance through Sianfu, over the mountains to Lanchow, then pushing onwards to the desert come to Hami and to Urumchi, laying rails, building roads, developing the country's resources. Some day, perhaps I shall sit comfortably in a luxurious *wagon-lit*, and see again the Central Asian wastes that I had once crossed with so much toil and hardship. The old inns will be gone, and the city walls will have crumbled before the rising tide of a new life, but the sun will still sparkle on the snow-capped peaks of the Tian Shan, and pour down upon the grey and yellow distances of the great Gobi.

INDEX

Lightning Source UK Ltd.
Milton Keynes UK
UKHW040705250820
368761UK00001BA/57

9 781845 748111